MULTILINGUAL MATTERS 30
Series Editor: Derrick Sharp

Introspection in Second Language Research

Edited by

Claus Færch and
Gabriele Kasper

MULTILINGUAL MATTERS LTD
Clevedon · Philadelphia

Library of Congress Cataloging-in-Publication Data

Færch, Claus.
Introspection in second language research.

(Multilingual matters ; v. 30)
Bibliography: p.
Includes index.
1. Language and languages—Study and teaching—
Psychological aspects. 2. Second language acquisition—
Methodology. 3. Introspection. I. Kasper, Gabriele.
II. Title. III. Series.
P53.7.F34 1987   401'.9   87–7647
ISBN 0–905028–73–2
ISBN 0–905028–72–4 (pbk.)

British Library Cataloguing in Publication Data

Introspection in second language research.—
(Multilingual matters; 30)
1. Second language acquisition
I. Færch, Claus II. Kasper, Gabriele
III. Series
418'.007   P118.2

ISBN 0–905028–73–2
ISBN 0–905028–72–4 Pbk

Multilingual Matters Ltd,

Bank House, 8a Hill Road,   &   242 Cherry Street,
Clevedon, Avon BS21 7HH   Philadelphia, PA 19106–1906,
England.   U.S.A.

Typeset by Photo·graphics, Honiton, Devon.
Printed and bound in Great Britain by
Short Run Press, Exeter, EX2 7LW.

Claus
my permanent co-author

Contents

In Memoriam

When this book was under production, Claus Færch died after a long illness. He had already lost his health in the summer of 1985, when we held the symposium on which the volume is based. However, dedicated and gifted as he was in his profession, he took his full share in preparing both the symposium and the book. Even though his physical resources were fading, he would not let our contributors down, nor would he let me take over — his strong sense of responsibility and consideration for others did not allow him to take the care of himself that he needed and deserved.

Working with Claus was a rewarding experience. His thinking was creative and systematic, analytic and integrative. He was good at spotting the weaknesses in his fellow researchers' work and formulating his criticism constructively and gently. He was a willing listener to criticism of his own work and profited from the suggestions made by others. He was sceptical of easy solutions and willing to develop and accept new insights when the final manuscript had already been typed — even before we had a computer. We sometimes disagreed about that!

Claus was a hard worker, and we were a hard-working couple. Now that he is not with me anymore I am asking myself whether we should have used our precious time differently, instead of investing so much of it in research. Yet on reflection, I come to the conclusion that we used it well after all. For very little of what made us write all those papers and give all those talks was for the benefit of a presentable product and the possible rewards connected with that. The main thing had always been the process of working together, and the fun we had of it.

Risskov, May 15th, 1987   Gabriele Kasper

Introduction

Several of the chapters contained in this collection were first read at a symposium on Introspective Methods in Second Language Research in connection with the First International Conference on Applied Psycholinguistics, Barcelona, June 1985. The first half of the symposium took place at the University of Barcelona, the second half in the breakfast room of the Hotel Regina due to a one-day general strike in Catalunya.

The book is the first to survey an important new development in second language (SL) research: the use of introspective methods. As can be seen from the table of contents, introspective methods have been adopted in numerous SL research domains, and there is now sufficient experience to offer specific suggestions for how and why to adopt these methods — and just as importantly, when and how not to! Yet it would be premature to venture an evaluation of the contribution of introspective procedures of data collection to SL research methodology in general. We hope that both the theoretically-oriented chapters and those in which empirical investigations are presented will put the reader in a good position to shape his or her own views upon the validity of these methods.

The first chapter, by Færch & Kasper, partly provides some historical context to the emergence of introspective methods in SL research, and partly surveys how these methods are currently being put to use. In the historical part, focus is on the product-process dichotomy which has always been of central concern to SL researchers, and it is shown how different methodologies have been adopted to reconstruct learners' processes. The use of introspective methods represents one promising way of achieving this, and the paper suggests a number of classification criteria according to which introspective methods can be compared.

Chapters 2–4 clarify the theoretical foundation of these methods and demonstrate how they may be applied to specific research questions. Ericsson & Simon's publication in 1980 of the article "Verbal Reports as Data" in *Psychological Review* and their subsequent publication of *Protocol Analysis* in 1984 have engendered much of the current interest in the use of introspective methods. In Chapter 2 they offer a detailed account of the stages involved in the planning and execution of an empirical design including introspective methods. In addition to the practical information provided, Ericsson & Simon argue that in principle there is no difference in validity between introspective methods and the received psychological methods: *any* empirical method needs to be critically scrutinized and its relevant domain identified before it is applied.

Whereas Ericsson & Simon's point of departure is experimental cognitive psychology, Grotjahn sees introspective methods from the more general perspective of a research methodologist working in the social sciences. A number of research paradigms are carefully described, and the difference between type of data and type of analysis is strongly emphasized. The chapter leaves no doubt that the commonly adopted dichotomy between quantitative and qualitative methods is a gross simplification, unsuitable to characterize introspective methods (or, indeed, other empirical procedures).

Cohen's chapter has both a theoretical and an empirical dimension. He partly discusses a number of criteria according to which introspective methods can be classified, partly makes a strong plea for adopting them in an investigation into how SL learning is brought about. In this way, the chapter can also be seen as a summary of some of the points made in the previous three chapters and as an exemplification from a central area of SL research.

The remaining chapters contain accounts of empirical investigations in which introspective methods are a major procedure of data collection. Two observations can be made with respect to the majority of the chapters:

1. Irrespective of which specific area the chapter deals with, *problems* in SL use as experienced by the informants loom large (translation problems, reading problems, etc.). This is a clear reflection of the theoretical foundation upon which most of the chapters are based, viz., Ericsson & Simon's model which establishes as a *sine qua non* for the use of introspective methods that information to be verbalized concurrently or retrospectively needs to be (or to have been) processed under the informant's *attention*. Unlike many other processes activated in the production, reception and learning of a SL, problem solving processes therefore lend themselves well to introspective reports.
2. Related to the preceding is that several chapters deal with *vocabulary*: high-level processes such as lexical search and lexical comprehension are likely to be more attended to than lower level processes that involve more highly automatized forms of linguistic competence. Hence, a

much-to-be-welcomed spin-off effect of adopting introspective methods may be that it boosts the study of one of the hitherto neglected areas of SL research.

The authors of Chapters 5–9 all use *translation* as their data elicitation technique, but with different research goals in view. Dechert makes the important observation, supported by his data, that a careful analysis of the temporal characteristics (pauses etc.) of the verbal protocol (e.g. a think-aloud protocol) must be included in the researcher's interpretation. Hölscher & Möhle demonstrate how a detailed model of speech production can explain the different phases in the production of a verbal protocol, thereby also exemplifying Dechert's main claim. Like Dechert and Hölscher & Möhle, Gerloff shows how think-aloud protocols can be analysed with a view to reconstructing production processes. Her objective, however, is different: by investigating how much of the original text is processed at a time, she is able to identify significant differences in the length of translation units between learners with different translation capabilities and between learners and a bilingual speaker. Krings, as well as Zimmerman & Schneider, is concerned with the strategies adopted by informants in order to solve translation problems, reconstructing the successive steps of their problem-solving patterns. The studies, however, differ in the type of introspective method employed.

The final four chapters illustrate how introspective methods can be applied to investigate comprehension, communication strategies, test-taking and language learning. Both Haastrup and Cavalcanti examine reading comprehension, though with the important difference that Haastrup identifies procedures in the decoding of lexical items unknown to the informants, whereas Cavalcanti's interest is to establish L2 reading processes in general. Poulisse, Bongaerts & Kellerman in their chapter describe an ongoing research project into compensatory strategies in oral speech production. The use of such strategies presupposes that learners are consciously aware of problems, i.e. a condition that fits the use of introspective methods very well. The chapter by Feldmann & Stemmer demonstrates how an aspect of language testing that has so far received surprisingly little attention, test-taking strategies, can be explored by a combination of think-aloud and retrospective techniques. This is a promising direction for future test research in that it provides important new information about test validity in addition to information obtained by means of traditional methods.

The final chapter by Gillette gives an account of an integrated study of SL learning, thus taking up some of the issues raised initially by Cohen.

By combining different introspective with observational methods, Gillette examines two SL learners in terms of their affective, social and cognitive characteristics, and the interaction of these factors with the informants' approaches to the task of SL learning. Her study exemplifies how introspective methods can help increase our understanding of what makes a good language learner.

From Product to Process — Introspective Methods in Second Language Research

CLAUS FÆRCH AND GABRIELE KASPER

Objects and Methods of Investigation in SL Research

This book is about a type of empirical method which is currently gaining ground in the exploration of the structure, use and development of non-native (foreign or second, henceforth: L2) language knowledge. As the majority of the chapters are concerned with L2 use rather than learning/acquisition, we have chosen to refer to the field of study as second language (SL) research, thus avoiding the bias towards developmental issues implicit in the more common term "second language acquisition research".

The objects and relationships that SL research describes, with the intention to eventually explain them, can roughly be sketched as in Figure 1.

One major task for SL research is to reconstruct learners' interlanguage (IL) development, i.e. to determine their changing states of competence ($C_1 \ldots C_n$) (cf. Nemser's "approximative systems", 1971, or Corder's "IL continua", 1978), referred to in Figure 1 as macroprocess$_c$. Various models and methods have been adopted to achieve this goal, for instance, establishing acquisition orders (see, for example, Burt & Dulay, 1980), developmental sequences (see, for example, Wode, 1984) or implicational acquisition scales (see, for example, Hyltenstam, 1977). What these rather different approaches have in common is that they (longitudinally or pseudo-longitudinally) compare states of IL performance ($P_1 \ldots$

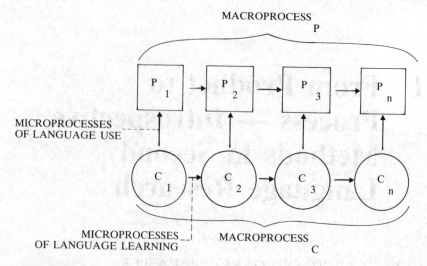

FIGURE 1. *Process levels in L2 learning and use*
(p = performance, c = competence)

P_n) under the assumption that these reflect essential characteristics of the underlying states of competence. In other words, L2 acquisition at the level of macroprocess$_c$ is established through developmental performance analysis at the level of macroprocess$_p$, i.e. an analysis of successive learner *products*. As has frequently been pointed out (for example, by James, 1980: 4), such investigations bear fundamental similarities to diachronic linguistics: where language change is phylogenetically reconstructed on the basis of texts (linguistic products evidencing different synchronic states) from different historical periods, its ontogenetic counterpart, an individual's language (L1 or L2) acquisition, is equally traced through samples of spoken or written products. Unlike diachronic linguistics, however, SL (and to some extent L1) acquisition research has a methodological alternative to developmental product analysis: learners' underlying knowledge can directly be probed by means of metalinguistic judgement tests (see below) or by other elicitation procedures that force them to reveal aspects of their IL competence. By using such methods longitudinally or pseudo-longitudinally, a more immediate access to macroprocess$_c$ is provided (for example, Jordens, 1977; Kellerman, 1977; Lightbown & Barkman, 1978).

However, such observations still remain descriptive rather than explanatory in that they establish *that* IL development proceeds in a specific way rather than *why* it takes the identified route. In order to account for how learners arrive at the next stage of their IL competence, we have to assume an interface between C_x and C_{x+1}. This interface is constituted by the microprocesses of learning. There is no need in the present context to specify these processes, suffice it to say that the conversion of one state of competence to another (or rather, of one state of some *aspect* of competence to another, due to the differential developmental course and speed of different types of IL knowledge) can basically be brought about in three ways: (1) by reorganizing the present state of competence without any external influence or manifestation, i.e. by the use of prior knowledge; (2) by processing input and; (3) by outperforming competence through the use of productive communication strategies, compensating for lack of requisite IL knowledge. As is apparent from this characterization, the last two types of microprocesses operate not only as links between successive states of competence, i.e. as learning processes, but also as an interface between the underlying knowledge and observable performance (C_1 and P_1, C_2 and P_2, ... C_n and P_n), that is as reception and production processes (for the interaction between reception and learning, see Færch & Kasper, 1986c; Gass, forthcoming; for the interaction between production and learning, see Swain, 1985).

The level of microprocesses has attracted SL researchers' attention from early on. Thus, Selinker (1972) hypothesized "five central processes" (transfer, generalization, transfer of training, communication and learning strategies) to account for fossilization of IL competence. Similarly, Dulay & Burt (1974), emphasizing the process, rather than the product level, as the object of SL investigation, defined as the relevant process level entities learners' "second language production strategies". At the same time, the interest for the microprocesses of language use and learning entailed a major methodological problem: as these processes are not accessible to direct observation, they have, in one way or another, to be inferred from observable entities which for theoretical reasons are considered to reflect the microprocess level.

A look at some of the methodological paradigms of SL research which have been particularly influential during the last 20 years reveals how this shared problem of reconstructing the (micro)process from the product level has been dealt with. In the late 1950's and early 1960's, when a major concern was to determine L1 influence on L2 learning and use, the predominant method was *Contrastive Analysis* (CA): by linguistic comparison of (sub-systems of) L1 and L2, areas of similarity and difference were identified, on the basis of which psycholinguistic microprocesses were predicted, similarity resulting in "positive transfer" ("facilitation"), difference in "negative transfer" ("interference") (cf. James, 1980 for an overview, in particular for the relationship of CA and transfer theory; and Eckman, 1985 for a current version of CA). The method thus is to reconstruct learners' processes from learner-external sources, rather than using data produced by learners themselves. This is precisely what distinguishes CA from its successors, Error Analysis (EA) and Performance Analysis (PA). These procedures, EA coexisting with CA in the late 1960's and early 70's, PA emerging during the early 1970's, focused on the learner, using as evidence for both states of underlying IL competence, development at the level of macroprocess and for the microprocesses of IL use the learner's own oral or written products (cf. Svartvik, 1973; Richards, 1974 for some of the most influential papers about these methods and their theoretical foundation). The difference between EA and PA is that the former attempts to reconstruct learners' microprocesses on the basis of errors alone while the latter makes use of the whole of their performance, both correct and erroneous. The methodological requirements for PA were precisely formulated by Selinker (1972), who identified "the utterances which are produced when the learner attempts to say sentences of a TL [target language]" as "the only observable data to which we can relate theoretical predictions". Unfortunately, neither Selinker nor Corder or others who specify the methodological principles of PA (see the two readers referred to above) provide any specific suggestions how such performance data should best be analysed. As the most conspicuous manifestation of learner-specific knowledge and processing in performance data are overt errors, much of what purportedly is a description of (some aspects of) learners' performance turns out to be no more than an *error* analysis (see the analysis of communication strategies in Tarone, Cohen & Dumas, 1976 as an example). However, even if both correct and erroneous utterances are taken into account, this does not imply that all of the information present in a learner text is exploited for analysis. More often than not, the analysis is based on *regularized* versions of the original text, i.e. the text is cleansed from most of the performance features such as, for oral production, slips of the tongue, self-corrections, supra-segmentals and temporal variables (pauses, speed, rate and manner of articulation). For instance, Selinker & Gass's (1984) workbook on SL acquisition, providing performance data for micro-process level analysis, contains regularized data only: production traces which might have been indicative of underlying processing mechanisms are not included in the transcripts.

   That such traces can in fact yield valuable information about the organization and processing of linguistic knowledge was demonstrated by two approaches, developed in psycholinguistics with respect to L1 users:

Fromkin's (e.g. 1973) investigations into spontaneously produced speech errors, and Goldman-Eisler's (e.g. 1968) research into temporal variables in speech. Their methods have been applied successfully to, and further developed for, SL studies by the Kassel Research Group into Pragmatics and Psycholinguistics (see, for example, Dechert & Raupach, 1980; Dechert, Möhle & Raupach, 1984). Unfortunately, their significant contribution to SL methodology has not as yet had the impact it deserves on the way performance analysis is carried out in the international community of SL researchers.

If PA is based on explicit models of the organization and access of IL knowledge and incorporates relevant production features into the analysis, important insights can certainly be expected from this approach in the future. However, reconstructing unobservable phenomena from performance data will always entail situations where the ambiguity between product and process cannot be solved. Looking for methods that provide a more direct access to learners' processes and knowledge, SL researchers have found help from the disciplines whose empirical methodologies have traditionally been a significant source of inspiration for SL research: linguistics, sociology and psychology. One common denominator for the methods in question is that they use as data, informants' own statements about the ways they organize and process information, as an alternative or supplement to inferring their thoughts from behavioural events. Methods of this type will be referred to in the following as *introspective methods* (or, as stylistic variants, "verbal reports/statements/data/protocols").[1] Whereas there is quite a long tradition in SL research for borrowing introspective methods as employed in linguistics and sociology, the utilization of verbal reports similar to those in cognitive psychology is a fairly recent development. In linguistics, the elicitation of native speakers' intuitions about what is grammatical, acceptable or appropriate in their language has been an important empirical tool for linguists working in the Chomskyan tradition. Such metalinguistic judgements are assumed to provide more direct access to the ideal native speaker's competence than its distorted manifestation in language users' performance (see, also, 1b below). Traditional sociological methods such as rating scales and questionnaires have long been part of the methodological inventory of SL research, where they have been mostly used to investigate "learner factors" such as attitudes, motivation, learning styles, etc. More recently, interviews and group discussions have been introduced. Sociologists working with such interactive methods have particularly emphasized the impact on the informants' statements of the socio-psychological dynamics between the participants (see 1a below).

The latest methodological innovation in SL research comes from psychology. In this field, the validity of introspective reports as an empirical instrument to uncover informants' thought processes had been an issue of debate since William James introduced (his variety of) the procedure in 1890. Whereas the use of introspection was a methodological taboo during the era of behaviourism, the paradigm shift to cognitivism renewed researchers' interest in procedures alternative or supplementary to the received measures of behavioural indicators such as eye-movement and reaction time (see Ericsson & Simon, 1984: 48 ff; and Börsch, 1986a for a historical overview). What makes it possible today to use introspective reports as rigorously as the so-called objective methods (cf. Grotjahn, this volume, Chapter 3, for a discussion of different methodological paradigms) is that the validity of the elicited statements can be assessed in terms of explicit models of information processing (Ericsson & Simon, 1980, 1984, this volume, Chapter 2), the formulation and testing of which is assisted by computer simulation. The exploration of processes of L2 learning and use has profited considerably from this advancement, as will be evident from the contributions to this book.

Criteria for the Classification of Introspective Methods in SL Research

As there is a variety of introspective methods employed in SL research, it seems useful to establish criteria according to which such methods can be classified. A classificatory framework can serve to compare studies that use different methods, and represents a precondition for evaluating their validity. The classification, suggested below,[2] is based on three previous proposals: the criteria introduced by Ericsson & Simon (1980, 1984) on the basis of a cognitive-psychological model of information processing; the classification grid established by Huber & Mandl (1982) for the description of verbal data used in the educational and social sciences; and Cohen & Hosenfeld's (1981) and Cohen's (1984, this volume, Chapter 4) criteria for classifying introspective methods in SL research.

It should be noted that this classification takes into account procedures of data *collection* only, disregarding methods of data *analysis*. As argued by Grotjahn (this volume, Chapter 3), selecting a specific data collection method does not necessarily determine the choice of analytical procedure (and *vice versa*). Just as, for instance, conversational performance data can be subjected to both qualitative-interpretative and quantitative-statistical treatment, introspective reports, in principle, allow for both types of treatment. Furthermore, if the collected introspective reports themselves are spoken or written discourse, they should be analysed with reference to an explicit discourse model. As for the analysis of orally-produced verbal protocols, this should take into account the temporal dimension of speech production, as argued by Dechert (this volume, Chapter 5) and demonstrated by Hölscher & Möhle (this volume, Chapter 6).

1. Object of introspection:
   1a cognitive, affective or social aspects;
   1b declarative v. procedural knowledge;
   1c modality of language use (spoken v. written, receptive v. productive, combination, e.g. in translation);
   1d continuous process v. specific aspect.
2. +/− related to concrete action.
3. Temporal relationship to action (simultaneous, immediately consecutive, delayed consecutive).
4. +/− informant training.
5. Elicitation procedure:
   5a degree of structure;
   5b +/− media support;
   5c self-initiated v. other-initiated;
   5d +/− interaction between informant and experimenter, between informants;
   5e +/− integration with action;
   5f +/− interference with action.
6. +/− combination of methods.

1. Object of introspection

Within the first criterion, four distinctions are made according to which the reported information can be described.

1a Cognitive, affective or social aspects

A first distinction relates to the psychological dimension of L2 learning and use under study. Most of the research reported on below, as well as the contributions to this volume, focus on learners' linguistic knowledge and its activation, i.e. on aspects of their cognitive structure. The affective dimension has been a major concern for SL researchers in its relation to L2 achievement. Attitudes, motivation and other affective variables have been investigated with traditional sociological instruments such as interviews and questionnaires containing open or closed (e.g. multiple choice) questions and rating scales (see Gillette, this volume, Chapter 14; Solmecke & Boosch, 1981; Ely, 1986 for overviews and references; and Oller, 1981 for a critical evaluation of introspective measures of affective factors). In one study, however, the affective and social dimension of L2 learning and use is examined from a different vantage point and with a different type of introspective method: by means of group discussions, Börsch (1982, 1986b) explores the motives of female and male university students for studying a foreign language and the impact of experiences with L2 on their identity.

1b Declarative v. procedural knowledge

If the object of investigation is the learners' IL, we propose to distinguish between two types of knowledge (cf. Færch & Kasper, 1985). *Declarative* linguistic knowledge comprises IL rule knowledge at all linguistic levels (referred to as states of competence in Figure 1), organized in more or less analysed, i.e. structurally transparent and articulated form (see, for example, Bialystok, 1981; Færch & Kasper, 1986a). In order to activate such knowledge in communication, and to increase it through learning, we assume a second type of knowledge, intervening between the declarative knowledge and (observable) performance: *procedural* knowledge. It comprises the cognitive and interactional processes activated in reception, production and language acquisition (referred to as the microprocesses of language use and language learning in Figure 1). As most of these processes are activated automatically, i.e. do not enter short term memory (cf. the discussion in Ericsson & Simon, this volume, Chapter 2), they are not accessible for introspective report. However, activities that involve slow and controlled processing, e.g. certain types of written translation, open the possibility for introspecting on procedural knowledge. Furthermore, sudden breakdowns of automatic processing, such as when the learner is faced with a problem in reception or production due to a lack of relevant (declarative) linguistic or other knowledge, often initiate attended processing, e.g. the use of communication strategies. These attended processes are then available to introspective reports.

Inspired by the development within linguistics of techniques for the elicitation of native speakers' linguistic intuitions as evidence of their underlying competence, the use of metalinguistic judgements has been adopted in SL research since the middle of the 1970's, (cf. Chaudron's (1983) instructive review of the use of metalinguistic judgements). In addition to judgement tests and interviews, we are aware of two other introspective procedures used to disclose learners' declarative knowledge. Raabe (1982, 1986) analyses learners' questions about L2 grammar, lexis and pragmatics, directed to their teacher or fellow students in foreign language classes. These questions shed light on the learners' hypotheses about L2 regularities, i.e. on the current state of their IL declarative knowledge. By means of a translation task during which the (Danish) learner is thinking aloud, Færch & Kasper (1986b) examine the cognitive status (implicit—explicit) of her declarative knowledge of two foreign languages (English and German).

Investigations of aspects of procedural knowledge by means of introspective reports are carried out in the studies examining processes in reception, production and learning, referred to in 1c. As far as investigating learning by means of introspective data is concerned, Seliger (1983) has raised objections against the validity of the method, claiming that self-reports at most yield information about how IL knowledge is used rather than developed (see the discussion in Cohen, 1984 and this volume, Chapter 4).

1c Modality of language use

Aspects of oral production are examined in studies of communication strategies, e.g. in Poulisse, Bongaerts & Kellerman (this volume, Chapter 11) or, with a particular view to strategic transfer, in Mogensen (1984). While no introspective studies of listening comprehension have come to our attention, reading comprehension has been examined introspectively in a number of investigations, e.g. in Hosenfeld (1977) and Cavalcanti (this volume, Chapter 12). Finally, there are tasks combining reception and production. These are primarily translation tasks, designed to disclose different aspects of the translation process (Gerloff, 1986, this volume, Chapter 7; Hölscher & Möhle, this volume, Chapter 6; Krings, 1986a, b, this volume, Chapter 8; Lörscher, 1986). It is important to note that in all these studies, the informants are non-professional translators (foreign language learners). This has the methodological advantage that they carry out large parts of their tasks under conscious attention, which opens up the possibility for verbal report. A further writing activity that combines reception and production is the solution of written tests, as examined in Grotjahn & Stemmer (1985), Grotjahn (this volume, Chapter 3) and Feldmann & Stemmer (this volume, Chapter 13).

1d Continuous process v. specific aspect

Continuous introspection of the controlled processes activated during task completion typically has the form of simultaneous thinking aloud or talking aloud (cf. Ericsson & Simon, this volume, Chapter 2, for an account of the difference between these two procedures). The informants are instructed to verbalize what they think while doing the task. Hosenfeld uses this method in her analysis of reading processes; further examples are the translation and test studies mentioned in 1c. Continuous introspection is particularly informative about informants' global approach to a task, the levels of decision making they operate on, and the considerations that govern their decisions.

Specific aspects of task performance can be elucidated through direct questioning during or after the activity. Cohen & Aphek (1981) intervened with prepared questionnaires during ongoing foreign language lessons in order to capture how students take in the teacher's vocabulary explanations and grammatical rule formulations. Rattunde (1978), observing learners solving written foreign language tasks, intervened whenever an error was produced by asking the learners to identify the error source. The elicited information helped classify errors which, on the product level, were ambiguous between intra- and interlingual. Cohen & Robbins (1976), too, used an introspective technique for the purpose of error analysis: in a retrospective interview they asked their informants to identify and explain the errors they had produced in a previously written task. In this volume, probing for specific aspects can be illustrated by a number of studies focusing on problems in lexical comprehension and production (Haastrup; Poulisse, Bongaerts & Kellerman; Zimmermann & Schneider), and by the pause protocols elicited by Cavalcanti as indicators of problems in reading comprehension.

2. +/− related to concrete action

This distinction captures whether or not the cognitive information reported on via introspection is, or has been, related to a specific action. Most of the studies referred to in this overview, just as in the following chapters of this book, belong to the first category. Reports on cognitive states that are not action-related can be illustrated by metalinguistic judgement tests, probing for informants' declarative knowledge (cf. Chaudron, 1983, for an overview). Procedural knowledge without relationship to a specific action is in focus when learners report about general tendencies in their communication and learning behaviour (e.g. "I usually look up words I don't know", "I participate in conversation as much as possible", etc.). On the basis of such generalized self-reports, profiles of "the good language learner" have been established (e.g. Naiman, Fröhlich, Stern & Todesco, 1978; Rubin, 1981; Politzer, 1983; Gillette, this volume, Chapter 14).

3. Temporal relationship to action

When action-directing cognition is the object of an introspective report, the temporal distance between action and verbalization ("recency effect", Cohen, 1984 and this volume, Chapter 4) is decisive for the validity of the data. It can be viewed as an open continuum, at one pole of which the verbalization coincides with the cognitive activity, the distance between them increasing towards the other pole. In order to characterize introspective data along this dimension, it seems sufficient to distinguish three points on the continuum: (1) simultaneous; (2) immediately consecutive; and (3) delayed consecutive introspection. *Simultaneous introspection*, (1), in terms of concurrent talking or thinking aloud or verbalization of specific cognitions, presupposes that the modality of language use is not itself oral-productive. It thus lends itself to investigating listening and reading comprehension, writing, translation and written test-taking (see 1c above), but not speech production. (2) and (3) are also referred to as immediate and delayed retrospection, respectively. They can be applied to all types of language use. With *immediate retrospection*, (2), traces of the original cognition are still present in short term memory. Therefore, this procedure seems to be particularly suitable for studying aspects of speech production attended to under task completion, such as the use of communication strategies. *Delayed retrospection*, (3), can be exemplified by diary studies, documenting learners' experiences with L2 acquisition over some period of time (e.g. Bailey & Ochsner, 1983; Grandcolas & Soulé-Susbielles, 1986), and Börsch's (1982, 1986b) group discussions about learners' emotionally relevant experiences with L2.

4. +/− informant training

The bulk of the introspective SL investigations available today were carried out without previous training of the informants. In particular in the two types of retrospection, where cognition and verbalization are temporally separated, informants appear to be able to produce introspective reports without any special training. In the case of simultaneous introspection, however, it can prove necessary to accustom informants to verbalize while carrying out the task. Thus in Færch & Kasper's (1986b) study of IL knowledge by means of a translation task and concurrent thinking aloud, a practice phase preceded the data collection: first, the informant was shown a video recording demonstrating thinking aloud while translating, followed by the informant practising this procedure on a different text. Similar warming-up procedures are used by Cavalcanti, Chapter 12, Grotjahn, Chapter 3, and Feldmann & Stemmer, Chapter 13 (all in this volume). Even though Ericsson & Simon (1984: 82f and this volume, Chapter 2) claim that informant training has no effect apart from increasing the completeness of the verbalization, we feel that it should be further examined as to possible effects on *L2 learners'* introspective reports, and, in any case, be taken into account in the interpretation of the data.

5. Elicitation procedure

The diverse elicitation procedures that have been used in order to collect introspective data in SL research can be classified according to the following criteria.

5a Degree of structure

By degree of structure imposed by the data collection instrument, we refer to the extent to which it predetermines the content of the verbalization. The most highly structured instruments are rating scales and multiple choice questionnaires, determining not only the wider area, but also the concrete content of possible answers. Questionnaires with closed questions in a multiple choice format were used by Politzer (1983) in his study of learning strategies, while Zydatiss (1976) elicited learner judgements on the "expanded form" of the verb in English by means of closed and open questions as well as rating scales. These highly structured instruments are also the favoured measures of affective and social aspects of L2 learning (see 1a above). The least structured instruments are those which leave it to the informants to decide what, how much, when and how they provide introspective reports, as is the case with diary studies (Bailey & Ochsner, 1983; Grandcolas & Soulé-Susbielles, 1986) or in unelicited metalinguistic/metacommunicative learner statements, such as the learner questions about aspects of the foreign language analysed by Raabe (1982, 1986). Also located at the low end of the scale of structuredness is continuous thinking aloud, as this procedure requires that informants verbalize everything they are thinking of, without any predetermination of content or form of the introspective report (cf. 1d for studies using continuous thinking aloud). Interposed between the two poles are instruments eliciting reports on specific cognitive or affective processes, such as the retrospective interview (e.g. Mogensen, 1984; Poulisse, Bongaerts & Kellerman, this volume, Chapter 11), group discussions (Börsch, 1982, 1986b), pair discussions (Haastrup, 1985, this volume, Chapter 10; see also 5e below) and questionnaires with open questions (Cohen & Aphek, 1981): with these procedures, the object of the verbalization is restricted by the researcher's instruction or questions, whereas the specific content and form of the report is at the informants' discretion.

5b +/− Recall support

In the case of retrospection, reactivating cognitive (and/or affective) processes can be facilitated by confronting informants once again with the task situation, e.g. by means of an audio or video recording (cf. for the use of audio-tapes, Glahn, 1980; for the use of video-tapes, Mogensen, 1984; Poulisse, Bongaerts & Kellerman, this volume, Chapter 11). Zimmermann & Schneider (this volume, Chapter 9) support their informants' verbalization by again presenting to them the original "stimulus", the source text for their translation task. Such confrontations provide reactivate traces in short term memory and counteract informants' tendency to conflate different events or confound them in retrospect (but see Ericsson & Simon, this volume, Chapter 2, for some caveats).

5c Self-initiated v. other-initiated

By self-initiated introspection we refer to the informant herself or himself taking the initiative to verbalize—apart from global instructions by the researcher, such as to keep a diary or to report continuously or on specific cognitive aspects during task performance. The introspection is other-initiated if the informant verbalizes only when explicitly requested to do so by the experimenter during or after the task. All of the previously mentioned studies using continuous thinking aloud are based on self-initiated verbal reports. The purest example of self-initiated introspection is the learners' questions analysed in Raabe (1982, 1986), as they are not even preceded by a global instruction to verbalize. Other-initiated verbalization can be exemplified by Cohen & Aphek's (1981) and Rattunde's (1978) immediately consecutive interventions. A combination of self- and other-initiated retrospection is employed by Mogensen (1984): she leaves it to her informants to identify production problems in their (videotaped) performance and to reconstruct their cognitive processes, taking initiative only when the informants remain passive.

5d +/− Interaction between informant and experimenter/between informants

As is well known from empirical research in the social sciences, the interaction between informant and experimenter and, if relevant, between informants has considerable impact on the data (cf. Dreher & Dreher, 1982; Ulich, 1982; Weidle & Wagner, 1982). This is the case even if the verbalization occurs as a "monologue", without any immediate feedback, for instance with diaries written for research purposes, continuous thinking aloud and responding to questionnaires in the absence of the experimenter. In direct interaction with the experimenter, however, e.g. in the retrospective interview, this effect will be much stronger (cf. the extensive discussions in Mann, 1982 and Mogensen, 1984). As Haastrup (1985, this volume, Chapter 10) has demonstrated in her analysis of pair discussions, it is particularly difficult to interpret this type of introspective data from an interactional point of view, as both the interaction between the informants and their relation to the experimenter have to be taken into account. Likewise, Börsch (1982) emphasizes the effects of the socio-psychological dynamics of group discussions on the participants' self-reports.

5e +/− Integration with action

With very few exceptions, the levels of action and cognition on the one hand and introspection on the other, are clearly separated in the literature under discussion. We are aware of two studies, however, where action and verbalization are inseparably integrated: Raabe's (1982, 1986) research on learner questions in foreign language teaching and Haastrup's (1985) pair discussions of lexical comprehension problems. These integrated methods exhibit a high degree of authenticity; at the same time they require analysing the data within the action context.

5f +/− Interference with action

This criterion is meant to help assess whether, and to what extent, the verbalization has an influence on the task performance. Such an effect is ruled out if the introspection takes place consecutively to the action and has not been previously announced to the informant, e.g. in Mogensen (1984) or Poulisse, Bongaerts & Kellerman (this volume, Chapter 11). According to Ericsson & Simon (1984, this volume, Chapter 2), simultaneous thinking aloud has no impact on the task performance either, if the attended information is already verbally encoded. Yet we are somewhat sceptical in extending this hypothesis to IL tasks and their current introspection: in order to carry out the task informants frequently activate both their IL and their L1/L3 knowledge, the verbalization being conducted in L1. Whether or not this recoding has an impact on the way the task is carried out remains an issue for future research. Direct effects of the verbalization can be expected if the elicited report interferes with the action, as in Rattunde's (1978) intervention into the learners' writing process on the occurrence of errors, and Cohen & Aphek's (1981) intervention with questionnaires into the ongoing teaching process.

6. +/− Combination of methods

As has frequently been pointed out, e.g. by Deffner (1984), the validity of an investigation based on an introspective method can be considerably enhanced if it is supplied by data resulting from a different elicitation procedure. (Incidentally, we believe that this precaution measure should be applied to "objective" data collection instruments as well— but arguing this point further is beyond the scope of this paper.) In SL studies, the most common combination of methods is the use of performance data and a concurrent or consecutive report, such as the product of a translation task and simultaneous verbalization (cf. the work on translation referred to in 1c), or oral production (e.g. conversational) data and retrospective interview, as in the studies on communication strategies mentioned in 1c, *passim*. Different introspective methods have been combined in the investigations of affective aspects, Börsch (1982) using a questionnaire and group discussions, Gillette (this volume, Chapter 14) supplementing questionnaire data with open interviews and informal observation. Simultaneous thinking aloud followed by retrospective interviews is employed in Haastrup's study of lexical inferencing (1985, this volume, Chapter 10), Cavalcanti's research on reading (this volume, Chapter 12) and the investigations of test-taking referred to in 1c. In the latter case, the data base consists of three sources, viz. performance data (the completed test) and the two types of introspective reports.

A combination of methods seems to be needed if we wish to substantially improve our understanding of learners' declarative knowledge, their communication and learning processes and of the affective and social aspects that interact with the cognitive dimension. Furthermore, such approaches will enable us to assess the validity of different data gathering procedures and eventually lead to more appropriate choices of data collection instruments for specific SL investigations.

Notes to Chapter 1

1. We are aware of the conceptual difference between the classical introspective method of self-observation, as practised in Wundt's laboratory, and the verbalization of thought processes as performed in current studies (cf. Ericsson & Simon, 1984: 48ff). Our preference for 'introspection' has simply to do with the fact that in SL research, performing a task is itself a linguistic activity, producing 'verbal (performance) data'.
2. The original version of the proposed classification was presented at the symposium on "Sprachlehrforschung und Psychologie", Hamburg, July 1982 (see Færch & Kasper, 1987).

References

BAILEY, K. M. & OCHSNER, R. 1983, A methodological review of the diary studies: Windmill tilting or social science? In K. M. BAILEY, M. H. LONG & S. PECK (eds), *Second Language Acquisition Studies*. Rowley, Mass.: Newbury House, 188–98.
BIALYSTOK, E. 1981, The role of linguistic knowledge in second language use. *Studies in Second Language Acquisition*, 4, 31–45.
BÖRSCH, S. 1982, *Fremdsprachenstudium — Frauenstudium?* Tübingen: Stauffenberg.
— 1986a, Introspective methods in research on interlingual and intercultural communication. In HOUSE & BLUM-KULKA (1986) 195–209.
— 1986b, Some thoughts about the emotional dimension in foreign language learning. In KASPER (1986) 71–81.
— (ed.) 1987, *Die Rolle der Psychologie in der Sprachlehrforschung*. Tübingen: Narr.
BURT, M. K. & DULAY, H. C. 1980, On acquisition orders. In S. W. FELIX (ed.), *Second Language Development*. Tübingen: Narr, 265–327.
CHAUDRON, C. 1983, Research on metalinguistic judgements: A review of theory, methods, and results, *Language Learning* 33, 343–77.
COHEN, A. 1984, Studying second-language learning strategies: How do we get the information?, *Applied Linguistics* 5, 101–12.
COHEN, A. & APHEK, E. 1981, Easifying second language learning, *Studies in Second Language Acquisition*, 3, 221–36.
COHEN, A. & HOSENFELD, C. 1981, Some uses of mentalistic data in second language research, *Language Learning*, 26, 45–66.
COHEN, A. & ROBBINS, M. 1976, Toward assessing interlanguage performance: The relationship between selected errors, learners' characteristics, and learners' explanations, *Language Learning*, 26, 45–66.
CORDER, S. P. 1978, Language-learner language. In J. C. RICHARDS (ed.), *Understanding Second and Foreign Language Learning*. Rowley, Mass.: Newbury House, 71–93.

DECHERT, H. W. & RAUPACH, M. (eds) 1980, *Temporal Variables in Speech*. The Hague: Mouton.
DECHERT, H. W., MÖHLE, D. & RAUPACH, M. (eds) 1984, *Second Language Productions*. Tübingen: Narr.
DEFFNER, G. 1984, *Lautes Denken—Untersuchung zur Qualität eines Datenerhebungsverfahrens*. Frankfurt: Lang.
DREHER, M. & DREHER, E. 1982, *Gruppendiskussion*. In HUBER & MANDL (1982), 141–64.
DULAY, H. C. & BURT, M. K. 1974, You can't learn without goofing. In RICHARDS (1974), 95–123.
ECKMAN, F. 1985, Some theoretical and pedagogical implications of the markedness differential hypothesis, *Studies in Second Language Acquisition*, 7, 289–307.
ELY, C. M. 1986, An analysis of discomfort, risk-taking, sociability, and motivation in the L2 classroom, *Language Learning*, 36, 1–25.
ERICSSON, K. A. & SIMON, H. A. 1980, Verbal reports as data, *Psychological Review*, 87, 215–51.
— 1984, *Protocol Analysis*. Cambridge, Mass.: MIT Press.
FROMKIN, V. A. (ed.), 1973, *Speech Errors as Linguistic Evidence*. The Hague: Mouton.
FÆRCH, C. & KASPER, G. 1985, Procedural knowledge as a component of foreign language learners' communicative competence. In H. BOLTE & W. HERRLITZ (eds), *Kommunikation im Sprachunterricht*. Utrecht: Rijksuniversiteit, 169–99.
— 1986a, Cognitive dimensions of language transfer. In E. KELLERMAN & M. SHARWOOD SMITH (eds), *Cross-Linguistic Influence in Second Language Acquisition*. Oxford: Pergamon, 49–65.
— 1986b, One learner—two languages. In HOUSE & BLUM-KULKA (1986), 211–27.
— 1986c, The role of comprehension in foreign language learning. *Applied Linguistics*, 7, 257–74.
— 1987, Introspektive Methoden in der Lernersprachenanalyse. In S. BÖRSCH. (1987), 269–303.
GASS, S. M. forthcoming, An integrative model of second language acquisition.
GERLOFF, P. 1986, Second language learners' reports on the interpretive process: Talk-aloud protocols of translation. In HOUSE & BLUM-KULKA (1986), 243–62.
GOLDMAN-EISLER, F. 1968, *Psycholinguistics. Experiments in Spontaneous Speech*. London: Academic.
GLAHN, E. 1980, Introspection as a method of elicitation in interlanguage studies. *Interlanguage Studies Bulletin Utrecht*, 5, 119–28.
GRANDCOLAS, B. & SOULÉ-SUSBIELLES, N. 1986, L'analyse de la classe de langue étrangère, *Studies in Second Language Acquisition*, 8, 293–308.
GROTJAHN, R. & STEMMER, B. 1985, On the development and evaluation of a C-test for French, *Fremdsprachen und Hochschule. AKS Rundbrief*, 13/14, 101–20.
HAASTRUP, K. 1985, Lexical inferencing—a study of procedures in reception, *Scandinavian Working Papers on Bilingualism*, 5, 63–86.
HOSENFELD, C. 1977, A preliminary investigation of the reading strategies of successful and non-successful second language learners, *System* 5, 110–23.
HOUSE, J. & BLUM-KULKA, S. (eds) 1986, *Interlingual and Intercultural Communication*. Tübingen: Narr.

HUBER, G. L. & MANDL, H. (eds) 1982, *Verbale Daten.* Weinheim and Basel: Beltz.

HYLTENSTAM, K. 1977, Implicational patterns in interlanguage syntax variation, *Language Learning,* 27, 383–411.

JAMES, C. 1980, *Contrastive Analysis.* London: Longman.

JAMES, W. 1890, *The Principles of Psychology.* New York: Holt.

JORDENS, P. 1977, Rules, grammatical intuitions and strategies in foreign language learning, *Interlanguage Studies Bulletin Utrecht,* 2, 5–76.

KASPER, G. (ed.) 1986, *Learning, Teaching and Communication in the Foreign Language Classroom.* Aarhus: University Press.

KELLERMAN, E. 1977, Towards a characterization of the strategy of transfer in second language learning, *Interlanguage Studies Bulletin Utrecht,* 2, 58–145.

KRINGS, H. 1986a, Translation problems and translation strategies of advanced German learners of French (L2). In HOUSE & BLUM-KULKA (1986), 263–76.

— 1986b, *Was in den Köpfen von Übersetzern vorgeht.* Tübingen: Narr.

LIGHTBOWN, P. M. & BARKMAN, B. 1978, *Interactions among learners, teachers, texts, and methods of English as a second language. Progress Report 1977–78.* Montreal: TESL Centre, Concordia University.

LÖRSCHER, W. 1986, Linguistic aspects of translation processes: towards an analysis of translation performance. In HOUSE & BLUM-KULKA (1986), 277–92.

MANN, S. 1982, Verbal reports as data: A focus on retrospection. In S. DINGWALL, S. MANN & F. KATAMBA (eds), *Methods and Problems in Doing Applied Linguistic Research.* Lancaster: Department of Linguistics and Modern English Language, University of Lancaster, 87–104.

MOGENSEN, L. 1984, Transfer af kulturspecifikke begreber. Unpublished MA thesis, University of Aarhus.

NAIMAN, N., FRÖHLICH, M., STERN, H. H. & TEDESCO, A. 1978, *The Good Language Learner.* Toronto: Ontario Institute for Studies in Education.

NEMSER, W. 1971, Approximate systems of foreign language learners. *IRAL 9,* 115–23.

OLLER, J. W. JR. 1981, Research on the measurement of affective variables: some remaining questions. In R. W. ANDERSEN (ed.), *New Dimensions in Second Language Acquisition Research.* Rowley, Mass.: Newbury House, 14–27.

POLITZER, R. L. 1983, An exploratory study of self-reported language learning behaviours and their relation to achievement. *Studies in Second Language Acquisition 6,* 54–68.

RAABE, H. 1982, "Ist ne … pas denn keine doppelte Verneinung?" Die Analyse von Fragereaktionen in ihrer Bedeutung für die Vermittlung von Fremdsprachen. In C. GNUTZMANN & D. STARK (eds), *Grammatikunterricht.* Tübingen: Narr, 61–100.

RAABE, H. 1986, The influence of L1 and L3 in the foreign language classroom: An analysis of learners' questions in foreign language teaching. In KASPER (1986), 59–69.

RATTUNDE, E. 1978, Problèmes d'analyse de fautes: interprétation plausible v. interprétation autorisée. Paper read at the 5th AILA World Congress, Montreal, August 1978.

RICHARDS, J. C. (ed.) 1974, *Error Analysis.* London: Longman.

RUBIN, J. 1981, The study of cognitive processes in second language learning. *Applied Linguistics 2,* 117–31.

SELIGER, H. W. 1983, The language learner as a linguist: Of metaphors and realities. *Applied Linguistics* 4, 179–91.

SELINKER, L. 1972, Interlanguage. *IRAL* 10, 209–31.

SELINKER, L. & GASS, S. M. 1984, *Workbook in Second Language Acquisition*. Rowley, Mass.: Newbury House.

SOLMECKE, G. & BOOSCH, A. 1981, *Affektive Komponenten der Lernerpersönlichkeit und Fremdsprachenerwerb*. Tübingen: Narr.

SVARTVIK, J. V. (ed.) 1973, *Errata*. Lund: Gleerup.

SWAIN, M. 1985, Communicative competence: some roles of comprehensible input and comprehensible output in its development. In S. M. GASS & C. G. MADDEN (eds), *Input in Second Language Acquisition*. Rowley, Mass.: Newbury House, 235–53.

TARONE, E., COHEN, A. & DUMAS, G. 1976, A closer look at some interlanguage terminology: a framework for communication strategies. *Working Papers in Bilingualism* 9, 76–90.

ULICH, D. 1982, Interaktionsbedingungen von Verbalisation. In HUBER & MANDL (1982), 43–60.

WEIDLE, R. & WAGNER, A. C. 1982, Die Methode des Lauten Denkens. In HUBER & MANDL (1982), 81–103.

WODE, H. 1984, *Papers on Language Acquisition, Language Learning and Language Teaching*. Heidelberg: Groos.

ZYDATISS, W. 1976, *Tempus und Aspekt im Englischunterricht*. Kronberg/Ts.: Scriptor.

2 Verbal Reports on Thinking

K. ANDERS ERICSSON AND HERBERT A. SIMON

Introduction

After a long period of studying human performance and abilities, research in psychology is now seeking to understand the underlying cognitive processes. Researchers are looking for observations on thinking that would allow tracing the intermediate steps of the thought processes. Subjects' verbal reports on their thinking would appear to be a major source of information about detailed steps of thought processes. However, investigators have been reluctant to rely on such reports on thinking for historical reasons. After an early period in which psychologists made heavy use of verbal reports (introspection), they fell into disrepute during the era of behaviourism; but they have been revived since the 1970s as a major source of data for cognitive research.

In the course of this history, verbal reports have been used for widely varying purposes and have been gathered and interpreted according to quite different methodologies. In the earlier period, they were a mainstay of classical introspection (Titchener, 1912), the analysis of problem solving by Würzburg and Gestalt psychologists (Duncker, 1945; Selz, 1913, 1922; Wertheimer, 1945), clinical analyses of thought (Freud, 1914), and analyses of the development of children's thinking (Inhelder & Piaget, 1958). In the recent resurgence of their use (Newell, Shaw & Simon, 1958; Newell & Simon, 1972), they have been employed within an information-processing framework, chiefly in the study of problem solving.

With the growing use of verbal reports in psychology, it has become important to improve the methodology for collecting and interpreting verbal reports and to provide protocol analysis with a firm theoretical foundation. The early investigators uncritically regarded the verbal reports by trained subjects of their cognitive processes as immediate and direct observations of those processes, veridical and uncontroversial. Given the assumed immediacy of the observations, investigators asked subjects to report specific types of information without any regard for how cognitive processes generating such reports were feasible. When, as a result of these deficiencies, verbal reports collected in different laboratories were found to be mutually inconsistent, opponents of the introspective method, like Watson, argued that the method was unscientific and should be discarded.

The goal of this chapter is to outline a framework for studying thinking that is consistent with the current experimental methodology. Within this framework, verbal reports of subjects are seen as one of many types of observations that provide data on subjects' cognitive processes. This chapter will show how the information processing theory of human cognition can guide us in selecting tasks, recording observations and interpreting verbal reports as evidence or data on underlying cognitive processes. Let us first briefly describe the theory and our theoretical framework.

Theoretical Framework

The most general and weakest hypothesis we require is that human cognition is information processing: that a cognitive process can be seen as a sequence of internal states successively transformed by a series of information processes. An important, and more specific, assumption is that information is stored in several memories having different capacities and accessing characteristics: several sensory stores of very short duration, a short-term memory (STM) with limited capacity and/or intermediate duration, and a long-term memory (LTM) with very large capacity and relatively permanent storage, but with relatively slow fixation and access times compared with the other memories.

Within the framework of this information processing model, it is assumed that information recently acquired (attended to or heeded) by the central processor is kept in STM, and is directly accessible for further processing (e.g. for producing verbal reports), whereas information from LTM must first be retrieved (transferred to STM) before it can be reported.

Subjects' thought processes can therefore be described as a sequence of states of heeded information. A subset of this heeded information is stored in LTM and is retrievable after the thought processes are completed at the end of a task. It is important to note that any observable behaviour used as data for a thought process requires an explicit account of its relation to the states of the thought processes and any mediating additional cognitive processes.

Within the framework of information processing an account of thought processes used in tasks involves a model, often specified in the form of a computer program, which can take the tasks as input and generate the corresponding answers as responses. From an analysis of the relevant tasks (task analysis) it is often possible to enumerate a wide range of *a priori* acceptable models that generate desired answers as a result of sequences of processing steps. From the acceptable models, the best model is selected by collecting additional observations on the thought processes, like reaction times, eye movements, verbal reports, etc. The best model is the one that can *regenerate* these additional observations in addition to the desired answers. In the following section we will demonstrate how this framework of regeneration allows us to treat verbal report observations in the same way as more traditional data. The concept of regeneration of observations provides an important criterion for judging how informative the observations are. The amount of information associated with obser- vations is related to their ability to discriminate between many *a priori* acceptable models. A more detailed description of information-processing theory is given by Newell & Simon (1972).

Let us now discuss the implications of our theoretical framework for the study of thought processes. The first set of issues concerns how tasks should be selected to best allow us to study thinking. We will show how tasks can be selected to assure thinking and how a task analysis provides *a priori* expectations regarding the possible thought processes available for generating the answer to the task. The second set of issues concerns how observations relevant to the thought processes should be collected in order to provide valid evidence about the thought processes. This presentation follows a more extensive discussion by Ericsson & Oliver (in press).

Selection of Tasks

Let us first look at the earliest studies of thinking and, using the concept of regeneration, critically evaluate some of the tasks used. Con- siderable research was done on the free-association task, in which subjects are instructed to say the first word that comes to mind after hearing or seeing a particular word like "needle" or "father" (Jung, 1910). This task was thought to involve a single associative step (from the stimulus word to the response word) and hence correspond to the simplest form of thinking that could be studied using introspective reports. Other tasks were designed by Karl Bühler (1951) to get at processes of comprehension by having subjects respond as quickly as possible if they did or did not understand sentences, such as: "We depreciate everything that can be explained". Other types of question testing general knowledge were also used, such as: "Do you know where our other stop-watch is now?".

When one attempts to propose a model for the thought processes involved in free-association and sentence comprehension, it becomes clear how uninformative such responses are in the regeneration sense. In both cases one could conceive of models in which the response was selected prior to the presentation of the task or by some task-irrelevant procedure. Any response in the free-association task is acceptable even though it may be unusual. The early investigators used this methodology because they felt they could trust their subjects to follow the instructions. However, a methodology can be devised where subjects need not be trusted by making their responses to a task more informative.

More modern methodology avoids these problems by determining *a priori* what is the correct answer. For example, the question, "Is Stockholm the capital of Sweden?", has only one correct answer, i.e. "yes". However, in all tasks that require choosing among a few alternative answers, the possibility exists that subjects might simply guess and hence give correct answers by chance. If the two possible responses are "yes" and "no", correct answers would be obtained about half of the time purely by chance. In studies of thinking it is not uncommon that only correct responses are analysed and the data from subjects with high error rates (more than 10–20%) are completely discarded. A different approach is to request a more informative answer or response: for the instruction "Name the capital of Sweden", the correct answer "Stockholm" would be unlikely to occur as a result of guessing.

Recent studies of thinking have primarily used tasks in logic (Guyotte & Sternberg, 1981; Johnson-Laird & Steedman, 1978), mathematics (Ginsberg, 1983), probability (Estes, 1976), and so on, where a given task has a single correct answer. Using tasks in a formalized domain has many advantages. It is easy to generate a large number of different problems among which only the surface elements differ. In addition, the investigator can make a careful analysis of the task, which may suggest what kinds of theory may be reasonable before observations of people performing the task are gathered.

Analysis of Tasks and Strategies

For those tasks for which we know the correct answers or responses, we also know a fair amount about the procedures, methods and knowledge available for producing the answers. A systematic analysis of such information for a certain task or domain of tasks is called a task analysis with a specification of possible strategies.

It is important to realize that a task analysis should be made prior to the collection and analysis of observations. Although the term task analysis is relatively new, experimental psychologists have always been concerned with how subjects generate their responses. The emphasis was on eliminating the possibility that the subject may rely on information that is not associated with the experimental variables. A well-known example is the use of nonsense syllables, like *qub* or *teg*, in memory experiments to eliminate the possibility that subjects could rely on previous knowledge when committing the syllables to memory (Ebbinghaus, 1885). As it turned out, subjects actually do draw on their knowledge of words and common spelling patterns when they memorize this material (Montague, 1972). Thus, empirical evidence showed that the initial task analysis was inadequate in that subjects used information not considered in advance to be important. This example shows that task analyses are always provisional and should be modified in the light of new findings.

It is particularly important to explicate the knowledge necessary to generate successful solutions when we study tasks that cannot be easily performed with simple strategies, like guessing. In such task domains as mathematics, logic, statistics, etc. clearly defined procedures exist for generating correct solutions. These procedures can be described as a sequence of steps, which in turn can be described with flow charts or even computer programs.

Tasks like translation of a particular sentence to a different language can be subjected to a similar task analysis, although the number of different acceptable translations will complicate the analysis. If one can assume that the sentence is translated in strict left-to-right order, the analysis will be considerably simplified. Of particular interest is the availability of linguistic rules as opposed to exceptions and idiomatic constructions. A description of the similarity of the two languages with respect to particular grammatical rules and specific lexical items is likely to be of major importance for assessing plausible cognitive representations and processes. Words with multiple lexical meanings are also likely to be particularly revealing with respect to the translation processes.

An *a priori* analysis of the possible thought sequences generating an answer to a task is essential. Such a task analysis often reveals that an answer can be generated by several alternative processing sequences. In many cases slight changes in the task or the specific problem can dramatically reduce the number of alternative accounts and provide more informative observations. The task analysis has another important function. It specifies a number of sequences of processing steps with specifications of the information processed at each step. These sequential accounts of possible thought processes are necessary for analysing a wide range of observations of behaviour observed during the thought processes, like sequences of eye-fixations and "think-aloud" reports.

Selecting Types of Observations to be Recorded

Once a task is selected for study, we may ask what observations can be recorded to provide information on the cognitive processes used in that task. The central issue is how these observations reflect underlying cognitive processes. Within the framework of information processing theory we can interpret a wide range of observations as providing information about the order and duration of processing steps. Figure 1 illustrates schematically the temporal sequence of thought processes in generating a solution to a task.

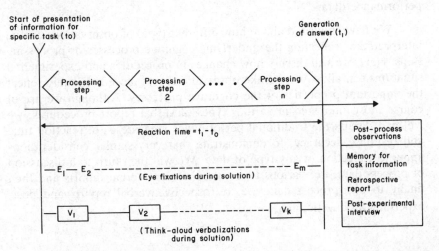

FIGURE 1. *Overview of different types of observations that are potentially available for a thinking process for a given task* (From Ericsson & Oliver, in press).

The reaction time, which is the duration measured from the presentation of the problem to the production of the answer, will then consist of the sum of the durations of individual processing steps. If the generated answer is correct, it is likely that one of the sequences of processes specified by our task analysis was used. If the generated answer is incorrect, the subject either lacked some crucial knowledge or made an error in executing one or more of the processing steps. We will call observations that bear on the total performance of a task, i.e. reaction time and accuracy of the response, *performance observations*.

There are also several types of observations that give information about the individual processing steps, such as spontaneous verbalizations and eye-movement sequences during the solution of the task. By instructing subjects to think aloud, i.e. verbalize their thoughts, during the solution of the task, one can get a sequence of verbalizations corresponding to the sequence of generated thoughts. We will call this type of observation *process observations*.

In addition, we can collect data after a task is completed, such as memory for thought-processes during the task, memory for presented information, and recollections of the strategies used. We will call this final type of observation *post-process observations*. Investigators have traditionally been reluctant to collect process data and post-process observations since they were concerned that procedures used to collect such data might change the subject's thought processes and, indirectly, the performance data.

We have indicated above how different types of observations can be interpreted as reflecting the underlying cognitive processes or processing steps. Next, we will discuss how changes in procedures and experimental situations can allow us to make observations that more accurately reflect the important properties of the cognitive processes. Although we are of course most interested in various types of verbal report procedures, we will first discuss the traditional performance measures, i.e. reaction time and response accuracy, to demonstrate that very similar considerations apply to collection of any type of data. We will then turn to a discussion of process data, i.e. various types of concurrent verbal reports and then finally to post-process data, i.e. retrospective verbal reports and post-experimental questioning.

Performance Observations

It is important to realize that, in a normal context, reaction times can be recorded relatively unobtrusively. But in most studies measuring reaction time as an indicator of underlying processes, several additional steps are taken to obtain a pure estimate of the necessary cognitive processes for that type of task.

It is easy to imagine a subject having a longer reaction time than necessary due to lapses of attention or additional checking on the correctness of a generated answer. In that case, the observed reaction time will not be a pure estimate of the durations of necessary processing steps but will reflect the durations of these extraneous cognitive activities as well. Hence, in studies measuring reaction time, subjects are usually instructed to respond as rapidly as possible without being inaccurate. Under these conditions experimenters should obtain a reasonably accurate reaction time of the necessary processing steps with any extraneous processing eliminated, or at least reduced.

The correct answers for some types of tasks can be generated by quite different methods and strategies. In most research using reaction-time measures, subjects are given some initial practice (warm-up) on the types of tasks used in the experiment. It is often assumed that the subjects use this warm-up time to come up with the strategy that is most efficient for them. Practice also gives them a chance to decide how careful they must be in order to be both accurate and fast. It is assumed that reaction times at the end of the warm-up phase give reasonably consistent estimates of the time necessary to perform particular sequences of cognitive processes.

The responses in the form of answers given by subjects can also be viewed as summary observations of sequences of cognitive processes in a given task. From a correct answer we can infer correct processing of all of the individual steps, and from an error we can infer incorrect processing of at least one of those steps. These inferences apply to an entire sequence of steps and leave unspecified what might be going on during the individual steps. We will now discuss observations on elements or individual steps of these processing sequences.

Concurrent Verbal Reports

A wide range of procedures may be used to elicit verbal reports on ongoing cognitive processes. We will first outline some theoretical considerations on various characteristics of such procedures and then discuss how some of the desirable procedures can and have been implemented. We will then discuss a broader range of concurrent verbal report procedures with reference to the recommended procedures.

Theoretical considerations

According to our information processing model described earlier, we can define a cognitive process as a sequence of states in which each state corresponds to information (thoughts) in attention and STM, i.e. heeded information (thoughts). To obtain verbal reports, as new information (thoughts) enters attention, the subjects should verbalize the corresponding thought or thoughts. According to this verbal report procedure the new incoming information is *maintained* in attention until the corresponding verbalization of it is completed. The crucial aspect of this procedure is that the sequence of states, i.e. the information contained in attention and STM, remains the same with the verbal report procedure as it would be without the reporting procedure, that is, when the cognitive processes proceed silently. The top panel of Figure 2 shows a normal (silent) cognitive process with its associated states of heeded information. The middle panel illustrates a "talk-aloud" report in which the subject simply vocalizes "silent speech". The bottom panel illustrates a "think-aloud" report in which subjects must convert the heeded information into a verbalizable form to vocalize it. In each of these three examples the *same* sequence of states is retained.

Before proceeding to some of the complications of our model let us illustrate the types of verbal reports observed. In Table 1 the observed verbalizations of a subject mentally multiplying 36×24 are given.

The observations in this case consist of a sequence of verbalizations each of which can be segmented on the basis of brief pauses and intonation patterns. These verbalizations are relevant to our task analysis that predicts a wide range of intermediate steps depending on the solution process. By matching these logically possible intermediate states against the verbalizations we can identify the specific solution process used for this particular task.

The verbal report procedures preserve the sequences of states, and hence the cognitive processes should not change as a result of the additional instruction to verbalize. Ericsson & Simon (1984) made an exhaustive review of studies comparing silent subjects' performance with

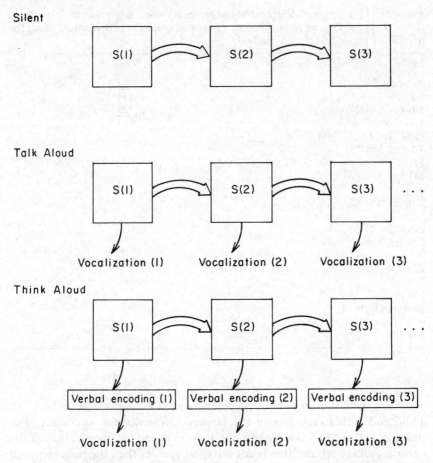

FIGURE 2. *The states of heeded information in a cognitive process and their relation to verbalizations under three different conditions.*

the performance of "talk-aloud" and "think-aloud" subjects. They found no consistent differences in the generated responses (accuracy). However, several studies indicated that subjects with "think-aloud" instructions required more time to complete their solutions. Let us therefore consider in more detail the temporal relation between thinking and verbalization.

The rate of heeding ("silent speech") has been found to be quite similar to the rate of overt speech (Landauer, 1962; Weber & Bach, 1969), and hence we can assume that overt vocalization occurs in parallel to the internal heeding without any requirement for additional time.

TABLE 1   *A transcript of a thinking-aloud protocol from a subject mentally multiplying 36 times 24.* On the right side, the same multiplication is performed using the traditional paper and pencil method.

OK	36
36 times 24	24
um	144
4 times 6 is 24	720
4	864
carry the 2	
4 times 3 is 12	
14	
144	
0	
2 times 6 is 12	
2	
carry the 1	
2 times 3 is 6	
7	
720	
720	
144 plus 72	
so it would be 4	
6	
864	

The situation is rather different for thinking aloud, where an additional verbal encoding of the heeded information is necessary. For that case we need to assume that the time required for vocalization of the corresponding verbalization is considerably greater than the time required for heeding in the silent case. The silent case is illustrated in the upper panel of Figure 3. In a recent study, Deffner & Ericsson (1985) proposed that the additional time required for full vocalization in "think-aloud" corresponded to maintained attention to the information verbalized. "Think-aloud" would then correspond to initial heeding, as in the silent case, and then maintained heeding during the verbalization, as illustrated in the lower panel of Figure 3. Hence, to produce the verbalization, the corresponding thought would have to remain heeded and subsequent states would not emerge until the verbalization was completed. An empirical test of this hypothesis could be made by estimating the actual time subjects vocalize, and then subtracting this time from their total solution time. Deffner & Ericsson (1985) found that verbalizations occurred in relatively short speech bursts, and by subtracting this vocalization time

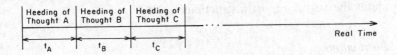

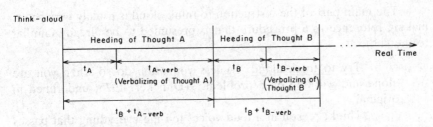

FIGURE 3. *The temporal characteristics of heeding of thoughts for silent thought and "think-aloud".*

they eliminated previously found differences in solution time between thinking-aloud subjects and silent control subjects.

If the additional time required for verbalization in thinking aloud corresponds to maintenance of attention to the information being verbalized, it means that the attention cannot be diverted without interrupting the verbalization. Thinking aloud is, therefore, not well suited to the study of cognitive processes with real-time attentional demands involving motor skills, and tasks requiring intermittent rehearsal of information. In such cases "talk-aloud" or post-process observations like retrospective reports should be preferred. A more complete discussion is given in Ericsson & Simon (1984, Chapter 5).

Methodology to elicit "talk-aloud" and "think-aloud"

The above theoretical considerations have led us to a verbal report procedure which should provide optimal information about the thought sequence with minimal interference. In this section we will discuss a methodology for eliciting such behaviour in subjects. We will first discuss the initial instruction to subjects, then we will discuss a warm-up procedure, and then, finally, something about how one should remind subjects about the verbal report instructions.

Instructions

We will begin by examining the instructions given by the two psychologists, Duncker and Claparède, who are usually credited with introducing the method of thinking aloud.

The main part of the instruction to think aloud is usually very short, making reference to a procedure that is presumed to be already familiar to the subjects.

"<u>Try to think aloud</u>. I guess you often do so when you are alone and working on a problem." (Duncker, 1926; underlined in original)

"Think, reason in a loud voice, tell me everything that passes through your head during your work searching for the solution to the problem." (Claparède, 1934)

Thus, in Duncker's instructions, although the word "think" is used, the subjects are asked just to vocalize their thoughts, which are apparently presumed to have the form of inner speech. If the presumption is correct, it is not surprising that such short instructions could elicit the desired behaviour. Verbalizing, under this assumption, would be quite simple, because of the oral code and sequential structure of the internal speech.

In Claparède's instructions, however, the subject is asked to verbalize "everything that passes through [his] head", whether encoded orally or not. In order to comply with such an instruction, the subject would in many cases have to label and encode the content of attention, thus requiring the kinds of recoding process that are postulated in think-aloud verbalization.

Although subjects appear to understand what "thinking aloud" means, they sometimes tend to fall into other forms of verbal communication with which they are more familiar. In a school situation with mathematics tasks, where the students were accustomed to explaining their solutions aloud, Krutetskii (1976) took special pains to warn his subjects against confusing the instruction to think aloud with that of explaining the solution:

"Do not try to explain anything to anyone else. Pretend there is no one here but yourself. Do not tell about the solution but solve it." (Krutetskii, 1976)

Ericsson & Simon (1984) have developed complete instructions for "thinking aloud" which have been successfully used by many investigators with occasional changes and adaptations to the particular tasks.

Warm-up

In many TA experiments, the subject is given initial warm-up problems to acquaint him with the experimental situation and accustom him to the microphones and tape recorders. Another important reason for a standardized procedure with warm-up is that we need some means to establish that all subjects are using the same verbal report procedure. Investigators using eye-movement equipment ask subjects to look at objects in different locations in the display to assure agreement between subjects' fixation points and the output of recording devices. Analogously, Ericsson & Simon (1984) recommend that subjects be asked to solve a series of standardized problems while thinking aloud. On the basis of the think-aloud reports on these problems an investigator can assess whether the subjects verbalize in a manner consistent with the instructions. If not, the subject can be reinstructed and given additional warm-up problems. Performance on such selected problems provides a means to distinguish differences in method of verbalization from differences in thought sequences, which cannot be easily separated in protocols on new problems.

Reminders

The experimenter is generally, though not always, present during TA experiments. In the earlier studies, the experimenter had to be present, since there was no other means for recording the subject's verbalizations. Although tape recorders are now used almost universally, the experimenter is still usually present, primarily to monitor the verbalizations by reminding the subject to speak, when he lapses into silence. These reminders, given after 15 second to one minute pauses (the interval being different in different studies), are generally standardized, taking the form of "keep talking" or "what are you thinking about?".

Reminders to verbalize of the "keep talking" variety should have a very small, if any, effect on the subject's processing. In fact, according to our theoretical model, subjects will invariably verbalize their thoughts when talking is initiated. However, a reminder of the type, "what are you thinking about?" is more likely to elicit a self-observation process or produce an other-oriented description as a response.

Other types of concurrent verbal reports

For "talk-aloud" and "think-aloud" reports we have attempted to identify a theoretical foundation by explicating the corresponding verbalization processes and their relation to the heeded information. In this section we will try to extend these considerations to the larger class of concurrent verbal report procedures.

In order to understand better the motivation for the other forms of concurrent report it is better to take on a more "naive" view. When concurrent verbal reports are collected it is desirable to gain as much information as possible about the subjects' cognitive processes. In addition to instructing subjects to think aloud, investigators often ask subjects to describe what they are doing physically or what they are perceiving visually. Another kind of complementary instruction is a request for *explanation*. In order to get as full an understanding as possible of the subjects' processes, they are asked to explain their thinking:

> "In order to follow your thoughts we ask you to think aloud, explaining each step as thoroughly as you can." (Smith, 1971)

These explanations allow the investigator to get an explicit description of general rules and methods used in the generation of the process. These requests for additional information may appear completely legitimate until we ask what kind of cognitive processes would be required to produce this additional information.

If the requested information would be produced with normal "think-aloud" instructions (and the associated cognitive processes) then these additional instructions would be unnecessary. However, if the instructions force subjects to report information not normally heeded, it means that the sequences of heeded states must be changed to bring the additional information into attention for subsequent verbalization. Such changes in the sequence of states are illustrated in Figure 4. The sequence of states for silent thinking is given in the upper panel, while the sequence of states associated with an instruction to verbalize additional information is shown in the lower panel. To simplify the comparison we assume that the first state of both sequences, $S(1)$, is identical. After the extra states necessary for the additional verbalization of description or explanation have been generated, it is conceivable that the subject could reinstate the original state, $S(1)$, and proceed with the next steps in the cognitive process (marked as alternative A), especially when a familiar procedure is followed. It is more likely that in tasks requiring productive thinking the state following the additional verbalizing will differ from the state encountered

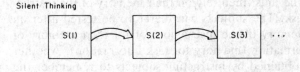

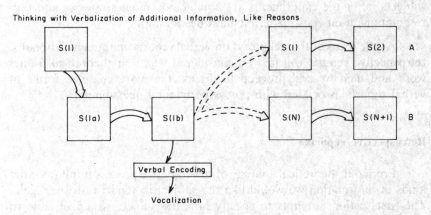

FIGURE 4. *A comparison of the states of heeded information for silent thought (upper panel) and for thinking with instruction to verbalize reasons for every step (lower panel).*

during silent thought (marked as alternative B). In a review of research comparing silent subjects' performance to the performance of subjects with a requirement to verbalize additional information (especially explanations and reasons) (Ericsson & Simon, 1984, Chapter 2), a large proportion of the studies showed reliable differences between the two groups even in accuracy and characteristics of generated solutions. A requirement to verbalize additional information leads to changes in the sequence of thoughts compared to silent control subjects.

Post-Process Observations

Once subjects have performed a task, one might think that no further information about their cognitive processes could be recorded. However, testing subjects' memory can provide three additional types of observation. In experiments on thinking, the same information may not always be continuously available to subjects. For instance, instructions may be given only once to subjects who must then rely on their memory of the instructions to perform the task. The subjects can therefore be tested after an experiment for their memory of the instructions or for their memory of other types of task information (memory for task information). Another type of observation is obtained by instructing subjects to remember the specific thoughts they had while generating the response (retrospective reports). And a final category of observations is obtained by questioning subjects, after the experiments are completed, about strategies and representations used (post-experimental questioning).

As the focus of this chapter is on verbal reports on thought processes, retrospective reports will first be considered from our theoretical framework and then we will proceed to discuss the more complex forms of verbal reports associated with post-experimental questioning.

Retrospective reports

From our theoretical analysis of the cognitive process it follows what kinds of information we would like the subject to report retrospectively. The first section attempts to specify how the subject would be able to retrieve such information, and we will also discuss briefly the recommended procedures for eliciting such reports. Finally, we will discuss the broader range of verbal report and interviewing procedures.

Theoretical considerations

Within our theoretical framework the cognitive processes are represented as sequences of states of heeded information (thoughts). Hence, even when subjects are giving verbal reports after the completion of a task or tasks, we want the subject to recall these sequences as accurately and directly as possible.

In the ideal case the retrospective report is given by the subject immediately after the task is completed, while much information is still in STM or otherwise directly accessible, and can be directly reported or used as a retrieval cue. It is clear that some additional cognitive processing is required to make certain that the particular memory structures of interest are heeded. Our model predicts that retrospective reports on the immediately preceding cognitive activity can be accessed and specified without the experimenter having to provide the subject with specific information about what to retrieve. In this particular case, the subject will have the necessary retrieval cues in STM after a general instruction is given "to report everything you can remember about your thoughts during the last problem". This form of retrospective verbal report should give us the closest approximation to the actual memory structures.

Even in this favourable case, some problems arise that are common to all kinds of verbal reports from LTM. First, the retrieval operation is fallible, in that other similar memory structures may be accessed instead of those created by the just-finished cognitive process. The probability of this occurring increases markedly if the subjects have just solved a series of similar problems. However, since most accessed memory structures contain redundant information beyond the cues used for retrieval, subjects may use this additional information to validate the retrieval as well as to increase their confidence in the veridicality of the retrieved information. In a subsequent section we will discuss this type of evaluation further and examine the relevant theoretical and empirical literature.

A second general problem when retrieving cognitive structures is to separate information that was heeded at the time of a specific episode, from information acquired previously or subsequently that is associated with it (Müller, 1911). For example, if a picture reminds one of an old friend, it may be tempting to use the stored information about that friend to *infer* what the person in the picture looked like. It may be possible to eliminate this artifact by instructing subjects only to report details that they can remember heeding at the time of the original episode (Müller, 1911). By imposing a requirement of determinable memory as a basis for reporting, we can avoid many subjects' tendency to fill in information that they can't remember but "must" have thought. It is possible to distinguish such inferred information from the remembered information by showing that such inferences would not be part of the possible sequences of thoughts. Hence, an analysis of the content and temporal characteristics of the generated retrospective reports allows us to assess that the instructions are followed, and we need not rely on simply trusting the subjects.

In analogy with the procedures for instructing subjects to "think-aloud", it appears to be essential to provide warm-up tasks which are particularly suited for retrospective reports. It is easy to monitor the instruction to report specific thoughts. The subject is instructed to think aloud during the solution of the warm-up problems; then the subject's retrospective report is compared to his think-aloud report.

From our theoretical perspective the retrospective reports will contain a sequence of heeded thoughts quite similar to that elicited with "think-aloud" instructions. When the studied cognitive process is of long duration, it is likely that many steps of the cognitive process will not be recalled at the end of the task and will be omitted from the retrospective report.

There are several methods available to reduce the level of omissions. A commonly used procedure is to break down the original task into smaller components with a retrospective report following each. For example, in studies of text comprehension, several investigators have divided the text into sentences. The subject reads the sentences one-by-one and gives a retrospective report after each. This procedure has been found to provide rich information, which allows monitoring concurrent expectations and comprehension, uncontaminated by subsequent events and information contained in the text (Olson, Mack & Duffy, 1981; Waern, 1979). Another possibility discussed in Ericsson & Simon (1984, Chapter 5) is to disrupt the cognitive processes at particular points in the solution of the task and ask for an immediate retrospective report. This last method is obviously quite intensive and should only be used on small proportions of randomly selected trials to ensure that the subject maintains normal task performance.

A rather different method attempts to increase subjects' recall by providing better retrieval cues at the time of giving retrospective reports. Asking subjects to recall thoughts of specified kinds is not recommended, unless the experimenter has previously established that thoughts of such kinds occur with all subjects. Otherwise it might bias subjects toward accepting low-confidence memories or even toward fabricating such thoughts. Furthermore, on trials following such probing, subjects might change their cognitive processes in order to effectively monitor further occurrences of such thoughts.

In the absence of a detailed description of a subject's thoughts it is hard to provide helpful and non-biasing retrieval cues. However, many investigators have collected concurrent eye-movements of subjects during the solution of tasks. Several studies (Deffner, 1984; Winikoff, 1967) have shown that concurrent verbal reports referring to perceptually available objects and information is reliably related to eye-fixations of the areas containing the corresponding information. Hence, displaying the sequence of eye-fixations recorded during the solution should provide effective cues for the subject's recall of the concurrent thoughts. Such aided recall has been used by several investigators, and retrospective verbal reports under these conditions have been found to be longer (measured by a word count) than normal retrospective reports. However, such aided recall raises an important methodological problem. Do the subjects actually recall their thoughts *or* do the subjects infer what they might have, or must have, thought given the displayed sequences of eye-fixations? We are not aware of any studies that have systematically explored this question. It would be possible to test whether subjects could reliably recognize parts of their sequences of eye-fixations from other subjects' for the same task, as well as subjects' ability to predict directly subsequent thoughts and corresponding eye-fixations. Let us now discuss other types of retrospective questioning and interviewing techniques, where the issue of memory versus inference becomes critical.

Other types of retrospective questioning and interviewing

According to our theoretical assumptions, even a complete retrospective report will only contain a sequence of states of heeded information, as is illustrated in Figure 5. Many investigators of human thought have tried to probe subjects for additional information. At the turn of the century, Titchener and other analytic introspectionists sought to describe the individual thoughts as completely as possible. Each thought should be described in terms of its smallest element, i.e. its sensory components, as is illustrated in the middle panel of Figure 5. A different type of information often sought are the relations or connections of states of heeded information. This additional information corresponds to asking why a given heeded thought emerged or why some heeded thought followed another heeded thought, as is illustrated in the lower panel of Figure 5.

Analysis of individual thoughts

The method of introspection, or observing the contents of one's mind, has been used frequently to gain information about thinking and the structure of thought. According to the theoretical assumptions of the analytic introspectionists, each thought could be described by enumerating its sensory elements. Hence, an analysis of a sequence of thoughts during a task should be made through a careful description of the elements of each thought. William James criticized such descriptions because the sensory elements were not immediately available — only the object of thought — and, hence, the sensory component could only be extracted through additional analysis. Later, this view became generally recognized, as concurrent analysis of thought into elements was found to disrupt and change the thought process (Lindworsky, 1931).

The problem of disruption was avoided by postponing the analysis of the thoughts until the cognitive processes were completed, i.e. retro-

Silent Thought

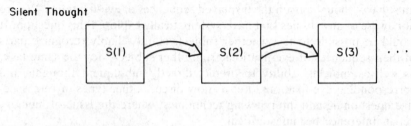

Analytic Introspection

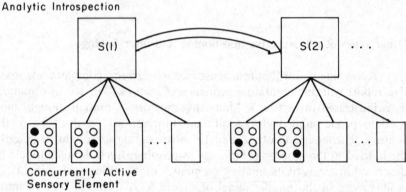

Concurrently Active
Sensory Element

Verbal Reports of Causes of Heeded Thoughts

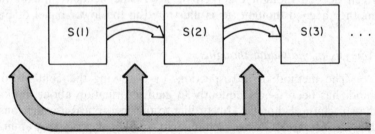

FIGURE 5. *A contrast between the information contained in a retrospective report after silent thought (upper panel) and the information requested by analytic introspection (middle panel) or by studies requesting causes or reasons for thoughts and actions (lower panel).*

spective analysis of thought. Within our framework such analysis would correspond to recall of each of the heeded thoughts, but in addition all recalled thoughts need to be processed further to extract their components, preferably their sensory elements. This subsequent analysis of a recalled thought will require additional retrievals, which may or may not yield information related to the originally heeded thought. Even long after the demise of analytic introspection, investigators have asked subjects questions about image characteristics of their thoughts, which would require a similar retrospective analysis for their answers. Although the current research on such issues is quite active, no clear account of the relationship between imagery reports and thinking/memory has emerged (Sheikh, 1983). For our present purposes the important conclusion is that the subsequently retrieved elements of a thought were not heeded initially and, therefore, not part of the information heeded originally.

Establishing reasons and causes of thoughts and actions

It has been traditional in many experiments to ask subjects *why* they did something, or why they preferred some alternatives over others. In a very important review, Nisbett & Wilson (1977) showed that subjects' reasons frequently were inaccurate in accounting for the experimental variables that actually influence their behaviour. The article raised a number of methodological issues that have been discussed in detail elsewhere (Ericsson & Simon, 1980; Nisbett & Ross, 1980; Smith & Miller, 1978; White, 1980). For our current purposes it is sufficient to note that giving a reason for one's thought or thought sequence (ideally, a cause relating to external stimuli) is quite different from reporting the thought sequence as remembered. Let us illustrate this point with an example.

When asked to generate a word starting with the letter "A" most undergraduates respond with "apple". If asked for a retrospective report they say that it simply "popped up" or "came", and are unable to report any intermediate thoughts. When asked why they thought of "apple" rather than any of thousands of words, they are quite willing to speculate, "I had an apple for lunch", "In grade school I learned 'A as in apple'", etc. One likely strategy for arriving at these inferred reasons is to use the response word, i.e. "apple", as a retrieval cue to find any pertinent episodes or associative relations to the given cue, i.e. starting with the letter "A". These generated characteristics have to be judged for plausibility and can be readily used for inferring "reasons" for other people's behaviour.

Even for cognitive processes involving several intermediate states or thoughts, similar problems exist. Subjects solving mental multiplication problems correctly are essentially unable to tell us why they did, or didn't, use a familiar short cut in a calculation procedure. In recognition of perceptually available objects, or during memory retrieval, there is considerable evidence for processes without intermediate heeded steps where the subject is only aware of the results of the processes. In sum, asking subjects to give more information than they can recall, as part of their retrospective report, is likely to lead to additional inferential processing with no obvious relation to a particular observed cognitive process.

Determining general strategies and procedures of subjects

Most investigators seek to identify the general strategies or procedures used by subjects in performing the experimental tasks. Hence, it has been a long-standing tradition in psychology to interview subjects after the experiment, where questioning cannot possibly bias the earlier recorded performance data. Subjects are often asked to describe how they solved the tasks, etc. The implicit assumption is that the subjects relied on a single strategy throughout the experiment and that they are able to recall this general strategy. However, there is considerable evidence that subjects' cognitive processes change during the experiment as a function of practice, and different cognitive processes and methods are used for problems in the same task domain. In cases of such diversity of cognitive processes, how do subjects describe their procedures? This question has not been seriously considered by investigators using post-experimental questioning.

Ericsson & Simon (1980) argued that this procedure is questionable if one wants to gain access to subjects' specific memory of their cognitive processes. After a large number of trials, subjects' memory for cognitive processes on individual tasks is quite poor due to interference from many similar solutions and the relatively long delay. Ericsson & Simon (1984) proposed that subjects might rely on their memory for a few, possibly unrepresentative, trials and attempt to abstract some general characteristics. Another possibility is that subjects would recall some of the tasks and retrieve or generate methods for solving these tasks. Regardless of the cognitive processes proposed for generating these verbal descriptions of strategies, it is clear that they would not be a veridical summary of all cognitive processes used in the experiments. Hence, the fact that some investigators have found inconsistencies between post-experimental interview data and actual performance data during the experiments is not surprising.

Summary

In analogy with our discussion of concurrent reports, we have argued for collecting retrospective reports consisting of memory for sequences of heeded thoughts. These reports constitute observations on the cognitive processes on a par with other types of data. After a comprehensive task analysis has been completed, these retrospective reports can then be encoded to supply data on the sequence of cognitive processes employed in a given solution. Analysis of reliable connections between states of heeded information and use of general strategies can be converted into empirically testable hypotheses regarding sequences of heeded information and we need not ask the subject to provide such information. It should be stressed that these other reporting instructions are not judged to be scientifically invalid. With a better understanding of the cognitive processes used to access this additional information, and of the relation between this additional information and the information heeded during the solutions, such reports should provide converging information on thinking.

Protocol Analysis

Up to this point we have been primarily concerned with task analysis and methodology for collecting verbal reports. The analysis and encoding of reports can be quite straightforward within our theoretical framework. In the most favourable case the task analysis has provided a large number of possible *unique* states with heeded information. In the encoding phase the verbal reports are segmented into verbalizations of heeded thoughts and the corresponding unique state from the task analysis is identified. However, in most actual studies using protocol analysis the mapping between verbal reports and states in the task analysis is not unambiguous and unique, due to the similarity of the heeded information in different states and lack of specificity of the verbal reports. Ericsson & Simon (1984) discuss many methods to deal with such situations. One very general method is to encode selectively a small number of unique and distinct states corresponding to alternative processing models, among which the investigator wants to determine the best one. Further discussion of such methods is not possible within the scope of this chapter. Instead, two examples of encoding and analysis of verbal reports will be presented. The first example demonstrates encoding of think-aloud protocols for a case in which the number of possible thoughts is too large and explicit enumeration is not feasible. The second discusses an analysis of cognitive processes using retrospective reports.

Think-Aloud Protocols from Anagram Problem Solving

In the anagram task, subjects are presented with a scrambled sequence of letters and asked to generate an English word using all the letters. From previous published work reporting thinking-aloud protocols collected for the anagram-solving task (Mayzner, Tresselt & Helbock, 1964; Sargent, 1940), we know that subjects heed several different kinds of information while solving these problems. Two types of information are especially prominent in protocols.

First, subjects select likely combinations of letters (sequences that occur frequently in English) and use these as constraints for generating longer strings or as probes to LTM to evoke words that contain those combinations. We encode mentions of such combinations in the protocols as C: L1–L2–...–L3 (Position), where C signifies Constraint, L1, L2, L3 are letters, and Position refers to the beginning, middle, or end part of the word.

Second, subjects generate alternative possible solution words. These can derive from attempts to sound out letter combinations or can be related words evoked from LTM. These possible solutions are encoded as A: (spelling of word or combination of syllables), where A signifies Alternative. In Table 2 we give several short protocols of subjects solving the anagram "NPEHPA". (The first two of these protocols are reproduced from Sargent, 1940.)

These protocols depend heavily upon recognition processes and evocation of information from LTM. A computer model could be programmed to produce qualitatively similar protocols, but it is impossible, in the absence of detailed knowledge of how subjects have information stored and indexed in LTM, to predict the sequence of events in any particular subjects' thinking-aloud protocol. In spite of the use of common processes, different subjects arrive at the anagram solution along different routes.

Retrospective Reports

Ericsson & Simon (1984) reviewed the relatively extensive evidence showing that subjects' retrospective verbal reports provide reliable information to predict the latencies for a variety of task domains. The validity of retrospective verbal reports extended to tasks with average latencies of less than two seconds. Systematic attempts to derive a processing model to predict the observed reaction times, on the basis of retrospective

TABLE 2   *Transcript of three thinking-aloud protocols from subjects solving the anagram 'NPEHPA'. The first two protocols were recorded by Sargent (1940). On the right side encodings of the verbalized thoughts are given. (From Ericsson & Simon, 1985.)*

Protocol 1
N–P, neph, neph
Probably PH goes together   C:PH
Phan   A:phan
Phanny   A:phanny
I get phan-ep   A:phan-ep
no. Nap-   A:nap
Phep-an, no   A:phep-an
E is at the end   C:E(end)
Phap-en   A:phap-en
People, I think of   A:people
Try PH after the other letters   C:PH(end)
Naph, no   A:naph
I thought of paper again   A:paper
E and A sound alike
couldn't go together without a conson-
ant
Try double P   C:PP
happy   A:happy
Happen   A:happen

Protocol 2
Start with P   C:P(beginning)
No, it doesn't
the two P's go together   C:PP
Happen   A:happen

Protocol 3
All right
Let's see
NPEHPA
Let's try what letters go together
Do you want to tell me when I miss,
okay
PH go together   C:PH
but they're not very likely
so how about APP   C:APP
Oh, happen   A:happen
Got it

---

reports, are much rarer. Two English investigators, Hamilton & Sanford (1978), studied subjects who made simple judgements of whether two presented letters, like "RP" or "MO", were in alphabetical order or not. In accord with previous investigators, they found that the reaction times were longer when the two presented letters occurred close together in the alphabet than when they were far apart. From the reaction time data alone, one would infer a uniform retrieval process, where factors internal to the retrieval process required more time for order decisions for letters occurring close together in the alphabet. Retrospective verbal reports, for subjects doing individual decisions, indicated two types of cognitive processes. For some of the trials, subjects reported no mediation or direct access of their order judgment. For other trials, subjects reported they ran through brief segments of the alphabet before making a decision of order. For example, when the letter-pair "MO" was presented, a subject reported retrieving "LMNO" before the subject reached the decision that the letters were in alphabetical order. In another case, a subject reported retrieving "RSTUV" before rejecting the letter-pair "RP" as not being in alphabetical order. In a subsequent analysis of the reaction times, Hamilton & Sanford (1978) found very different relations for trials with direct access, versus trials with retrieval of segments of the alphabet. For trials with retrieval, the observed reaction time was a linear function of the number of retrieved letters. The estimated rate of retrieval corresponded closely to rates obtained in studying simple recital of the alphabet. For trials with reports of direct access, no relation of reaction time to the amount of separation of the two letters was found. Hamilton & Sanford (1978) concluded that the original effect was due to a mixture of two quite different processes, and that closeness of the letters influenced the probability that recall of letters would be necessary before an order decision could be made.

Summary and Conclusions

The goal of this chapter was to analyse verbal reports on cognitive processes and explicate their relation to those processes. The information-processing theory was used as a theoretical framework for describing thinking. Within this framework, thinking can be represented as a sequence of states of heeded information (thoughts). From a task analysis it is possible to specify a number of *a priori* plausible thought sequences, which are sufficient to generate the correct answer. By collecting observations on the thought processes and by specifying how these observations reflect the sequence and durations of processing steps, many alternative accounts of the thought processes can be eliminated.

Procedures for collecting concurrent and retrospective verbal reports were described, where the verbal reports consist of verbalizations of the sequence of heeded thoughts. These verbalizing procedures allow the thought processes to proceed along their normal course and, with only one exception, at their normal rate. When subjects "think aloud" the rate of thinking has to be slowed down to allow for the additional time required for verbalization of the heeded thought. Concurrent and retrospective verbal reports contain sequences of verbalized thoughts, which can be matched against the *a priori* plausible thought sequences given by the task analysis.

Other procedures for eliciting concurrent verbal reports were analysed and changes in the thought processes could be identified as a function of complying with the instructions. The problems with other types of retrospective report procedures concerned requests for information beyond memory for heeded thoughts. Attempts were made to specify the information retrieved by these other types of reporting procedures.

Within the framework of information processing we have been able to describe the thought process as a sequence of thoughts and show how a wide range of observations reflect its characteristics. It is important to note that observations in the form of verbal reports are analysed in a manner analogous to other observations, like eye-movements and reaction times. In fact, a considerable number of studies have used the redundancy between observations, like eye-movements and verbal reports, to provide convergent validation of the description of the thought processes.

To build an adequate theory of a dynamic system, like the human brain solving problems, observations must be made on that system at a temporal density commensurate with the speed of its processes. Although they are not fully adequate for catching the fine grain of thought processes, verbal protocols and recordings of eye movements have provided data at the highest densities we have as yet attained. For this reason, they have been, and remain, indispensable experimental tools in contemporary cognitive science.

Note to Chapter 2

This chapter is, for the most part, a summary of ideas developed in more detail in Ericsson & Simon (1984, 1985) and Ericsson & Oliver (in press). We would like to sincerely thank Victor Schoenberg for his helpful comments and suggestions on earlier drafts of this chapter.

References

BÜHLER, K. 1951, On thought connections. In D. RAPAPORT (ed.), *Organization and Pathology of Thought*. New York: Columbia University Press.

CLAPARÈDE, E. 1934, Genese de l'hypothèses. *Archives de Psychologie 24*, 1–155.

DEFFNER, G. 1984, Lautes Denken-Untersuchung zur Qualität eines Datenerhebungsverfahrens. Frankfurt: Lang.

DEFFNER, G. & ERICSSON, K. A. 1985, *Sprechtempo und Pausen bei lautem Denken*. Paper presented at Tagung experimentell arbeitender Psychologen. Wuppertal, West Germany.

DUNCKER, K. 1926, A qualitative (experimental and theoretical) study of productive thinking (solving of comprehensible problems). *Pedagogical Seminary* 33, 642–708.

— 1945, On problem solving (Entire issue). *Psychology Monographs*, 58:5.

EBBINGHAUS, H. 1964, *Memory: A Contribution to Experimental Psychology*. H. A. RUGER & C. E. BUSSENIUS, trans. New York: Dover Publications, Inc. (Originally published 1885).

ERICSSON, K. A. & OLIVER, W. in press, Methodology for laboratory research on thinking: Task selection, collection of observations and data analysis. Invited chapter in R. J. STERNBERG & E. E. SMITH (eds), *The Psychology of Human Thought*. New York: Cambridge University Press.

ERICSSON, K. A. & SIMON, H. A. 1980, Verbal reports as data. *Psychological Review* 87, 215–51.

— 1984, *Protocol Analysis*. Cambridge, Mass.: MIT Press/Bradford.

— 1985, Protocol analysis. In T. A. VAN DIJK (ed.), *Handbook of Discourse Analysis*, Vol. 2. New York: Academic Press, 259–68.

ESTES, W. K. 1976, The cognitive side of probability learning. *Psychological Review* 83, 37–64.

FREUD, S. 1914, *Psychopathology of Everyday Life*. New York: Macmillan.

GINSBERG, H. (ed.) 1983, *The Development of Mathematical Learning*. New York: Academic Press.

GUYOTTE, M. J. & STERNBERG, R. J.1981, A transitive-chain theory of syllogistic reasoning. *Cognitive Psychology* 13, 461–525.

HAMILTON, J. M. E. & SANFORD, A. J. 1978, The symbolic distance effect for alphabetic order judgments: A subjective report and reaction time analysis. *Quarterly Journal of Experimental Psychology* 30, 33–43.

INHELDER, B. & PIAGET, J. 1958, *The Growth of Logical Thinking from Childhood to Adolescence*. New York: Basic Books.

JOHNSON-LAIRD, P. N. & STEEDMAN, M. 1978, The psychology of syllogisms. *Cognitive Psychology* 10, 64–99.

JUNG, C. G. 1910, The association method. *American Journal of Psychology* 21, 219–69.

KRUTETSKII, V. A. 1976, *The Psychology of Mathematical Problem Solving*. Chicago, Ill.: University of Chicago Press.

LANDAUER, T. K. 1962, Rate of implicit speech. *Perceptual and Motor Skills* 15, 646.

LINDWORSKY, J. 1931, *Experimental Methodology*. New York: Macmillan.

MAYZNER, M. S., TRESSELT, M. E. & HELBOCK, H.1964, An exploratory study of mediational responses in anagram problem solving. *Journal of General Psychology* 57, 263–74.

MONTAGUE, W. E. 1972, Elaborative strategies in verbal learning and memory. In G. H. BOWER (ed.), *The Psychology of Learning and Motivation* (Vol. 6). New York: Academic Press.

MÜLLER, G. E. 1911, Zur Analyse der Gedächtnistätigkeit und des Vorstellungs-verlaufes: Teil I. *Zeitschrift für Psychologie, Ergänzungsband* 5.
NEWELL, A., SHAW, J. C. & SIMON, H. A. 1958, Elements of a theory of human problem solving. *Psychological Review* 65, 151–66.
NEWELL, A. & SIMON, H. A. 1972, *Human Problem Solving.* Englewood Cliffs, N.J.: Prentice-Hall.
NISBETT, R. E. & ROSS, L. 1980, *Human Inference: Strategies and Shortcomings of Social Judgment.* Englewood Cliffs, N.J.: Prentice-Hall.
NISBETT, R. E. & WILSON, T. D. 1977, Telling more than we can know: Verbal reports on mental processes. *Psychological Review* 84, 231–59.
OLSON, G. M., MACK, R. L. & DUFFY, S. A. 1981, Cognitive aspects of genre. *Poetics* 10, 283–315.
SARGENT, S. S. 1940, Thinking processes at various levels of difficulty. *Archives of Psychology* 249, 5–58.
SELZ, O. 1913, *Über die Gesetze des geordneten Denkverlaufs.* Stuttgart: Spemann.
— 1922, *Zur Psychologie des produktiven Denkens und des Irrtums.* Bonn: Friedrich Cohen.
SHEIKH, A. A. (ed.) 1983, *Imagery: Current Theory, Research, and Application.* New York: Wiley.
SMITH, C. O. 1971, *The Structure of Intellect Processes Analyses System. A Technique for the Investigation and Quantification of Problem Solving Processes.* Unpublished doctoral dissertation, University of Houston.
SMITH, E. R. & MILLER, F. S. 1978, Limits on the perception of cognitive processes: A reply to Nisbett & Wilson. *Psychological Review* 85, 355–62.
TITCHENER, E. B. 1912, The schema of introspection. *American Journal of Psychology* 23, 485–508.
WAERN, Y. 1979, *Thinking Aloud during Reading: A Descriptive Model and Its Application* (Report No. 546). Stockholm: Department of Psychology, University of Stockholm.
WEBER, R. J. & BACH, M. 1969, Visual and speech imagery. *British Journal of Psychology* 60, 199–202.
WERTHEIMER, M. 1945, *Productive Thinking.* New York: Harper & Row.
WHITE, P. 1980, Limitations on verbal reports of internal events: A refutation of Nisbett & Wilson and of Gem. *Psychological Review* 87, 105–12.
WINIKOFF, A. 1967, *Eye Movements as an Aid to Protocol Analysis of Problem Solving Behavior.* Unpublished doctoral dissertation, Carnegie-Mellon University.

3   On the Methodological Basis of Introspective Methods

RÜDIGER GROTJAHN

Introduction

In this chapter I shall discuss some basic methodological issues involved in the use of introspective methods in empirical research. In this context I shall first characterize some mainstreams of current empirical methodology and discuss various metatheoretical criteria which have been proposed for evaluating empirical research. Part of the discussion will pertain to all empirical science (including natural science) because I hold some of the metatheoretical criteria to be valid for all empirical research. I shall then try to elucidate the status of introspective methods within current empirical methodology. I think this is necessary because either the relationship of these methods to the various theories of current philosophy of science is not made clear, or an affinity to a certain methodological position is simply posited without sufficient substantiation, as when, for example, Cavalcanti (1982) and Börsch (1986) suggest a close kinship between introspective methods and qualitative methodology. Furthermore, I hope to inform a wider audience of some important methodological issues which have been discussed in German language publications. In the last part of my chapter, I shall present some information about the methodological basis of a research project,[1] in which we use introspective methods to validate a language test. It should be noted that this part of my chapter is also intended to introduce and in some way to supplement the chapter by Ute Feldmann & Brigitte Stemmer (this volume, Chapter 13), who provide much more concrete information about our project.

Since the term "introspection" is not always understood in the same sense in the literature, some preliminary terminological clarification seems necessary. For the purpose of this chapter, I shall use the term "introspective methods" (also: "introspective procedures" or "introspective data collection methods") to refer collectively to the procedures of self-report, self-observation and self-revealment, as defined by Cohen (1984b; this volume). The term "introspective methods" thus also covers terms such as thinking-aloud or retrospection. It is, however, not synonymous with "verbal report" or "verbal data" — terms with a much broader meaning (cf. Ericsson & Simon, 1984: 7 and the different types of verbal data discussed in Huber & Mandl, 1982: 23). Nevertheless, much of what will be said is valid not only for introspective methods but for all kinds of (verbal) data analysis.

Methodological Paradigms and Criteria for Evaluation of Empirical Research

Scientific activity is oriented on certain criteria, just as are the activities of day-to-day life. Indeed, according to the paradigm of analytical-nomological methodology,[2] the orientation on recognized criteria of judgement is decisive for regarding a research activity as scientific (cf. for example, Groeben & Westmeyer, 1975: 24ff). The attempt to establish evaluation criteria for introspective methods thus also involves the question whether and to what extent working with these methods can be regarded as scientific.

Just as research can be judged by means of evaluation criteria, so can, and should, evaluation criteria be judged by means of metacriteria, such as relevance for theory construction or for coping with practical problems (cf. Iseler & Perez, 1976). Correspondingly, the problem of evaluation criteria should, in my opinion, not be discussed with respect to introspective methods in general, but has to take into account the objectives pursued in the data collection process. I shall therefore first distinguish various objectives of (introspective) data collection which I think to be important for the discussion of possible evaluation criteria. On this basis several methodological paradigms will then be distinguished.

In accordance with the well-known distinction between the context of discovery, the context of justification and the context of utilization of empirical statements (cf. for example, Friedrichs, 1973: 50ff), it is possible to distinguish three main objectives of data collection:

a) exploration of a certain domain of reality with the aim of hypothesis formation;

b) collection of empirical information with the aim of hypothesis testing;
c) theory application in diagnosing (interlanguage phenomena, for instance) and/or theory-based application with the aim of changing certain (social) phenomena.

By means of these distinctions various methodological paradigms can be characterized. For disciplines that are primarily oriented on analytical-nomological philosophy of science, especially (Popperian) critical rationalism (cf. for example, Lakatos, 1970), as, for example, experimental psychology or quantitative social research, the exploration of a domain of reality with the aim of hypothesis formation only plays a minor role, and is to be carefully distinguished from what is considered to be the genuine task of empirical science, namely hypothesis testing. Well confirmed general hypotheses — also called nomological hypotheses — can then be applied to reality in the form of explanation, prediction and technology. These disciplines will subsequently be referred to collectively as the analytical-nomological paradigm.

In contradistinction to the hypothesis testing approach of the analytical-nomological paradigm, conceptions of science such as hermeneutic sociology, communicative social research or ethnomethodology — subsequently referred to in first approximation as the exploratory paradigm — take as unbiased an exploration as possible to be of decisive importance. The division between hypothesis formation and hypothesis testing is then often suspended. This is the case when, for example, as Glaser & Strauss (1974) suggest, instead of the usual practice of establishing a representative sample, once and for all, at the beginning of an investigation, the sample is constantly extended in accordance with the insights gained in the course of hypothesis formation so that hypothesis formation and hypothesis testing can be performed simultaneously.

Within the exploratory paradigm, data analysis is often carried out exclusively by means of interpretative procedures (such as text interpretation or qualitative content analysis) and subsequent statistical analysis is dispensed with (cf. Brunner, 1982; Soeffner, 1979; Terhart, 1982). In such cases I shall speak of an exploratory-interpretative paradigm.

It should be noted that I use the term "interpretative" here only with regard to data analysis and not to refer to an entire research paradigm, as does Wilson (1970, 1973) with his well-known distinction between a normative and an interpretative paradigm. His concept of "normative" is very close to "analytical-nomological" as used in this paper. While the normative paradigm proceeds from the assumption that actions and definitions of situations are to be considered as either explicitly or implicitly determined once and for all, according to the interpretative paradigm they are based on interpretations which in the course of interaction are continually reformulated and mutually agreed upon. In accordance with this basic ontological assumption the researcher does not gain access to actions and definitions of situations via deductive-nomological explanations, but alone via an interpretative approach, that is by himself interpretatively describing the interpretations of the actors.

Again, within interpretative methodology several variants can be distinguished. Thus, for example, Terhart (1983: 157) differentiates an ethnographic-descriptive variant, a communicative-emancipatory variant and a structuralistic-reconstructive variant, whose adherents criticize each other.

Closely related to the exploratory-interpretative paradigm is the concept of action research (cf. for example, Treiber & Groeben, 1981; Moser, 1983; König, 1983). The trichotomy of context of discovery, context of justification and context of utilization is definitively suspended here. The aim is not a pseudo-neutral description and explanation of reality and technological control of reality in the sense of the analytical-nomological tradition, but a theory-based modification of reality which is initiated in the exploratory phase and often involves a practical-emancipatory interest (sensu Habermas, 1971).

Instead of the distinction between the exploratory-interpretative and the analytical-nomological paradigm, the dichotomy between qualitative and quantitative research can often be found (cf. for example, Reichardt & Cook, 1979; Mohler, 1981; Wilson, 1982; Nußbaum, 1984; Van Buer, 1984; Silverman, 1985; Thomae, 1985). In my opinion this usage should be avoided unless the terms "qualitative" and "quantitative" are explicitly defined.

On the one hand, the term "qualitative" is used in at least two different senses; it frequently remains unclear which sense is being referred to in the discussion. With regard to concepts and data used to grasp a certain domain of reality, the term "qualitative" designates either a certain type of concept or the level of measurement of the data to be collected. In general, classificatory concepts and thus, also, data measured on a nominal scale are considered to be qualitative, whereas metrical concepts or data measured at least on an interval scale are regarded as quantitative. With regard to comparative concepts and thus, also, to data measured on an ordinal scale, usage is not unified. These are sometimes termed quantitative, sometimes qualitative; I shall follow the latter usage. As a consequence, the term "measurement" is also inconsistently used. Some speak of "measurement" only if at least an interval scale is meant, others use the term "measurement" also in the case of an ordinal scale, still others even in the case of a nominal scale. I, too, shall speak of "measurement" in the case of a nominal scale (for a justification see Gigerenzer, 1981: 131ff).

On the other hand the term "qualitative" is often used in a much wider sense to designate an entire research paradigm (for a justification see Filstead, 1979). It then refers simultaneously to the manner of data collection, of theory construction and of data analysis as well as to the social and philosophical orientation of the investigation in question. But it often remains unclear what precisely is meant by "qualitative", as for example in Cavalcanti (1982) or Börsch (1986). Furthermore, the label "qualitative" is controversial among advocates of qualitative research methods (cf. for example, Hopf & Weingarten, 1979; Mohler, 1981; Kleining, 1982; Wilson, 1982; Küchler, 1980, 1983; Achtenhagen, 1984). Sometimes the use of "qualitative" coincides more or less with what I have called "exploratory-interpretative"; sometimes, however, it is used in a much wider sense, even to refer to hypothesis testing procedures (e.g. Kleining, 1982). Furthermore, the demand for social criticism and action is also often associated with the label "qualitative" (cf. for example, Jüttemann, 1985: 10f; Mayring, 1985: 190ff).

On examining the use of the dichotomy "qualitative v. quantitative" in the literature, one can, with Reichardt & Cook (1979: 10), distinguish the following manners of characterizing this opposition (cf. also Mohler, 1981: 726f and Patton, 1980: 39ff):

1. phenomenology and verstehen v. logical positivism;
2. naturalistic (unobtrusive) and uncontrolled observation v. obtrusive and controlled measurement;
3. subjective v. objective;
4. close to the data v. removed from the data;
5. discovery-oriented, exploratory, descriptive and inductive v. verification-oriented, confirmatory, inferential and hypothetico-deductive;
6. process-oriented v. outcome-oriented;
7. valid, "rich" and "deep" data v. reliable, "hard" and replicable data;
8. ungeneralizable, single case studies v. generalizable, multiple case studies;
9. holistic v. particularistic;
10. assumption of a dynamic reality v. assumption of a stable reality.

Similar lists are given by Aschenbach, Billmann-Machecha & Zitterbarth (1985: 33–37) and, in the form of 10 critical questions addressed to advocates of "qualitative" positions, by Van Buer (1984) with reference to classroom observation. Reichardt & Cook (1979) and Mohler (1981) have attempted to show that none of the dichotomies listed above bears critical examination (cf. however, the discussion in Aschenbach, Billmann-Machecha & Zitterbart, 1985). In view of this situation I shall use "qualitative" and "quantitative" only with regard to scaling or measurement as discussed above and shall refrain from using these terms to characterize research paradigms.

Qualitative data can be analysed both interpretatively and statistically: statistically, for example, by means of the well-known chi-square method. Verbal data can be both qualitative and quantitative; collection of qualitative verbal data such as different word classes or different communication strategies is, however, much more common than the collection of quantitative verbal data such as the type-token ratio or sentence length as measured by the number of words.

In addition to the form of the data (qualitative v. quantitative) and the method of analysis (interpretative v. statistical), Patton (1980: 111–17) suggests that the manner of data collection be taken into account, namely non-experimental design (e.g. naturalistic inquiry) v. (quasi-)experimental design. Thus, in addition to the pure exploratory-interpretative paradigm, which Patton refers to as "pure qualitative", and the pure analytical-nomological paradigm, which he calls "pure hypothetical-deductive", six mixed forms can be distinguished (cf. also Rudinger, Chaselon, Zimmerman & Henning, 1985: 12f), yielding a total of eight possible paradigms:

PURE FORMS

Paradigm 1: exploratory-interpretative
   1. non-experimental design
   2. qualitative data
   3. interpretative analysis

Paradigm 2: analytical-nomological
   1. experimental or quasi-experimental design
   2. quantitative data
   3. statistical analysis

MIXED FORMS

Paradigm 3: experimental-qualitative-interpretative
   1. experimental or quasi-experimental design

2. qualitative data
3. interpretative analysis

Paradigm 4: experimental-qualitative-statistical
1. experimental or quasi-experimental design
2. qualitative analysis
3. statistical analysis

Paradigm 5: exploratory-qualitative-statistical
1. non-experimental design
2. qualitative data
3. statistical analysis

Paradigm 6: exploratory-quantitative-statistical
1. non-experimental design
2. quantitative data
3. statistical analysis

Paradigm 7: exploratory-quantitative-interpretative
1. non-experimental design
2. quantitative data
3. interpretative analysis

Paradigm 8: experimental-quantitative-interpretative
1. experimental or quasi-experimental design
2. quantitative data
3. interpretative analysis.

Paradigms 7 and 8 are not considered by Patton (1980) or Rudinger, Chaselon, Zimmermann & Henning (1985). It is characteristic of these two paradigms that although quantitative data are collected, the method of analysis is primarily interpretative. Such an approach is probably very rare in social science and psychology, in which statistics plays an integral role in the training of researchers. But in second language acquisition research it is not as rare, so that it may here be justified to speak of methodological paradigms. Since the current methodological controversy is primarily taking place between the two pure methodological paradigms, that is, the analytical-nomological and the exploratory-interpretative, I shall restrict myself to these in the following discussion.

Evaluation Criteria for the Analytical-Nomological Paradigm

According to analytical-nomological methodology the aim of empirical science is to construct theories with as high an information content as possible, that is, theories that make valid statements about as large a section of reality as possible (for a critique of this view with regard to psychology see Wottawa, 1981). With respect to theory formation the general methodological criterion of *objectivity* is of central importance. In this connection we have to distinguish at least three different uses of "objectivity" and its antonym "subjectivity" (cf. Scriven, 1972; Patton, 1980: 336ff; Schaff, 1980): all three may be referred to simultaneously if someone speaks, for example, of an "objective approach". In the first place "objective" means that phenomena exist independently of the knowing subject. Consequently knowledge is considered to be objective if the knowing subject adequately reflects objective reality, or, in other words, if the knowledge is true. In the second place "objective" means the same thing as "in principle replicable by any subject". Frequently, this use is also referred to by the term "intersubjectivity". Thirdly "objective" stands for neutral and impartial.

If one ignores primarily emancipatory conceptions of research, the demand for objectivity in its first two meanings is broadly recognized also by researchers not adhering to the analytical-nomological paradigm and is often considered to be even a criterion for regarding empirical research as scientific. However, whether objectivity in the third sense has to be considered a necessary precondition for the first two kinds of objectivity, and whether the demand for objectivity implies the requirement of strict separation of researcher and research object, continues to be a matter of debate, although, in contradistinction to exploratory-interpretative methodology, most researchers adhering to the analytical-nomological paradigm will probably answer in the affirmative.

Closely connected to the criterion of objectivity is the requirement of the *reproducibility* of the results. In part derived from the criteria just mentioned is the requirement to use quantitative concepts in theory construction and thus also to use quantitative data and statistical methods of analysis in theory testing (cf. for example, Opp, 1976).

The *measurement criteria* of objectivity, reliability and validity of classical test theory are closely related to these general methodological requirements. The axioms and evaluation criteria of classical test theory have been applied to all kinds of data collection procedures and measurement instruments, including introspective methods. These criteria can be characterized in simplified form as follows (cf. Lienert, 1969; Nunnally, 1978; Leichner, 1979; Upshur, 1983; Feger & Bredenkamp, 1983).

Objectivity (as a measurement criterion) designates the extent to which the results of measurement are independent of the researcher and of those who score and interpret the data. (Measurement is to be understood to include data collection here and in all that follows.) A measure of objectivity is for example the correlation between the interview results of two different interviewers working with one and the same sample. Objectivity is closely related to and often regarded as being a special case of reliability.

Reliability refers to the precision of a measurement instrument, irrespective of whether it really measures what it is supposed to measure. Reliability coefficients allow us to estimate the measurement error of an instrument and simultaneously also to estimate the reproducibility of measurement results.

The requirement of *standardization* of the research conditions is derived from the evaluation criteria of objectivity and reliability. The aim of standardization is to reduce social interaction between the researcher and the subject as much as possible. It is considered to be a necessary precondition for reproducibility of research results and thus, also, for high retest reliability.

The *validity* of a measurement instrument indicates to what extent it actually measures what it is supposed to measure. Just as in the case of reliability, a number of subtypes can be distinguished. To estimate *criterion-oriented validity* the measurement results of a group of subjects are compared with their scores on an external criterion which is assumed to be valid and which has to be a manifest, that is, directly observable variable (cf. Leichner, 1979: 73ff). A criterion-oriented validation of an introspective interview of teachers regarding their *potential* reactions to students' behaviour in certain situations, for instance, could be attempted as follows: the *actual* reactions of the teachers in the corresponding situations (external criterion) are registered and compared with their responses in the interview. A substantial correlation could then be interpreted as evidence of the validity of the introspective interview.

In contradistinction to criterion-oriented validity, *construct validity* refers to the extent to which research results are consistent with certain theory-based expectations. For example, if one wishes to validate a new second language test, one can correlate scores from that test with scores from a well-established intelligence test. On the theoretical assumption that intelligent people, all other things being equal, are also better able to learn a second language, scores on the language test should correlate highly with those on the intelligence test.

According to classical test theory the relationship between objectivity, reliability and validity is as follows (cf. Lienert, 1969: 19ff). Objectivity of administration and scoring is regarded as a necessary, but not a sufficient, condition of the reliability of a measurement instrument. Reliability and objectivity of interpretation are, in turn, regarded as a necessary, but not a sufficient, condition of validity. Furthermore, reliability constitutes a numerical upper bound of validity, that is, data can only be valid to the extent that they are reliable. According to this view introspective methods cannot yield valid results if, for instance, they are not sufficiently reliable or if they depend on the researcher or if there is no intersubjectively accepted interpretation.

A further evaluation criterion of analytical-nomological methodology is the *representativity* of the results both with respect to a certain reference population of persons as well as with respect to a certain reference population of behaviour or action patterns.

Analytical-Nomological Evaluation Criteria and Research Practice

The application of the evaluation criteria characterized above has a number of serious consequences for research practice. Since a high degree of objectivity and reliability is regarded as a necessary precondition of validity, researchers very often try to meet the criteria of objectivity and reliability first. The demonstration of validity, and especially construct validity, being substantially more difficult, is then often not attempted, although the analytical-nomological paradigm also prescribes that validity must be secured.

In order to fulfil the criteria of objectivity and reliability, an effort is made to eliminate the reactivity of the measurement instrument as far as possible. Furthermore, the attempt is made to keep the amount of necessary inference on the part of the researcher, subject and scorer as low as possible. Consequently, standardized data collection methods, such as the standardized interview with closed questions, are preferred. In many cases the use of standardized data collection procedures with the aim of hypothesis testing results in a drastic reduction of the quantity and quality of the information obtained.

Furthermore, a theory of measurement error based on classical test theory is used to try to cope with the reactivity of measurement instruments such as interview or participant observation. Such a theory of error makes predictions about the effects of various variables on objectivity, reliability and validity and, thus takes account, for instance, of the well-known tendency of respondents to give affirmative or socially desirable answers in interviews (cf. for example, Scheuch, 1967: 136ff; Esser, 1975).

Moreover, striving for representativity and quantification often leads us to neglect the individual case: the individual subject is valued only for his contribution to the overall statistical tendency of the data. It should, however, be noted that the research practice just mentioned is not necessarily a consequence of the application of the analytical-nomological evaluation criteria. Recent attempts to develop a methodology of single subject research based on the analytical-nomological paradigm (cf. for example, Huber, 1984 for a survey) and research strategies such as that proposed by Wottawa (1981) offer evidence for this view.

In the methodological discussion in the literature, analytical-nomological research practice is the subject of fierce dispute. It is for instance argued that the methodology of critical rationalism leads to an empiristic research practice that produces primarily trivial and fortuitous results (cf. Holzkamp, 1972 or Köckeis-Stangl, 1980). A very lucid and in my opinion quite adequate characterization of the analytical-nomological research practice is offered by Köckeis-Stangl (1980: 341):

"As regards the principles, there is wide unanimity that the research problem should first be established and that only then an appropriate research method should be chosen (or developed). But *de facto*, admittedly important problems are often put aside with the justification that there are no 'scientifically sound' methods available to explore them; less interesting or more limited topics that seem to be susceptible to treatment with familiar methods are chosen instead. Or a theoretically significant problem is trimmed and reduced until it can finally be forced into a strictly logical-deductive pattern and can be handled with objectivistic-quantitative means.... The traditional canonical methodology thus becomes an obstacle, if not a strait-jacket, particularly since ... its application provides us with by no means especially secure results, but does cause many researchers to fancy themselves secure, to pay attention only to observing rules established in advance, and not to undertake an independent critical examination of their method themselves." (translated by Rüdiger Grotjahn)

Much of this and other criticism seems to me to be generally valid. However, this undesirable state of affairs should in my opinion not be attributed exclusively to fundamental deficiencies of the analytical-nomological paradigm. Rather, it should be imputed primarily, as Rudinger,

Chaselon, Zimmermann & Henning (1985: 13) suggest, to the unreflected application of this paradigm in research practice.

Some Evaluation Criteria of Exploratory-Interpretative Methodology

As already mentioned, the concept of exploratory-interpretative methodology is used to refer collectively to a number of different although fundamentally convergent research conceptions. Hence it is not correct to speak of *the* evaluation criteria of exploratory-interpretative methodology. Rather, there are a few widely accepted criteria as well as some less widely accepted ones, which I shall not discuss.

Although researchers adhering to the exploratory-interpretative paradigm for the most part do not want to appear inexact and subjective, the criteria of reliability and also of objectivity — in particular in its third meaning as well as in its test theoretical sense — play a rather minor role. Their primary interest is to ensure validity, although, however, this concept is modified to a certain extent, as will become clear in this chapter. The primary prerequisite for obtaining valid data is observance of the criterion of *openness* (cf. Hartwig & Dearing, 1979; 9ff; Hoffmann-Riem, 1980: 343ff). According to this criterion, a theoretical structuring of the object of research is avoided until it is structured by the informants themselves. The criterion of openness thus implies the renunciation of hypothesis formation *ex ante*. Glaser & Strauss (1974: 37) go so far as to suggest that one should refrain from a study of the literature prior to the exploratory examination of reality.

The criterion of openness is closely connected to the criterion of *communication* (cf. Arbeitsgruppe Bielefelder Soziologen, 1976; Hoffmann-Riem, 1980: 346ff). Whereas the analytical-nomological methodology regards communication and interaction between the researcher and the subject as a potential source of bias, exploratory-interpretative methodology postulates that valid data can only be obtained when an appropriate relationship is built up between the researcher and the subject. The aim is a "data collection" situation that is as free of dominance relationships as possible. Thus the subject is no longer regarded as an object of research, as in analytical-nomological methodology, but as a knowing subject — significantly also referred to as "informant" — who, in principle, has equal rights with the researcher and whose subjective theories are of central importance for the process of theory construction.

The change in the method of research thus goes hand-in-hand with a change of the central assumptions about the human subject: the behavioural object model of pure analytical-nomological methodology is replaced by an epistemological subject model (cf. Groeben & Scheele, 1977; Treiber & Groeben, 1981).

Whereas analytical-nomological methodology stresses *explanation* in terms of relating facts to each other by means of theory-based assumptions of regularities, exploratory-interpretative methodology strives for *understanding* (Verstehen) in terms of a reconstruction of how the informant relates facts to each other by means of his own assumptions of regularity (cf. Groeben & Scheele, 1977: 116). The aim is the interpretative reconstruction of structures of sense, of the view of the world and of self, as well as of everyday knowledge.

The criteria of openness and communication have an immediate effect on the practice of research. Standardized data collection methods have been replaced by open or unstructured methods such as the focused interview or the narrative interview (cf. Hron, 1982 with regard to these interview techniques).

The focused interview is centred on a certain area by interview guide lines. At the same time, the interviewee is permitted to express freely what is significant for him or her and to present it from his or her own subjective perspective. The narrative interview goes a step further. Only an initial topic is given. Aside from this restriction, the interviewer does not make any pre-planned interventions to control the course of the interview. He must then attempt to reconstruct the meaning of the interviewee's utterances interpretatively.

But inasmuch as, in unstructured methods such as the narrative interview and thinking aloud, the researcher himself becomes a research instrument by virtue of his role as interpreter (cf. Weidle & Wagner, 1982 or Ericsson & Simon, 1984: 228ff for the method of thinking aloud), interpretative methods are in great danger of violating not only the criteria of objectivity and reliability, but of validity as well.

As has already been mentioned, most researchers adhering to the exploratory-interpretative paradigm (in contradistinction to adherents of the analytical-nomological paradigm) aim primarily at securing validity. Nevertheless, they also try to observe the criterion of objectivity — at least in its first and second meaning — and, to a lesser degree also, that of reproducibility.

A series of attempts has been made to limit the degree of subjective discretion in interpreting by developing *methods of controlled understanding of others* (cf. the indications given by Köckeis-Stangl, 1980: 347f; Brunner, 1982; Kade, 1983; Terhart, 1983; Schneider, 1985). Among these attempts, the so-called method of *communicative validation* is in my opinion worthy of particular attention (for the following discussion cf. Treiber & Groeben, 1981, 1983; Lechler, 1982).

Communicative validation attempts to ensure validity by examining to what extent the informant agrees with the interpretation of his or her utterances. A similar suggestion has been made by Mehan (e.g. 1977, 1978) within his framework of constitutive ethnography (cf. also Long, 1980: 25ff). Essential to communicative validation is a criterion of truth based on consensus, as proposed in particular by Habermas (e.g. 1973). Since this criterion presupposes a symmetrical dominance-free dialogue between researcher and research subject, appropriate conditions must be created to ensure that this prerequisite is met as far as possible.

However, if one accepts the arguments adduced by Groeben & Scheele (1977) or by Treiber & Groeben (1981, 1983), which I hold to be valid, then communicative validation has only a restricted range. Only the *adequacy of interpretation and reconstruction*, that is, the adequacy of the researcher's interpretation of the introspective statements of the subject and the adequacy of his reconstruction of the subject's cognitions and personal theories, can be decided on the basis of the subject's agreement. Communicative validation only serves to confirm so-called descriptive constructs (see Herrmann, 1969: 69 for the distinction between descriptive and explanatory constructs). But cognitions and personal, subjective theories also have, at least, potential explanatory force as regards the actions of the subject, and are thus explanatory constructs, whose *adequacy to reality* is to be investigated. Such an investigation cannot, however, be founded on a consensus theory of truth but, rather, requires an examination based on external observational data in terms of the correspondence theory of truth as presupposed by the falsification methodology of the analytical-nomological paradigm (cf. Lakatos, 1970 for different versions of falsification methodology).

One possible approach consists, for instance, in the collection of supplementary psycho-physiological data (cf. Rösler, 1983, 1984). Another approach is based on the concept of *behavioural validation*, which in turn is based on analytical-nomological falsification methodology. According to this concept, introspective statements about cognitions — that is, about mental states not intersubjectively observable — are checked against, and possibly falsified by, directly observable behaviour. Treiber & Groeben (1981: 127) claim that although behavioural validation is temporally subsequent to communicative validation, it takes precedence over it because of its wider epistemological range. According to Wahl (1982: 259), behavioural validation can be achieved by:

> "(1) computing correlations between cognitions and observable behaviour; (2) predicting future observable behaviour with the help of the reconstructed cognitions; and (3) modifying the subjective theories by means of reflective training procedures and examining whether observable behaviour also changes." (translated by Rüdiger Grotjahn)

If one regards the criterion of behavioural validity in abstraction from the criterion of communicative validity and from the underlying view of the person, then it has to be ascribed to analytical-nomological methodology. But if one takes the fact into account that behavioural validation is preceded by communicative validation and that authors such as Groeben & Scheele do not work in terms of an object-oriented behaviouristic model but, rather, a subject-oriented epistemological model, then it becomes clear that the concept of behavioural validation is an attempt — in my opinion a fruitful one — to combine exploratory-interpretative and analytical-nomological methodology meaningfully.

The Methodological Status of Introspective Methods

In the course of the history of psychology the methodological status of introspective methods has been the subject of fierce controversy, especially between behaviourists and cognitivists (cf. Boring, 1953; Liebermann, 1979; Danzinger, 1980; Feger & Graumann, 1983; Ericsson & Simon 1984: 48–61; Börsch, 1986). A similar controversy is taking place in linguistics and second language acquisition research, in which introspective methods have recently received increased attention (cf. Itkonen, 1981; Ringen, 1981; Mann 1982; Schnelle, 1981; Seliger, 1983; Cohen 1984b; Færch & Kasper, 1987). Most of the arguments adduced in the discussion refer to the epistemological-methodological status of introspective methods. The principal argument put forward against introspective methods has been that they are not objective in the second sense of the word, i.e. that they do not provide intersubjectively replicable results. In addition, ontological arguments have been adduced; they are closely related to the epistemological arguments and can be regarded as prior to them. (The philosophical aspects of introspective methods are discussed in greater detail by Natsoulas, 1967, 1970 and Holenstein, 1980.)

Thus, for example, the question as to the ontological status of interlanguage can be raised: is interlanguage a state of mind (cf. Bialystok & Sharwood Smith, 1985) and hence, at least in principle, accessible to introspection, or is it a theoretical construct that can only be physicalistically interpreted in terms of correspondence rules (that is, in terms of observational phenomena) but which is not accessible to introspection?

Similarly, the conception of language (cf. Bunge, 1984: 109ff) plays a central role in evaluating the scope of introspective methods. If one proceeds on the basis of an exclusively neurolinguistic conception of language, introspective methods can be excluded from the very beginning as a data collection instrument. The same holds true of a structuralistic conception of language in Harris' sense. But if we proceed, as does Chomsky, from a mentalistic conception of language, such that the intuition of an (idealized) speaker/hearer plays a central role instead of induction on the basis of a linguistic corpus (as does Harris), then introspective methods in a broad sense become an important data collection instrument.

If the accessibility of the research object to introspection can, at least in principle, be presupposed because of its ontological status, and the epistemological status of introspective methods is examined, one has to decide which of the evaluation criteria should be applied to introspective methods and which methodological paradigm they should be ascribed to. Since a precise answer to this question depends on the aims of an investigation using introspective methods, I shall restrict myself to a few general remarks; further comments are given in the following discussion of the use of introspective procedures in the validation of language tests.

Among the investigations using introspective methods discussed by Ericsson & Simon (1984) and Færch & Kasper (1987), both exploratory and hypothesis testing research can be found. Ericsson & Simon (1984: 275) refer to these as "data-driven research" and "theory-driven research" respectively and explicitly stress that both procedures are legitimate. Correspondingly, some investigations tend more towards naturalistic inquiry (such as foreign language learning research in a normal teaching situation in school classes), and some more towards experimental design; in psychological literature experimental design seems to be preponderant. As far as the method of analysis is concerned, both purely interpretative procedures (especially in second language acquisition research) and primarily statistical procedures are used. Moreover, both qualitative data (e.g. various problem solving strategies) and quantitative data (e.g. pause length as an indicator of problem solving processes) can be found; qualitative data are, however, preponderant.

As these remarks indicate, it is not possible to attribute all introspective procedures to one methodological paradigm. In my opinion it is equally unjustified to assume an affinity to so-called qualitative methodology — all the more so when the fact is taken into consideration that although a practical-emancipatory epistemological interest is usually connected with the concept "qualitative", quite a few introspective investigations are based on a primarily technological-epistemological interest (as, for instance, our project described below). Rather, introspective methods can be used in all eight of the paradigms distinguished above. Correspondingly, all evaluation criteria discussed can be applied to introspective methods, provided that the aim of the investigation in question (e.g. exploratory or hypothesis testing) and the restrictions mentioned in the above discussion of the evaluation criteria are taken into account.

A central problem of the application of introspective methods is the fact that introspection yields *verbal* data, in which case the problem of validity presents itself in two respects. In the first place, assuming that we are not restricted to a pure analysis of performance data, we always have to ensure *interpretative validity*, that is, to attempt a valid interpretative reconstruction of both the propositional content and the intended meaning. In the second place, our verbal data are always reports of something and thus have a representational function; their *representational validity* must therefore also be ensured.

Ericsson & Simon's "model of human information processing" (1980, 1984) is certainly an important contribution to the evaluation of validity, although it may be questioned whether it is directly applicable to second language research, in particular if we do not investigate problem solving but language production (cf. Dechert, this volume, Chapter 5). Another approach consists in the collection of supplementary observational data such as psycho-physiological reactions or eye movements. Deffner (1984), for example, used this last procedure; his data confirmed predictions made on the basis of Ericsson & Simon's model (see also the discussion in Ericsson & Simon, this volume, Chapter 2).

A further important contribution is made by the concepts of communicative validation and behavioural validation discussed above. But as the research done, for instance, by Oevermann and his collaborators (cf. for example, Oevermann, Allert, Konau & Krambeck, 1979), as well as our own experience has shown (see below), the attempt to ensure the validity of introspective data is very often extremely time consuming and results in immense amounts of data that can hardly be evaluated in any detail within a small research project (cf. Küchler, 1980: 383). If the cost-benefit ratio is considered as a metacriterion (cf. the above remarks on the metacriterion of relevance), the question can be asked whether the increment of knowledge or sometimes only of certainty justifies the additional effort.

Thinking Aloud and Retrospective Interview in C-test Validation

The C-test was introduced in 1981 by Christine Klein-Braley and Ulrich Raatz. It is based on the same test-theoretical and psycholinguistic principles as the Cloze test, but has a different test format (for more information about the C-test, cf. for example, Klein-Braley & Raatz, 1984; Klein-Braley, 1985; Grotjahn & Stemmer, 1985; and Feldmann & Stemmer, in this volume, Chapter 13). Research into the validity of the C-test carried out so far has been, except for three studies, restricted to a statistical analysis of the correlations of the C-test with, for instance, other language tests, intelligence tests or school grades. Although I find such investigations very important, I also think that this type of investigation will not suffice to provide us with a satisfactory answer to the problem of validity.

There are at least two reasons for this. First, validation of a language test with the help, for example, of other language tests presupposes the construct validity of these tests, which is normally at best partially established, and if so, then only with the help of correlational analysis. The potential circularity of this approach should be obvious. Second, validation by correlational analysis tells us nothing about the individual mental processes going on in a learner when he or she takes a test. For instance, as has been shown by Cohen (1984a) with the help of introspective methods, the correct solution to an item can be based on a wrong hypothesis, and an incorrect solution on a correct hypothesis. Furthermore, the correct solution to one item can be the result of various underlying mental processes (cf. Ericsson & Simon, 1984). Therefore the usual approach, namely to consider mainly statistical properties in test validation, is very problematic.

Consequently, when validating a test we have to analyse the mental processes in the test-taking subject in order really to understand the nature of constructs such as "general language proficiency" or "pragmatic expectancy grammar" (cf. Vollmer, 1981: 115 for a similar suggestion). We have therefore undertaken a corresponding research project in which we are using introspective methods to uncover the mental processes going on in a learner when he or she is doing a C-test.

Up to now only a few attempts have been made to use methods such as thinking aloud, introspection or retrospection in validating language tests. A first survey is given by Cohen (1984a). With regard to the C-test there are only three studies of this kind, namely Cohen, Segal & Weiss (1985), Grotjahn & Stemmer (1985) and Feldmann & Stemmer (in this volume, Chapter 13) — the latter two discussing some results from our research project.

In this project we have attempted to approach the problem of test validation by combining analytical-nomological and exploratory-interpretative methodology in a sort of triangulation approach (cf. Denzin, 1978; and Patton, 1980: 108ff, 329ff for a discussion of the concept of triangulation). The following three basic types of triangulation are employed in our project: 1) *data triangulation*, i.e. we make use of a variety of data sources to study the same problem; 2) *theory triangulation*, i.e. we try to interpret a single set of data from different theoretical perspectives; and 3) *methodological triangulation*, i.e. we make use of multiple methods to study the same problem. In this way we hope to get a less biased and more complete picture of our research object.

Following the analytical-nomological research paradigm, we have first carried out various statistical analyses with more than 500 university students (cf. Grotjahn & Stemmer, 1985). In these investigations our French C-test turned out to be a very practical, economical, and at the same time highly reliable testing device. Similar analyses are currently being done on a Spanish C-test. However, the question as to what the C-test precisely measures could not be satisfactorily answered by these analyses. Furthermore, as already mentioned, the statistical approach to test validation tells us nothing about the individual mental processes going on in the testees when doing a test.

On the basis of suggestions made for instance by Ericsson & Simon (1980), Huber & Mandl (1982), Wahl (1982) and Treiber & Groeben (1981, 1983), we, therefore, developed a research design combining the methods of thinking aloud and retrospective interview, in order to examine more thoroughly what the C-test really measures. Since this was the first investigation of this kind into the C-test, we had almost no pre-established hypotheses. Therefore, this part of our project has to be regarded as primarily exploratory. Our research design can be characterized as follows:

In separate sessions, each subject (our subjects were mainly university students) was individually given three different French or four different Spanish C-test texts arranged in order of increasing difficulty. According to our pilot studies the texts differed markedly in mean item difficulty. As has also been shown in these studies, the instructions with regard to the experiment had to be relatively extensive. This is in accordance with experiences in other cognitive-psychological investigations using a similar design. In order to ensure that the subjects completely understood what they were supposed to do, they were first informed about the objectives of our study. In this way we also hoped to make the subjects feel they were competent collaborators in the sense of Huber & Mandl (1982).

Subsequently, they were given a written description of the task. In this description they were, for example, instructed to say everything they thought and felt while filling in the blanks. Furthermore, they listened to a recording illustrating thinking aloud during C-test solving. The exemplary nature of this recording had been made clear to them. Finally, the subjects were given a trial C-test text in order to familiarize them with the task and to make sure that they had understood everything correctly.

After this instructional phase, which lasted about 20 minutes, the subject was left alone in the room and worked on the C-test while thinking aloud. The utterances were audiotaped. Preliminary investigations had shown that this part should be limited to about 30 minutes for the three French and 40 minutes for the four Spanish C-test texts. However, if necessary, more time was allowed.

After this thinking-aloud phase, the interviewer and the subject listened to the audiotape together. In this retrospective phase, the subject could spontaneously comment on his or her thinking-aloud utterances and behaviour during the previous test phase or answer the interviewer's questions concerning his or her utterances or behaviour. In order to meet the criterion of openness, the questions were not prepared in advance. The objectives of this retrospective interview phase were two-fold. First, it was intended to provide immediate communicative validation of the interpretation of the thinking-aloud data by the interviewer. Its second objective was to elicit additional information about the problem-solving processes during the thinking-aloud phase. We hoped that listening to the audiotaped utterances immediately after thinking aloud would enable the subject to recall information that really pertains to the problem-solving processes and thus prevent him from giving *a posteriori* rationalizations. This retrospective phase took about two hours for French and three hours for Spanish, and was also audio-taped. Finally, the subjects filled in a questionnaire to provide us with some background information. In all, each individual session lasted about three hours in the case of French and four hours in the case of Spanish. In this way data from 30 subjects for French and 40 for Spanish were collected.

We then transcribed literally the audio-taped verbalizations obtaining for each subject a written transcript of about 20 pages in the case of French and about 35 pages in the case of Spanish. Subsequently several of the transcripts have been analysed interpretatively with regard to the strategies used by the learner when doing the C-test (for details see Grotjahn & Stemmer, 1985; and Feldmann & Stemmer, in this volume, Chapter 13). So far, no statistical analysis of the frequency of the different strategies identified has been carried out. However, such an analysis will be done in the near future. Hence the final methodological orientation of the introspective part of our project will not be on a pure exploratory-interpretative research paradigm (Paradigm 1 above), but rather on an exploratory-qualitative-statistical paradigm (Paradigm 5 above).

The final transcript of all verbal protocols will consist of more than 2000 pages. We thus face the problem already mentioned of how to proceed in view of the immense amounts of data. Since a detailed analysis of all the material will not be possible in a small research project such as ours, we are currently discussing whether the information already obtained in the course of our exploratory data analysis should be used to formulate specific hypotheses to be examined in more detail on the basis of the remaining data.

Conclusions

In addition to the interpretative analysis of the verbal protocols, the following four types of analysis are being carried out (cf. also Feldmann & Stemmer, in this volume, Chapter 13):

1) *A descriptive analysis of the solutions to the C-test items.* In this context, the items are analysed, for example, with regard to the frequency of acceptable, unacceptable and missing solutions or with regard to the linguistic properties of the solutions attempted.

2) *An analysis of the task the subjects are requested to do.* With regard to task analysis (cf. Stephens, Bhaskar & Dillard, 1981; Bromme, 1985), we are currently examining the applicability of information processing models such as those proposed by Ericsson & Simon

(1984) or by Van Dijk & Kintsch (1983) as well as an information statistical approach.

3) *An explanatory analysis of the solutions to the C-test items on the basis of our verbal protocol data.* In this context, the solutions are considered as indicative of the learner's interlanguage and explained with the help of various psycholinguistic processes. In so doing we no longer follow the limited paradigm of "classical" interlanguage research, but use an approach which we consider to be more adequate in view of the complexity of interlanguage.

4) *Behavioural validation of protocol data.* Following the paradigm of behavioural validation described earlier in this paper, the validity of our verbal protocol data and of our interpretative analyses is examined by:

a) computing correlations between strategies so far identified and observable behaviour (e.g. scores on the C-test);

b) predicting future observable behaviour (such as the solution to a specific item) on the basis of the identified strategies;

c) teaching our students strategies identified as characteristic for successful C-test solving in order to see whether their scores on the C-test will then improve.

Although only some of these analyses have been carried out so far, we already feel secure enough to draw at least the following two general conclusions:

1) The objection of epiphenomenality, that is, the argument that there is no correspondence between verbal reports and cognitive processes (cf. Nisbett & Wilson, 1977), has to be rejected, at least with regard to our data.

2) Our approach, namely combining the usual statistical methodology of test validation with an introspective methodology in a sort of triangulation strategy, will lead us to a much more thorough understanding of what the C-test really measures.

Notes to Chapter 3

1. We thank the *Deutsche Forschungsgemeinschaft* (German Research Foundation) for the financial support granted since the beginning of 1986.
2. I use the concept of paradigm following Kuhn (1962, 1970) in the sense of a set of assumptions which provides a philosophical and conceptual framework for the study of the world. I use the term "paradigm" only because it is very often referred to in the literature discussed in this paper. It should, however, be noted that it has been severely criticized because of its vagueness and

ambiguity (see Masterman, 1970 for a listing of 21 different uses of the term "paradigm" by Kuhn himself) and that Kuhn (1974) in view of this and other criticism has modified his original conception. Furthermore it has been argued that the concept of "paradigm", used by Kuhn to describe the history of mature sciences such as physics, is inapplicable to disciplines such as psychology or social science (cf. the discussion and references in Westmeyer, 1981). Esser, Klenovits & Zehnpfennig (1977: 161ff) differentiate between two main meta-scientific paradigms, an analytical-nomological and an hermeneutical-dialectical. Esser, Klenovits & Zehnpfennig's analytical-nomological paradigm embraces such various schools as (logical) empiricism, (neo-)positivism, falsificationism and fallibilism. Their hermeneutic-dialectical paradigm embraces a critical-emancipatory school, the Frankfurt school, (Neo-)Marxism, dialectical-materialism, historicism, the Verstehen approach and the hermeneutical approach. With regard to the various schools of metascience see also Radnitzky (1973) and Ochsner (1979); the latter deals with second language acquisition research.

References

ACHTENHAGEN, F. 1984, Qualitative Unterrichtsforschung. Einige einführende Bemerkungen zu einer kontrovers diskutierten Problematik. *Unterrichtswissenschaft* 12, 206–17.

Arbeitsgruppe Bielefelder Soziologen (ed.) 1976, *Kommunikative Sozialforschung. Alltagswissen und Alltagshandeln*. München: Fink.

ASCHENBACH, G., BILLMANN-MACHECHA, E. & ZITTERBARTH, W. 1985, Kulturwissenschaftliche Aspekte qualitativer psychologischer Forschung. In G. JÜTTEMANN (ed.), *Qualitative Forschung in der Psychologie: Grundfragen, Verfahrensweisen, Anwendungsfelder*. Weinheim and Basel: Beltz, 25–44.

BIALYSTOK, E. & SHARWOOD SMITH, M. 1985, Interlanguage is not a state of mind: An evaluation of the construct for second-language acquisition. *Applied Linguistics* 6, 101–17.

BÖRSCH, S. 1986, Introspective methods in research on interlingual and intercultural communication. In J. HOUSE & S. BLUM-KULKA (eds), *Interlingual and Intercultural Communication*. Tübingen: Narr.

BORING, E. G. 1953, A history of introspection. *Psychological Bulletin* 50, 169–89.

BROMME, R. 1985, Aufgaben- und Problemanalyse bei der Untersuchung des problemlösenden Denkens. In G. JÜTTEMANN (ed.), *Qualitative Forschung in der Psychologie: Grundfragen, Verfahrensweisen, Anwendungsfelder*. Weinheim and Basel: Beltz, 259–81.

BRUNNER, E. J. 1982, Interpretative Auswertung. In G. L. HUBER & H. MANDL (eds), *Verbale Daten*. Weinheim and Basel: Beltz, 197–219.

BUNGE, M. 1984, Philosophical problems in linguistics. *Erkenntnis* 21, 107–73.

CAVALCANTI, M. 1982, Using the unorthodox, unmeasurable verbal protocol technique: Qualitative data in foreign language reading research. In S. DINGWALL & S. MANN (eds), *Methods and Problems in Doing Applied Linguistic Research*. University of Lancaster: Department of Linguistics, 72–85.

COHEN, A. 1984a, On taking language tests: what the students report. *Language Testing* 1, 70–81.

— 1984b, Studying second-language learning strategies: how do we get the infor-
mation? *Applied Linguistics* 2, 101–12.
COHEN, A. D., SEGAL, M. & WEISS BAR-SIMAN-TOV, R. 1984, The C-test in
Hebrew. *Language Testing* 1, 221–25.
DANZINGER, K. 1980, The history of introspection reconsidered. *Journal of the
History of the Behavioural Sciences* 16, 241–62.
DEFFNER, G. 1984, *Lautes Denken—Untersuchungen zur Qualität eines
Datenerhebungsverfahrens*. Frankfurt: Peter Lang.
DENZIN, N. K. 1978, *The Research Act*. New York: McGraw-Hill.
ERICSSON, K. A. & SIMON, H. A. 1980, Verbal reports as data. *Psychological
Review* 87, 215–51.
— 1984, *Protocol Analysis. Verbal Reports as Data*. Cambridge, Mass.: MIT Press.
ESSER, H. 1975, *Soziale Regelmäßigkeiten des Befragtenverhaltens*. Meisenheim
am Glahn: Hain.
ESSER, H., KLENOVITS, K. & ZEHNPFENNIG, H. 1977, *Wissenschaftstheorie. Bd 1:
Grundlagen und Analytische Wissenschaftstheorie*. Stuttgart: Teubner.
FÆRCH, C. & KASPER, G. 1987, Introspektive Methoden in der Lernersprache-
nanalyse. In S. BÖRSCH (ed.), *Die Rolle der Psychologie in der Sprachlehrfor-
schung*. Tübingen: Narr. 269–303.
FEGER, H. & BREDENKAMP, J. (eds) 1983, *Forschungsmethoden der Psychologie.
Band 3: Messen und Testen*. Göttingen: Hogrefe.
FEGER, H. & GRAUMANN, C. F. 1983, Beobachtung und Beschreibung von Erleben
und Verhalten. In H. FEGER & J. BREDENKAMP (eds), *Forschungsmethoden
der Psychologie. Band 2: Datenerhebung*. Göttingen: Hogrefe, 76–134.
FILSTEAD, W. J. 1979, Qualitative methods. A needed perspective in evaluation
research. In T. D. COOK & C. S. REICHARDT (eds), *Qualitative and Quantitative
Methods in Evaluation Research*. Beverly Hills: Sage, 33–48.
FRIEDRICHS, J. 1973, *Methoden empirischer Sozialforschung*. Reinbek: Rowohlt.
GIGERENZER, G. 1981, *Messung und Modellbildung in der Psychologie*. München
and Basel: Reinhardt.
GLASER, B. G. & STRAUSS, A. L. 1974, *The Discovery of Grounded Theory:
Strategies for Qualitative Research*. Chicago: Aldine.
GROEBEN, N. & SCHEELE, B. 1977, *Argumente für eine Psychologie des reflexiven
Subjekts*. Darmstadt: Steinkopff.
GROEBEN, N. & WESTMEYER, H. 1975, *Kriterien psychologischer Forschung*.
München: Juventa.
GROTJAHN, R. & STEMMER, B. 1985, On the development and evaluation of a C-
test for French. *Fremdsprachen und Hochschule. AKS Rundbrief* 13/14,
101–20. (Ruhr-Universität Bochum: AKS).
HABERMAS, J. 1971, *Knowledge and Human Interests*. Boston: Beacon Press.
— 1973, Wahrheitstheorien. In H. FAHRENBACH (ed.), *Wirklichkeit und Reflexion.
Walter Schulz zum 60. Geburtstag*. Pfullingen: Neske, 211–65.
HARTWIG, F. & DEARING, B. E. 1979, *Exploratory Data Analysis*. Beverly Hills:
Sage.
HERRMANN, T. 1969, *Lehrbuch der empirischen Persönlichkeitsforschung*. Göt-
tingen: Hogrefe.
HOFFMANN-RIEM, C. 1980, Die Sozialforschung einer interpretativen Soziologie—
Der Datengewinn. *Kölner Zeitschrift für Soziologie und Sozialpsychologie* 32,
339–72.

HOLENSTEIN, E. 1980, Introspektion. In E. HOLENSTEIN (ed.), *Von der Hintergehbarkeit der Sprache: kognitive Unterlagen der Sprache*. Frankfurt: Suhrkamp, 84–155.

HOLZKAMP, K. 1972, Zum Problem der Relevanz psychologischer Forschung für die Praxis. In K. HOLZKAMP (ed.), *Kritische Psychologie: vorbereitende Arbeiten*. Frankfurt: Fischer, 9–34.

HOPF, C. & WEINGARTEN, E. (eds) 1979, *Qualitative Sozialforschung*. Stuttgart: Klett-Cotta.

HRON, A. 1982, Interview. In G. L. HUBER & H. MANDL (eds), *Verbale Daten*. Weinheim and Basel: Beltz, 119–40.

HUBER, G. L. & MANDL, H. 1982, Verbalisationsmethoden zur Erfassung von Kognitionen im Handlungszusammenhang. In G. L. HUBER & H. MANDL (eds), *Verbale Daten*. Weinheim and Basel: Beltz, 11–42.

HUBER, H. P. 1984, Entwicklungstendenzen in der Einzelfallstatistik. *Psychologische Beiträge* 26, 348–62.

ISELER, A. & PERREZ, M. (eds), 1976, *Relevanz in der Psychologie: zur Problematik von Relevanzbegriffen, -forderungen und -behauptungen*. München and Basel: Reinhardt.

ITKONEN, E. 1981, The concept of linguistic intuition. In F. COULMAS (ed.), *A Festschrift for Native Speaker*. The Hague, Paris and New York: Mouton, 127–40.

JÜTTEMANN, G. 1985, Vorbemerkungen des Herausgebers. In G. JÜTTEMANN (ed.), *Qualitative Forschung in der Psychologie: Grundfragen, Verfahrensweisen, Anwendungsfelder*. Weinheim and Basel: Beltz, 7–22.

KADE, S. 1983, *Methoden des Fremdverstehens*. Bad Heilbrunn: Julius Klinkhard.

KLEIN-BRALEY, C. 1985, A cloze-up on the C-test: A study in the construct validation of authentic tests. *Language Testing* 2, 76–104.

KLEIN-BRALEY, C. & RAATZ, U. 1984, A survey of research on the C-test. *Language Testing* 1, 134–46.

KLEINING, G. 1982, Umriss zu einer Methodologie qualitativer Sozialforschung. *Kölner Zeitschrift für Soziologie und Sozialpsychologie* 34, 224–53.

KÖCKEIS-STANGL, E. 1980, Methoden der Sozialisationsforschung. In K. HURRELMANN & D. ULICH (eds), *Handbuch der Sozialisationsforschung*. Weinheim and Basel: Beltz, 321–70.

KÖNIG, E. 1983, Methodenprobleme der Handlungsforschung—Zur Diskussion um die Handlungsforschung. In P. ZEDLER & H. MOSER (eds), *Aspekte qualitativer Sozialforschung*. Opladen: Leske and Budrich, 79–94.

KÜCHLER, M. 1980, Qualitative Sozialforschung. Modetrend oder Neuanfang? *Kölner Zeitschrift für Soziologie und Sozialpsychologie* 32, 373–86.

— 1983, "Qualitative" Sozialforschung — Ein neuer Königsweg? In D. GARZ & K. KRAIMER (eds), *Brauchen wir andere Forschungsmethoden? Beiträge zur Diskussion interpretativer Verfahren*. Frankfurt: Scriptor, 9–30.

KUHN, T. S. 1962, *The Structure of Scientific Revolutions*. Chicago: University of Chicago Press (revised edition 1970).

— 1974, Second thoughts on paradigms. In F. SUPPE (ed.), *The Structure of Scientific Theories*. Urbana, Ill.: University of Illinois Press, 459–82.

LAKATOS, I. 1970, Falsification and the methodology of scientific research programmes. In I. LAKATOS & A. MUSGRAVE (eds), *Criticism and the Growth of Knowledge*. London: Cambridge University Press, 91–196.

LECHLER, P. 1982, Kommunikative Validierung. In G. L. HUBER & H. MANDL (eds), *Verbale Daten*. Weinheim and Basel: Beltz, 243–58.

LEICHNER, R. 1979, *Psychologische Diagnostik: Grundlagen, Kontroversen, Praxisprobleme*. Weinheim and Basel: Beltz.

LIEBERMANN, D. A. 1979, Behaviorism and the mind. A (limited) call for a return to introspection. *American Psychologist*, 34, 319–33.

LIENERT, G. A. 1969, *Testaufbau und Testanalyse*. Weinheim, Berlin and Basel: Beltz.

LONG, M. H. 1980, Inside the "black box": Methodological issues in classroom research on language learning. *Language Learning* 30, 1–42.

MANN, S. J. 1982, Verbal reports as data: A focus on retrospection. In S. DINGWALL & S. J. MANN (eds), *Methods and Problems in Doing Applied Linguistic Research*. University of Lancaster: Department of Linguistics, 87–104.

MASTERMAN, M. 1970, The nature of a paradigm. In I. LAKATOS & A. MUSGRAVE (eds), *Criticism and the Growth of Knowledge*. London: Cambridge University Press, 59–89.

MAYRING, P. 1985, Qualitative Inhaltsanalyse. In G. JÜTTEMANN (ed.), *Qualitative Forschung in der Psychologie: Grundfragen, Verfahrensweisen, Anwendungsfelder*. Weinheim and Basel: Beltz, 187–211.

MEHAN, H. 1977, Ethnography. In: *Bilingual Education: Current Perspectives. Vol. 1: Social Science*. Arlington, Va: Center for Applied Linguistics, 73–89.

— 1978, Structuring school structure. *Harvard Educational Review* 48, 32–64.

MOHLER, P. P. 1981, Zur Pragmatik qualitativer und quantitativer Sozialforschung. *Kölner Zeitschrift für Soziologie und Sozialpsychologie* 33, 716–34.

MOSER, H. 1983, Zur methodologischen Problematik der Aktionsforschung. In P. ZEDLER & H. MOSER (eds), *Aspekte qualitativer Sozialforschung*. Opladen: Leske and Budrich, 51–78.

NATSOULAS, T. 1967, What are perceptual reports about? *Psychological Bulletin* 67, 249–72.

— 1970, Concerning introspective knowledge. *Psychological Bulletin* 73, 89–111.

NISBETT, R. E. & WILSON, T. D. 1977, Telling more than we can know: Verbal reports on mental processes. *Psychological Review* 84, 231–59.

NUNNALLY, J. C. 1978, *Psychometric Theory* (2nd ed.). New York: McGraw-Hill.

NUßBAUM, A. 1984, Quantitative oder qualitative Unterrichtsforschung? *Unterrichtswissenschaft* 12, 218–31.

OCHSNER, R. 1979, A poetics of second language acquisition. *Language Learning* 29, 53–80.

OEVERMANN, U., ALLERT, T., KONAU, E. & KRAMBECK, J. 1979, Die Methodologie einer "objektiven Hermeneutik" und ihre allgemeine forschungslogische Bedeutung in den Sozialwissenschaften. In H.-G. SOEFFNER (ed.), *Interpretative Verfahren in den Sozial- und Textwissenschaften*. Stuttgart: Metzler, 352–434.

OPP, K.-D. 1976, *Methodologie der Sozialwissenschaften: Einführung in Probleme ihrer Theoriebildung*. Reinbek: Rowohlt.

PATTON, M. Q. 1980, *Qualitative Evaluation Methods*. Beverly Hills: Sage.

RADNITZKY, G. 1973, *Contemporary Schools of Metascience*. Chicago: Henry Regnery.

REICHARDT, C. S. & COOK, T. D. 1979, Beyond qualitative versus quantitative methods. In T. D. COOK & C. S. REICHARDT (eds), *Qualitative and Quantitative Methods in Evaluation Research*. Beverly Hills: Sage, 7–32.

RINGEN, J. D. 1981, Quine on introspection in linguistics. In F. COULMAS (ed.), *A Festschrift for Native Speaker*. The Hague, Paris and New York: Mouton, 141–51.

RÖSLER, F. 1983, Physiologisch orientierte Forschungsstrategien in der Differenti-
ellen und Diagnostischen Psychologie: I. Zur Konzeption des psychophysiol-
ogischen Untersuchungsansatzes. *Zeitschrift für Differentielle und
Diagnostische Psychologie* 4, 283–99.
— 1984. Physiologisch orientierte Forschungsstrategien in der Differentiellen und
Diagnostischen Psychologie: II. Zur Systematisierung psychophysiologischer
Untersuchungen. *Zeitschrift für Differentielle und Diagnostische Psychologie*
5, 7–36.
RUDINGER, G., CHASELON, F., ZIMMERMANN, E. J. & HENNING, H. J. 1985,
Qualitative Daten, Neue Wege sozialwissenschaftlicher Methodik. München,
Wien and Baltimore: Urban and Schwarzenberg.
SCHAFF, A. 1980, Objektivität. In J. SPECK (ed.), *Handbuch wissenschaftstheore-
tischer Begriffe* (Vol. 2). Göttingen: Vandenhoeck and Ruprecht, 460–64.
SCHEUCH, E. K. 1967, Das Interview in der Sozialforschung. In R. KÖNIG (ed.),
*Handbuch der empirischen Sozialforschung. Band 2: Grundlegende Methoden
und Techniken. Teil 1.* Stuttgart: Enke, 66–190.
SCHNEIDER, G. 1985, Strukturkonzept und Interpretationspraxis der objektiven
Hermeneutik. In G. JÜTTEMANN (ed.), *Qualitative Forschung in der Psycho-
logie: Grundfragen, Verfahrensweisen, Anwendungsfelder.* Weinheim and
Basel: Beltz, 71–91.
SCHNELLE, H. 1981, Introspection and the description of language use. In F.
COULMAS (ed.), *A Festschrift for Native Speaker.* The Hague, Paris and New
York: Mouton, 105–26.
SCRIVEN, M. 1972, Objectivity and subjectivity in educational research. In L. G.
THOMAS (ed.), *Philosophical Redirection of Educational Research: the Seventy-
First Yearbook of the National Society for the Study of Education.* Chicago:
University of Chicago Press, 50–68.
SELIGER, H. W. 1983, The language learner as linguist: of metaphors and realities.
Applied Linguistics 4, 179–91.
SILVERMAN, D. 1985, *Qualitative Methodology and Sociology.* Aldershot: Gower.
SOEFFNER, H.-G. (ed.) 1979. *Interpretative Verfahren in den Sozial- und Textwissen-
schaften.* Stuttgart: Metzlersche Verlagsbuchhandlung.
STEPHENS, R., BHASKAR, R. & DILLARD, J. F. 1981, The role of task analysis in
understanding problem-solving behavior. *Instructional Science* 10, 23–45.
TERHART, E. 1982, Interpretative approaches in educational research. *Cambridge
Journal of Education* 12, 141–60.
— 1983, Schwierigkeiten mit der "Objektiven Hermeneutik". Eine Antwort auf
Ulrich Oevermann. In D. GARZ & K. KRAIMER (eds), *Brauchen wir andere
Forschungsmethoden? Beiträge zur Diskussion interpretativer Verfahren.*
Frankfurt: Scriptor, 156–75.
THOMAE, H. 1985, Zur Relation von qualitativen und quantitativen Strategien
psychologischer Forschung. In G. JÜTTEMANN (ed.), *Qualitative Forschung in
der Psychologie: Grundfragen, Verfahrensweisen, Anwendungsfelder.*
Weinheim and Basel: Beltz, 92–107.
TREIBER, B. & GROEBEN, N. 1981, Handlungsforschung und epistemologisches
Subjektmodell. *Zeitschrift für Sozialisationsforschung und Erziehungssozio-
logie* 1, 117–38.
— 1983, Vorarbeiten zu einer Reflexiven Sozialtechnologie — Die Integration
von dialog-konsenstheoretischem Wahrheits- sowie Falsifikationskriterium am
Beispiel subjektiver Theorien von Lehrern. In P. ZEDLER & H. MOSER (eds),
Aspekte qualitativer Sozialforschung. Opladen: Leske and Budrich, 163–208.

UPSHUR, J. A. 1983, Measurement of individual differences and explanation in the language sciences. In A. Z. GUIORA (ed.), *An Epistemology for the Language Sciences*. Michigan: University of Michigan, 99–140.

VAN BUER, J. 1984, "Quantitative" oder "qualitative" Unterrichtsbeobachtung? Eine falsche Alternative. *Unterrichtswissenschaft* 12, 252–67.

VAN DIJK, T. A. & KINTSCH, W. 1983, *Strategies of Discourse Comprehension*. New York: Academic Press.

VOLLMER, H. J. 1981, Why are we interested in "General Language Proficiency"? In C. KLEIN-BRALEY & D. K. STEVENSON (eds), *Practice and Problems in Language Testing 1*. Bern and Frankfurt: Lang, 96–123.

WAHL, D. 1982, Handlungsvalidierung. In G. L. HUBER & H. MANDL (eds), *Verbale Daten*. Weinheim and Basel: Beltz, 259–74.

WEIDLE, R. & WAGNER, A. C. 1982, Die Method des Lauten Denkens. In G. L. HUBER & H. MANDL (eds), *Verbale Daten*. Weinheim and Basel: Beltz, 81–103.

WILSON, T. P. 1970, Conceptions of interaction and forms of sociological explanation. *American Sociological Review* 35, 697–710.

— 1973, Theorien der Interaktion und Modelle soziologischer Erklärung. In Arbeitsgemeinschaft Bielefelder Soziologen (ed.), *Alltagswissen, Interaktion und gesellschaftliche Wirklichkeit* (Vol. 1). Reinbek: Rowohlt, 54–79 (revised German version of Wilson 1970).

— 1982, Qualitative "oder" quantitative Methoden in der Sozialforschung. *Kölner Zeitschrift für Soziologie und Sozialpsychologie* 34, 487–508.

WOTTAWA, H. 1981, Allgemeine Aussagen in der psychologischen Forschung: eine Fiktion. In W. MICHAELIS (ed.), *Bericht über den 32. Kongreß der Deutschen Gesellschaft für Psychologie in Zürich 1980* (Vol. 1). Göttingen and Toronto: Hogrefe, 131–36.

4 Using Verbal Reports in Research on Language Learning[1]

ANDREW D. COHEN

As researchers have become increasingly interested in investigating the strategies[2] used in learning a second or foreign language, there has been a growing interest in using learners' reports of their own intuitions and insights as a complement to classroom observation and other measures. In this chapter, I will consider the potential of such verbal reports and the ways they can be obtained.

First, let us look at some of the limitations of restricting our study to observation of the learner's behaviour in the classroom. These approaches assume that observable behaviour will reveal the learning process. They rely, in part, on detailed observation schedules (see, for example, Fanselow, 1977, 1985; Rubin, 1981). However, it has become apparent that it is difficult to obtain accurate insights about learners' conscious thought processes through conventional observations of teacher-centred classroom sessions. By "conscious thought processes", what is meant are all thoughts that are within the realm of awareness of the learner, whether they are attended to fully or not.[3]

Classroom observations can record the physical movements of students — nods of the head, smiles, eye movements, and what they say — but cannot easily capture what they are thinking about, how they are thinking, or how they feel. Hence, observations regarding language learning behaviour are generally limited to students who speak up. Such observations tell us nothing about those who remain quiet, and not a great deal about those who do not. Rubin would suggest that it is possible to make observations of student learning strategies, but that the approach is tedious and not so productive in most classrooms because teachers tend to focus on product rather than on process and because opportunities have to be created to verify the observers' interpretations of learner strategies (Personal Communication).

Consider what a strategy might be like. A student learning to conjugate a new verb might go through a thought process something like this one that I went through in dealing with a new Hebrew verb:

"Now, how am I going to learn how to conjugate the verb *rigel* 'to spy' in Hebrew? Oh, I see. It is conjugated just like *diber* 'to speak'. So now I know its forms — no problem."

In this case, I used the strategy of analogy to learn the appropriate forms of the verb. Sometimes the strategies seem obvious. Sometimes they are quite surprising. Thus, the outside observer has little chance of guessing accurately either the likelihood that a certain strategy is being used or the frequency with which it is used. Verbal reports from learners about the kinds of strategy that work well for them can be most helpful in learning training — in training learners to make more efficient use of their time spent learning a second language.

After a number of hours of classroom observation, Naiman *et al.* (1975) concluded that very few learning techniques were overtly displayed in the classroom. For example, although the researchers had hoped to investigate the extent to which learners used circumlocution in their utterances, they found very rare cases of its use. It was not that it did not occur, but, rather, that it was difficult for an outside observer to determine when the learner was, in fact, using circumlocution. Naiman and his colleagues did not feel that more time in the classroom would help. They suggested that students be interviewed directly regarding what were largely covert forms of learning behaviour in the daily classroom routine. They felt that only through interviews could one have access to techniques that were invisible to any observers — such as "attempting to answer to themselves every question asked by the teacher" (Naiman *et al.*, 1975: 68).

Because of these limitations on observational techniques, there has therefore developed a new focus in research on strategies: the collection of learners' reports of their own insights about the strategies they use.

Types of Verbal Report Data

What kinds of data can be obtained from learners' reports of the processes they use? At the outset it is important to point out that these reports are limited to that subset of *learning* strategies that the learner is conscious of. In other words, we can only learn about the conscious strategies that learners utilize in their efforts to master a language. We are not talking about what have been posited as separate second-language *acquisition* processes (Krashen, 1982) — namely, unconscious processes that lead to mastery. (There is still debate as to whether such a separation exists.) The learning strategies that interest us span a wide range of activities. They include: how learners attend to language input, how learners arrive at spoken utterances, how readers process a text, how writers generate text, and how vocabulary is learned initially and retrieved subsequently. These strategies may be effective or they may not work for the given learner. In other words, they may result in enhanced learning or they may not.

In order to tap the strategies involved in language learning, researchers have utilized three basic categories of learner report data. They will be referred to as "self-report", "self-observation", and "self-revelation" (see Table 1). The first refers to learners' descriptions of what they do, characterized by generalized statements about learning behaviour (e.g. "When I have a word I really want to learn, I say it over to myself several times and try to associate it with some other word I already know.") or labels they apply to themselves (e.g. "I'm a 'speed listener' in another language. I make a quick search for the key words, and if I don't know them, I try to figure out their meaning from context.") Such statements are usually based on beliefs or concepts that the learners have about the way that they learn language, and are often not based on the observation of any specific event.

"Self-observation", on the other hand, refers to the inspection of specific language behaviour, either while the information is still in short-term memory, i.e. introspectively, or after the event, i.e. retrospectively (usually after 20 seconds or so).[4] Retrospection can be immediate (e.g. within, say, an hour of the event) or delayed (a few hours, days, or even weeks after the event). It appears that the bulk of the forgetting occurs right after the mental event. Thus, data from immediate retrospection may only be somewhat more complete than data from delayed retrospection.[5]

The term "self-revelation" is introduced here to refer to a learner's report that is neither a description of general behaviours, nor based on inspection of specific ones. Rather it consists of "think-aloud" stream-of-consciousness disclosure of thought processes while the information is being attended to.[6] The data are basically unedited and unanalysed.

TABLE 1 Types of Data and their Descriptors

DESCRIPTORS

TYPE OF DATA	# Participants			Context		Recency	Mode				Formality	Degree of External Interven.
							Elic.		Resp.			
	Gp.	Indiv. + Invest.	Indiv. Alone	Dur. Class	Other		O	W	O	W		
Self-Report	X	X	X		X	LO-HI	X	X	X	X	LO-HI	LO-HI
Self-Observation: introspection	X	X	X	X	X	HI	X	X	X	X	LO	LO-MED
retrospection	X	X	X	X	X	LO-MED	X	X	X	X	LO-MED	LO-MED
Self-Revealment: think-aloud		X			X	HI	X		X		LO	LO

KEY:
 # Participants: group, individual + investigator, individual alone
Context: during class, other
Mode: elicitation—oral, written; response—oral, written

Any given report may have different types of data in it. For example, data from self-report studies may include learners' retrospections about specific language learning behaviours, just as data from retrospective studies can include generalized pronouncements, extending beyond the observation of a given event. Furthermore, it is sometimes difficult to establish whether students are actually *thinking aloud* — without analysis — or whether they are instead *observing* that behaviour, whether introspectively or retrospectively. For example, a student wants to learn a new word in Spanish, *sacar* "to take out", and is asked to think aloud while doing it. The report data may look like these data I collected on myself:

> "Let me see. It sounds like a 'sack', like in 'a sack of garbage'. Is that the best I can do? Will I remember it? Let me picture myself actually taking out the garbage. O.K. Did that work? Yeah, I think so. I think I managed to learn that word by its similarity in sound to a word in English that can be linked to it by meaning."

Most of this report contains think-aloud data, but at the end I was self-observing retrospectively — when analysing the process of finding a mnemonic association for remembering the word *sacar*.

Descriptors of Data Types

There are at least six major factors which characterize the data obtained from the three categories of verbal report described above. These include: the number of participants, the research context, the recency of the event, the mode of elicitation and response, the formality of elicitation, and the degree of external intervention (see Table 1). "The number of participants" refers to how many investigators and respondents take part in the data collection process. Informants may collect data by themselves, as in the case of diary studies when there are no directions provided by outside investigators (Schumann & Schumann, 1977; Bailey & Ochsner, 1983). Alternatively, one or more investigators can work with individual informants or with groups of informants at a time. The classroom teachers may be involved as investigators in this form of research, as long as their participation does not interfere with their teaching duties. Teachers, in fact, may be in a special position to encourage and train learners to report accurately on their learning.

"The research context" refers to the "when", "where", and to some extent the "how" of data collection. The data may be collected in the classroom — either during a class session, at a break, or after class.

Similarly the data can be collected elsewhere in an institutional setting — as in a language laboratory or a video studio. The data could also be collected in a variety of other places — as is customary of diary studies. More formal settings allow for data collection procedures not possible elsewhere. For example, it is possible to seat informants at booths in a language laboratory and have each one tape-record think-aloud data at given intervals during a discussion or while reading a passage.[7]

"The recency of the event" relates to the proximity of the verbal report to the actual learning event. Whereas think-aloud data is obtained at the time of the learning event, self-observational and self-report data can vary with respect to how soon after the learning event they take place. Researchers may wish to increase the recency by methodological procedures. For example, the teacher could stop a class session to find out how a student's thinking led to a certain utterance (Cohen & Aphek, 1981). In a like manner, students could note inferences made during class sessions at the moment that these inferences occur — by jotting them down in their notebooks along with their other notes (Rubin & Henze, 1981).

"The mode of elicitation and response" concerns whether the investigator elicits the verbal report data orally or by means of written instructions (if there is an external investigator), and whether the informants respond orally or in writing. Both oral and written responses can be videotaped, providing a visual record of the event. Such a record may help in subsequent analysis of think-aloud data — i.e. in checking the relationship between what learners were saying and what they were actually writing down on paper (see Jones, 1982; Tetroe & Jones, 1982).

"The formality of elicitation" has to do with the degree of formal structure imposed on the elicitation by an outside investigator. For example, self-report data could reflect a questionnaire with high formal structure, through a set of fixed questions (whether general or specific to a given learner) or with less structure through the use of a flexible questioning format, allowing for the respondents to provide information along the lines that they themselves determine. Oral interviews — more than written questionnaires — may cater to this flexible approach. In this case, the researcher later provides the structure to the responses through content analysis.[8]

The final factor, "the degree of external intervention", is the extent to which the investigator shapes the respondent's reporting process. Self-observational studies, for example, can be shaped through the types of instructions given to the informants. For example, informants could write a diary on language learning reflecting any behaviours that they wish to describe, or they could be requested to limit their insights to one or more areas of interest to the investigator. Even think-aloud data can be directed along certain lines according to the investigator's instructions.

Table 1 has been filled out to show which descriptor variables tend to apply to particular types of data, or the extent to which the descriptors apply. These ratings are meant to be suggestive. For example, think-aloud data are usually collected orally from an individual by an investigator, out of class, at the moment the thoughts are taking place, with a low degree of formality of elicitation, and with little external intervention by the investigator. It would be possible to find exceptions to this pattern, and such variations might provide useful research insights.

Issues of Controversy Regarding Verbal Report

For many years, psychologists have been debating the merits of verbal report data as a research tool. It appears that, at present, mentalistic approaches enjoy the modified support of a respectable group of cognitive psychologists (Bakan, 1954; Radford, 1974; Lieberman, 1979; White, 1980; and Ericsson & Simon, 1980, 1984). As such approaches have become more prevalent in second-language research, reservations have begun to appear concerning the merits of applying verbal report data to this field (Seliger, 1983). Whether such data can really be used as evidence regarding the inner workings of the learner's mind has been called into question.

An objection to using verbal reports as data rests on the assumption that much of language learning takes place at an unconscious level and is, therefore, inaccessible to mental probes. Seliger (1983) sees verbal reports as, at best, a source of information on how learners *use* what they have learned, and not as a means of describing how the systems responsible for interlanguage performance become internalized. The issue is raised as to how much of verbal report is a description of the actual processes used in learning to understand and produce second-language utterances and how much is *post hoc* guessing or inferencing based on comprehension or production.

It is true that much of the verbal report data in second-language research to date has concerned language *using*, rather than language *learning*. But this is not to say that data on the processing of language in language learning is necessarily inaccessible. It is also true that after the particular learning event, it need not be clear to an outside investigator whether the bit of information has, in fact, been learned, and if it has been learned, whether it really has been learned in the way that the learner says that it has. However, as we begin to accumulate descriptions of second-language learning events, patterns emerge which begin to take on a certain reality as they are corroborated by more learners.

Taking a somewhat historical perspective on this methodological approach, we note that, at the same time that learners' errors were being analysed to determine the nature of interlanguage, studies also began to appear which used learners as informants to better understand the process of rule learning (e.g. Cohen & Robbins, 1976). Although such studies generally focused on *what* had been learned or not learned, rather than on *how* it had or had not been learned, it was possible to use the learner's explanations of how they learned, to reconstruct the way the particular forms came into the learner's interlanguage.

In eliciting data on the language learning process, we are both asking someone to use language to do certain tasks and also to use language to describe how they did these tasks. We are, in effect, asking for a description of language processing while learners are performing their language competence. If there were some language learning involved, we would also be asking for a verbalization of the learning process as well. Thus, we are taxing the learner's capacity to remember a stage of performance once that stage is passed, and even to hold on to information within a single stage. Memory of mental events is problematic for the learner, and could lead to faulty reporting, but it then is the challenge for the researcher to tap this information while it is still available.

While it is true that much of what we process is done unconsciously, White (1980) would suggest that we underestimate the extent of conscious processing. The reason he gives is that we simply do not pay attention to all our conscious processes. It has also been pointed out that the nature of the verbal report task itself will dictate the degree of attention we pay to our mental processing.

Evidence from self-observational studies calling for introspection shows that, depending on the task, subjects may be successful at consulting their memory of cognitive processes and describing them. That is, subjects may have accessible memory for such processes and awareness of the information while the process is going on (Ericsson & Simon, 1980: 245–46). Their conclusion is based on an extensive review of the literature, involving a variety of cognitive tasks — e.g. learning lists of paired associates (A–B, B–C, than A–C), solving anagrams, verbalizing rules for sorting illustrated cards or other stimuli, discovering geometrical proofs, and solving a puzzle with disks and pegs or numbered tiles. We note that this series of tasks includes those requiring both linguistic and visual processes. In fact, it is not so unnatural to ask subjects to verbalize their reasoning dealing with nonverbal tasks since such tasks may well be accomplished with the assistance of linguistic processing.

For example, subjects may talk to themselves about why they are putting a disk in one place and not in another, or about why an illustrated card is being sorted into one pile and not into another. Such categorization tasks are an integral part of second-language learning, as in the learning of agreement between subject and verb in person, number, and gender. Just as cognitive psychologists may have subjects indulge in consciousness raising to try to determine how they accomplish tasks such as those listed above, so applied linguists can apply these methodological techniques to investigate the accomplishment of language learning tasks. As we will discuss in the next section, however, verbal report data must be collected with care.

Care in Collecting Verbal Report Data

In a study of the process of writing, Hayes & Flower (1983) corroborate a finding by Ericsson & Simon that introspective verbal reporting does not change or slow down the reporting of memory traces that are verbal.[9] They did find that if the respondents are asked to report information usually *not* attended to (i.e. within their realm of conscious awareness but receiving little or no attention), introspection does modify the normal sequence of mental processes. They also found in retrospective reporting that subjects forgot some information about processes that was available during the task performance: e.g. the writer would struggle with the choice of words and word order in a difficult sentence and then later deny having had a problem. As they put it, "... the delicate structure of goals and subgoals erected to construct the sentence was destroyed when the goal was accomplished" (Hayes & Flower, 1983: 215).

Poor verbal report data are often the result of poor methods of reporting. Ericsson & Simon give three instances where this might happen. First, they claim that faulty reporting can result if the information is not attended to, since for information to be available from short-term memory,[10] it must be attended to (1980: 224). Thus, in the case of probes requesting subjects to produce verbal reports about information not attended to, it is possible that the subjects will infer missing information and generalize incomplete memories. Secondly, they suggest that faulty reporting can result if not all the information which is in short-term memory at the time of the reporting, is actually reported. For this reason, it is important to utilize elicitation procedures that obtain reports that are as complete as possible. Finally, faulty reporting can result when not all information previously available in short-term memory has been retained in long-term memory, or is retrievable from long-term memory.

White (1980) adds that the reporting tasks should be easy — not requiring excessive concentration or effort. He also points out the need for the subjects and the researcher to conceptualize the situation the same way. In fact, faulty data may result from an inadequate understanding on the part of the respondents as to how they are supposed to report. Hosenfeld found, for example, that her respondents sometimes needed prodding in order for them to produce think-aloud data rather than retrospective data (Cohen & Hosenfeld, 1981). The fact is that respondents may need training in how to provide the desired form of data. It would appear that some pre-training and specific instructions may be necessary in order to have respondents reveal their learning processes.[11] For example, one researcher (Cavalcanti, 1982 and in this volume, Chapter 12) found that left to their own devices, subjects asked to think aloud while reading would actually read large chunks of text and then retrospect. To avoid this pattern, she trained them to give think-aloud data each time they noticed that they had paused in the course of reading.

From all these considerations, it emerges that verbal report data can be a useful research tool under certain conditions and with certain limitations. Ericsson & Simon (1980: 247) put it as follows:

> "For more than half a century...the verbal reports of human subjects have been thought suspect as a source of evidence about cognitive processes. ... verbal reports, elicited with care and interpreted with full understanding of the circumstances under which they were obtained, are a valuable and thoroughly reliable source of information about cognitive processes.... They describe human behavior that is as readily interpreted as any other human behavior."

Hayes & Flower (1983) point out that, whereas verbal report protocols are incomplete because many important psychological processes are completely unconscious, the collecting of verbal report data is still beneficial in that it provides direct evidence about processes that are otherwise invisible, yields rich data and thus promotes exploration of cognitive processes.

The potential value of verbal report data to the study of language learning is similarly great. It may well provide further important insights for enhancing learners' attention to language input, facilitating their efforts to speak fluently, assisting them in reading more efficiently, and guiding them in successful vocabulary learning. As we find out more about the processes that learners use, we are better equipped to test hypotheses about strategies that we would predict are likely to produce the greatest success for given types of learners. For example, as we learn more about the mnemonic devices that learners actually use to try to remember L2 vocabulary, we could perhaps design an experiment in which the learners would receive mnemonic aids which we hypothesize as most beneficial to them, given the vocabulary learning preferences we find them to exhibit (e.g. hearing a word v. seeing it in print, seeing a picture of a word v. hearing a description of the word). As the field of second language acquisition emerges, we will surely find more and more possible applications for verbal report data.

Notes to Chapter 4

1. An earlier version of this paper appears in Wenden & Rubin (1987). I would like to thank Anita Wenden, Joan Rubin, and Herb Seliger for their helpful comments and encouragement.
2. "Strategy" is used here to refer to those thought processes that learners consciously choose to utilize in accomplishing learning tasks. Some researchers prefer to reserve the term "strategy" for general categories of behaviour (e.g. "viewing language as a system", "monitoring L2 performance"). They refer to more lower-level activities within a given category (e.g. "classifying the verbs into groups that are conjugated similarly", "checking to make sure that nouns and adjectives agree in gender and number") as "techniques" (Naiman et al., 1975) or "tactics" (Seliger, 1984). For our purposes, we will refer to all such operations as strategies.
3. One set of models about how attention works, referred to as the "capacity" models, would suggest that all simultaneous inputs can be processed to one degree or another in parallel. If the number of stimuli requiring analysis exceeds a certain capacity, the learner sets priorities in processing. Consequently, some stimuli will be analysed fairly completely, while others will receive only superficial analysis. Some of the latter stimuli may still be available to conscious memory or awareness (Wingfield & Byrnes, 1981: 214–15). Thus, it is possible for one to be conscious of information but not attend to it.
4. Ericsson & Simon (1980) proposed a model for verbalization processes that is very similar to this one developed by Cohen & Hosenfeld (1981), with slight variations in terminology. They refer to "think-aloud probing", and to "concurrent" and "retrospective verbalizations", rather than to "introspective" and "retrospective self-observation", as in this chapter. In their more recent

book (Ericsson & Simon, 1984), as well as in their contribution to this volume, Chapter 2, they also distinguish "talking aloud" (i.e. directly into vocalization) from "thinking aloud" (i.e. from thinking to verbal encoding to vocalization).

5. One study had two groups of students retrospect about test items that they had taken — one group (n=18) within six hours of having taken the test and one group (n=23) three days later. In the first group, the first student started being interviewed 30 minutes after taking the test, the last student about five hours afterwards. The investigator noted few observable differences in the report data, other than a few memory lapses among students in the group doing more delayed retrospection (Larson, 1981).

6. Mann (1982) describes think-aloud data as that produced when the subject "externalizes the contents of the mind while doing something". Accordingly, an alternative to "self-revelation" could be "self-externalization".

7. I am aware of only two studies that have utilized the language laboratory for purposes of obtaining simultaneous verbal report about language learning from each individual in a group. One was an investigation of college-level reading in Spanish and English (Serrano, 1984) and the other an exploration of second-language composing aloud in a remedial ESL college writing class (Raimes, 1985).

8. Several research efforts on L2 learning strategies have utilized the semi-structured interview format, fashioning categories on the basis of content analysis of informants' responses. They include, for example, the interviewing of 34 learners by Naiman et al. (1975), four learners by Stevick (1981), and 25 learners by Wenden (1982).

9. This study investigated native-language writing processes. It is possible that introspective verbal reporting in *second-language* writing may change or slow down reporting in that it would require switching back and forth between languages if the reporting were in L1, and could cause difficulties in self-expression if the reporting were in L2.

10. Short-term memory is defined by Ericsson & Simon as "information that is heeded or attended to. The amount of information that can reside in short-term memory at one time is limited to a small number (four?) of familiar patterns (chunks)" (1980: 224).

11. There may sometimes be a fine line between providing enough external structure so as to produce the desired type of data and providing so much that the respondents feel inhibited. There is the further danger that the researcher might inadvertently plant ideas in the respondents' mind.

References

BAILEY, K. M. & OCHSNER, R. 1983, A methodological review of the diary studies: Windmill tilting or social science? In K. M. BAILEY, M. H. LONG & S. PECK (eds), *Second Language Acquisition Studies*. Rowley, Mass.: Newbury House, 188–98.

BAKAN, D. 1954, A reconsideration of the problem of introspection. *Psychological Bulletin,* 51: 2, 105–18.

CAVALCANTI, M. 1982, Using the unorthodox, unreasonable verbal protocol technique: Qualitative data in foreign language reading research. In S. DINGWALL,

S. Mann & F. Katamba (eds), *Methods and Problems in Doing Applied Linguistic Research*. Lancaster: Dept. of Linguistics and Modern English Language, University of Lancaster, 72–85.

Cohen, A. D. & Aphek, E. 1981, Easifying second language learning. *Studies in Second Language Acquisition*, 3: 2, 221–36.

Cohen, A. D. & Hosenfeld, C. 1981, Some uses of mentalistic data in second language research. *Language Learning*, 31: 2, 285–313.

Cohen, A. D. & Robbins, M. 1976, Toward assessing interlanguage performance: The relationship between selected errors, learners' characteristics, and learners' explanations. *Language Learning*, 26: 1, 45–66.

Ericsson, K. A. & Simon, H. A. 1980, Verbal reports as data. *Psychological Review*, 87: 3, 215–51.

— 1984, *Protocol Analysis: Verbal Reports as Data*. Cambridge, Mass.: MIT Press.

Fanselow, J. F. 1977, Beyond RASHOMON — conceptualizing and describing the teaching act. *TESOL Quarterly*, 11: 1, 17–39.

— 1985, "Could I ask you a couple of questions?" Episode 4 in *Breaking Rules: Alternatives in Language Teaching*. New York: Longman.

Hayes, J. R. & Flower, L. 1983, Uncovering cognitive processes in writing. In P. Mosenthal *et al.* (eds), *Research in Writing: Principles and Methods*. New York: Longman. 207–20.

Jones, S. 1982, Attention to rhetorical information while composing in a second language. Ottawa: Carleton University.

Krashen, S. D. 1982, *Principles and Practice in Second Language Acquisition*. Oxford: Pergamon.

Larson, K. 1981, A study of student test-taking strategies and difficulties. Course paper, ESL Section, Department of English, University of California, Los Angeles.

Lieberman, D. A. 1979, Behaviorism and the mind: A (limited) call for a return to introspection. *American Psychologist*, 34: 4, 319–33.

Mann, S. 1982, Verbal reports as data: A focus on retrospection. In S. Dingwall, S. Mann & F. Katamba (eds), *Methods and Problems in Doing Applied Linguistic Research*. Lancaster: Dept. of Linguistics and Modern English Language, University of Lancaster, 87–104.

Naiman, N., Fröhlich, M., Stern, H. H. & Todesco, A. 1975, *The Good Language Learner*. Toronto: Modern Language Center, Ontario Institute for Studies in Education.

Radford, J. 1974, Reflections on introspection. *American Psychologist*, 29: 4, 245–50.

Raimes, A. 1985, An investigation of how ESL students write. New York: Department of English, Hunter College/C.U.N.Y.

Rubin, J. 1981, The study of cognitive processes in second language learning. *Applied Linguistics*, 2: 2, 117–31.

Rubin, J. & Henze, R. 1981, The foreign language requirement: A suggestion to enhance its educational role in teacher training. *TESOL Newsletter*, 15: 1, 17, 19, 24.

Schumann, F. M. & Schumann, J. H. 1977, Diary of a language learner: An introspective study of second language learning. In H. D. Brown *et al.* (eds), *On TESOL '77. Teaching and Learning English as a Second Language*. Washington, D.C.: TESOL, 241–49.

SELIGER, H. W. 1983, The language learner as linguist: Of metaphors and realities. *Applied Linguistics*, 4: 3, 179–91.
— 1984, Processing universals in second language acquisition. In F. ECKMAN, L. BELL & D. NELSON, *Universals of Second Language Acquisition*. Rowley, Mass.: Newbury House, 36–47.
SERRANO, N. S. 1984, Patterns of reading in L1 and L2. In D. M. SINGLETON & D. G. LITTLE (eds), *Language Learning in Formal and Informal Contexts*. Dublin: Irish Association for Applied Linguistics, 165–76.
STEVICK, E. W. 1981, Learning a foreign language: The natural ways. In M. HINES & W. RUTHERFORD (eds), *On TESOL '81*. Washington, D. C.: TESOL, 1–10.
TETROE, J. & JONES, S. 1982, Transfer of planning skills in second language writing. Ottawa: Linguistics Department, Carleton University.
WENDEN, A. L. 1982, The processes of self-directed learning: A case study of adult language learners. Unpublished doctoral dissertation, Teachers College, Colombia University, New York.
WENDEN, A. L. & RUBIN, J. (eds) 1987, *Learner Strategies in Language Learning*. Englewood Cliffs, NJ: Prentice Hall, 31–40.
WHITE, P. 1980, Limitations on verbal report of internal events. *Psychological Review*, 87: 1, 105–12.
WINGFIELD, A. & BYRNES, D. L. 1981, *The Psychology of Human Memory*. New York: Academic Press.

5 Analysing Language Processing Through Verbal Protocols

HANS W. DECHERT

Introduction

A state-of-the-art resumé on the use and psychological validity of introspective data in psycholinguistic research has long been overdue, in spite of the seminal 1980 article by Ericsson & Simon. The Ericsson & Simon 1984 volume, to be sure, for many years to come will be taken as the generally appreciated realization of this desideratum.

Language processing is discussed in various portions of this book, explicitly and implicitly. However, the work that has been done in first and second language acquisition research is widely overlooked.

There may be various reasons for that. Cognitive scientists, unfortunately, have little contact with applied linguists and psycholinguists. Much of the work that has been done in this area has started in Europe only just recently and simply was not available at the time of the production of this book. Or is there a fundamental difference between the study of thinking and the study of language processing?

The most serious argument I have found in this respect is this:

"Ericsson and Simon (1980) have revived the method of *réflexion parlée* in the study of problem solving. The method does have its uses, for we do monitor some of the *results* of our ratiocinations, and we use these results to make deliberate choices of future strategies. Furthermore, we can be forced to articulate hypotheses about things we would ordinarily leave to inarticulate reasoning. But the method works best in problem solving; it hardly works at all as a method for exploring how language is produced." (Deese, 1984: 12, note 9).

Whether this is true or not may be decided in course of time by the readers of this volume and other researchers using introspective data in psycholinguistic research.

Facing this situation I shall attempt to:

1. exemplify and discern the function of verbal protocols in the analysis of language processing;
2. draw a preliminary implicit outline of a model of language processing with a focus on units of processing, spread of activation, and reconstruction of information in the case of translation.

This chapter is based on the following assumptions:

1. The human information processing system is a unified one. There are no fundamental differences between various types of processing.
2. The capacity of the human information processing system is limited. Information is stored in such a way that some of it in the focus of attention is immediately accessible for processing — and as such reportable — whereas some of it must be currently activated and reorganized in order to be accessible and reportable. It is especially this second type of information processing — the activation and reorganization of information — that is likely to be disclosed by verbal protocols.
3. Human information retrieval is partly declarative and, as such, accessible for verbalization, and partly proceduralized and, therefore, not accessible for verbalization.
4. Verbal protocols for this reason are incomplete.
5. Verbal protocols, nevertheless, as Ericsson & Simon have argued, do provide valid and useful data on language processing.

I shall argue that nevertheless there are differences between verbal reports described in cognitive science literature and verbal reports used in the analysis of language processing.

1. In cognitive literature, protocols serve to identify mental processes occurring during the solution of a cognitive task whose inherent structure and rules are completely known, as in a game of chess, logic problems, the Tower of Hanoi problem, the Missionaries and Cannibals problem, the Eight Puzzle, Duncker's Attack-Dispersion problem, etc (cf. Simon, 1979: 230–44, 246–49, 344, 447–50, 499; Anderson, 1983: 157–62). Verbal protocols disclose the movements and sequences of movements, i.e. the decision tree in the subject's strategic plan to solve the problem according to its structure and rules.

2. Verbal protocols in language processing research, on the other hand, are documents of processing whose inherent structure and rules are neither known to the processor nor to the researcher.[1] They are an instrument to shed light on the verbalization process itself so that it may be recognized as such and explained. Indications of the processing aspect of verbal protocols, the competition of plans, the units and levels of processing, etc. are especially found, as we have suggested for some time, in the temporal variables and speech errors in the language output.

Discussion of Data

Sample 1

The experiment reported by Gick & Holyoak (1980) aimed at the exploration and description of analogical problem solving from one domain (a fortress being attacked and captured by an army) to a semantically distant but structurally analogical domain (a tumour being attacked and destroyed by high-intensity rays without destroying the healthy tissue surrounding it).

Duncker's radiation problem

Attack-dispersion story

A fortress was located in the centre of the country.
Many roads radiated out from the fortress.
A general wanted to capture the fortress with his army.
The general wanted to prevent mines on the roads from destroying his army and neighbouring villages.
As a result the entire army could not attack the fortress along one road.
However, the entire army was needed to capture the fortress.
So an attack by one small group would not succeed.
The general, therefore, divided his army into several small groups.
He positioned the small groups at the heads of different roads.
The small groups simultaneously converged on the fortress.
In this way the army captured the fortress.

Radiation problem

A tumour was located in the interior of a patient's body.
A doctor wanted to destroy the tumour with rays.

The doctor wanted to prevent the rays from destroying healthy tissue.
As a result, the high-intensity rays could not be applied to the tumour
   along one path.
However, high-intensity rays were needed to destroy the tumour.
So applying one low-intensity ray would not succeed.
The doctor, therefore, divided the rays into several low-intensity rays.
He positioned the low-intensity rays at multiple locations around the
   patient's body.
The low-intensity rays simultaneously converged on the tumour.
In this way the rays destroyed the tumour.

The two concluding paragraphs in italics are the solution to the
problem which had to be found by the subjects in the experiment.
(Gick & Holyoak, 1980: 306–55)

Verbal protocols in this experiment were used to discover the mental
processes leading subjects to the discovery of the solution and its transfer
from the first to the second story as expressed in the final two paragraphs
of the radiation text. The result Gick and Holyoak achieved was that if
— and only if — subjects were given hints to use the military story to
solve the medical target problem they succeeded in doing so.

Protocol analysis for these investigators — as for other cognitive
scientists — served to provide data for the assessment of the role of
analogical reasoning in problem solving, that is, the analogical solution of
a *verbally* presented *abstract* cognitive task (the medical problem) in terms
of the *verbally* presented *abstract* solution of a structurally similar task
(the military problem).

According to the design of the experiment subjects were first provided with a story analogy, for instance, the attack-dispersion story, which
implicitly described the problem and then asked to think aloud while they
were trying to solve the target problem in the radiation story.

Since both stories, taken from Duncker (1945),[2] were constructed
for the purpose of representing two analogical but semantically different
versions of the attack-dispersion solution of the problem, the scoring of
the thinking-aloud protocols could be easily based on the number of
propositions relating to the solution, their combination and sequence, and
any statements disclosing the discovery of mapping relations between the
solution principle and the second story. The particular *language* in the
protocols — the *way* the discovery processes leading to the solution of
this *non-linguistic* cognitive task were verbalized and what problems and
deficiencies of *verbalization* occurred — was practically of no concern
for the investigators.

To put it another way: Information about mental processes in analogical problem solving as well as other cognitive activities has been gained mainly, if not exclusively, on *non-linguistic criteria*.

It is not language but thought that has been in the focus of protocol analysis so far.

Protocol for S15 (attack-dispersion condition)

Subject reads radiation problem.

S: Alright I, what I most, what I'd probably do is send in the ray at sufficiently high intensity and then taking the risk that the tissues, the healthy tissues that would be destroyed, could be repaired later on. Trying to relate this to the other problem, I could say that you could give multiple treatments of low-intensity ray. But from this problem it seems that they won't have effect on the tumour so ... so I don't think that would work.

Later ...

E: Okay. And as a last question can you give me a, tell me ways in which your solution would satisfy the constraints of the experiment?
S: What are the constraints of the experiment?
E: Okay, i.e. that the healthy tissue will not be destroyed, and the tumour will be?
S: Alright, in that way my first suggestion would probably not be the way to go at it. Because that way you're getting low intensity so it won't destroy the tissue and hopefully over a period of time the additive effect of low-intensity rays would kill the tumour. But from reading the article, I don't know if that would work or not, because it says that a low-intensity ray doesn't have any effect on the tumour at all. So I don't know. I don't know any other possible way of doing it.
E: Would it help to possibly go back to the story and see whether you can apply that?
S: Well, that's what I was trying to do here. It says here he divides his army into different small groups. Okay, may ... possibly. What they could do, but this is a whole new solution now, possibly what they could do is attack the tumour from a multiple of directions with lower intensity rays and then, since you're coming in from all different directions, the healthy, with small-intensity rays you're not going to be destroying the healthy tissue but you're, and they'll

all converge at the point of the tumour which will hopefully destroy the tumour.

(Gick & Holyoak, 1980: 306–55)

Actually, in spite of occasionally documenting speech errors such as false starts ("what I most"), self corrections ("the tissue — the healthy tissue"), and repetitions ("so ... so I don't think ...") this protocol, like the others Gick and Holyoak present, not only does not sound like natural speech, which is deficient and hesitant all over, but resembles a type of edited text from which almost all features characteristic of competitive verbal planning, as can be seen from the verbal protocols published in this volume, have been excluded for some reason or other.

In the cognitive literature on verbal protocols the verbalization processes as such are of little interest. Verbal protocols are usually taken as documents of mental problem solving in a problem space, i.e. revealing means-ends analyses and the breaking down of problems in sequences of sub-problems, etc. What counts is what is being verbalized, not so much how this is done.

If it is true that the human information processing system is a unified one, that mental processes underlying non-linguistic problem solving tasks, such as the transfer of a solution in one area to the solution of a structurally similar problem in a different area, and mental processes underlying linguistic tasks, such as the translation of a text from one language to another, are principally the same, verbal protocols should shed light on the underlying processes in the solution of verbal tasks as well. This is what this chapter and this volume are about. Whether a psycholinguistic analysis of verbal protocols in the solution of non-linguistic tasks might add to the quality and reliability of protocol analysis in general is a different question. I am convinced that it would.

Sample 2

The second sample to be discussed presents three brief excerpts from a long transcription of a thinking-aloud protocol recorded during the solution of a translation task of an expository text from the subject's L2 English into her L1 German. It is taken from a thesis of one of my graduate students. This thesis deals with the decomposition of the translation process with the method of thinking-aloud-protocols (Dechert & Sandrock, 1986).

The sample fully reprinted in the Appendix (cf. p. 110) is a much simplified modification of the original transcript used in the thesis as it neither represents the levels of translation in the original — one of the dimensions of decomposition — nor the exact temporal measures of the verbalization and writing passages of the TAP. What it does represent:

1. in the first excerpt is an almost totally proceduralized translation process with no introspective information whatsoever;
2. in the second excerpt is a minor syntactic search process on a sub-plan level (cf. Hölscher & Möhle, this volume, Chapter 6), which is only minimally revealed by introspective information;
3. in the third excerpt is the course of a comparatively long and complex lexical search process, the various attempts to initiate relevant sub-processes, i.e. to activate new knowledge sources and reorganize the accessible information in various sequences and units of translation.

The first excerpt

Reading of L2 source text passage: Moreover, some people speak a dialect ...
Protocol: Außerdem sprechen (0.90) einige Leute einen Dialekt (...)[3].

This first sentence in the sample is preceded in the original text by a number of statements in which the difference between standard written language and dialect oral speech in England is discussed. With the exception of the words "people" and "speak", all other lexemes do not occur in the passage preceding this excerpt.

After reading the source text sentence, the oral German translation is immediately initiated. There are no indications of processing problems. The simple syntactic structure of the sentence, almost identical in both languages, and its shortness quite obviously facilitate the direct translation. There is no hesitation between the oral translation of the sentence and the following writing it down which might signal a control or monitoring process after the translation. The three steps of the translation: the reading and comprehending of the source text as a whole, without decomposing it, the translation of it as a whole, and its final being written down as a whole follow each other immediately. Only the second part of the second step is interrupted by a pause which seems to serve the processing of the final portion of the sentence. No introspective information whatsoever gives us insight into the underlying processes. This first excerpt is an almost perfect example of proceduralized text processing which is hidden from introspective observation. The decoding of the meaning of the sentence and the finding of the translation equivalent is not only facilitated by its shortness and syntactic similarity, but additionally by the inherent etymological and phonological similarity of "speak–sprechen" and "dialect–Dialekt" which, in terms of a representation model of language processing, certainly have an island-function.[4] Such analogical processing reduces the task load considerably and contributes to an almost totally proceduralized whole translation which is indicated by a complete lack of concurrent verbalization. Or to put it another way, when no conscious attention must be paid to the translation process, no insight into the underlying mental processes is provided.

The second excerpt

Reading of L2 source text passage: *Today* regional accents *can* be heard in all the big towns and cities of England (0.57).

Protocol:	heutzutage	können (...)	können (0.16)	äh	nee
	nowadays	can (p1)	can (p1)	uhm	no
	heutzutage	kann man			
	nowadays	can one			

This second excerpt from the protocol, different from the first excerpt discussed before, exemplifies a decomposition process after the reading of the whole source text sentence. A step by step translation of comparatively small units follows. We shall only deal with the first of these units: "Nowadays can" (in its plural function with reference to the L2 sentence subject "accents" v. in its singular form with reference to the L1 target language transformation of the L2 passive construction into the L1 active construction and the corresponding shift of the subject to the singular "one").

The subject sets out with a translation of the equivalent plural "können" (can), following the adverb "today". She is so convinced that this is a safe hypothesis that she begins writing right away. What is completely automatized is the finding of the translation equivalent for "today", for "can", as well as the syntactic inversion processor with a postponement of the sentence subject "regional accent". The repetition of the plural "können" after the first unit has been written down signifies a control or monitor mechanism. Whether it is activated as a kind of afterthought or in the process of searching for the following subject of the sentence, we do not know. In any case, the subject suddenly becomes aware that an additional mechanism must be activated: the transformation of the English passive construction into the more adequate German active construction with a change of subject, from "accents" to "one". This transformation is easily effectuated after the very short silent pause, the filled pause "äh" and the introspective denial "nee" of the preceding hypothesis. There are no other introspective items of information which might give us more hints about this reorganization process.

What the protocol reveals, however, is the sequence of steps just discussed, and the final decision that takes place when the subject drops the L2 governed first plan and chooses the L1 governed active construction instead "nowadays can one (hear) (...)". Once again, the translation process that occurs in this very brief passage is highly automatized, as is the case in the first excerpt. However, this time it proceeds less smoothly and takes some time and reorganization. The introspective decision marker "no" closes a competition of plans triggered by the source text and the target translation, which is finally decided upon in favour of the active L1 version. The protocol in connection with the false starts "nowadays can ... can" clearly discloses the underlying mental activity of competitive planning, finally leading to an acceptable translation, in spite of the fact that practically no introspective information about this competition is given by the verbalization found in the protocol.

The third excerpt

Reading of the L2 source text passage: where there is less (0.30) movement (0.24) of the (0.12) local population.
Protocol: cf. Appendix, p. 111f.

The subject begins by rereading the subordinate clause "*where there is ...*" which in the course of the translation of the immediately preceding main clause has been read once before. Syntactic units such as main clauses and subordinate clauses may be, but need not be, the kind of unit to initiate a translation process (cf. Gerloff, this volume, Chapter 7). As the pauses in the second reading indicate, the repetition of the subordinate clause not only serves to perceive and comprehend the text, but also to scan it in order to identify the forthcoming translation problems. The pauses before and after the words "movement" and "local population" make us anticipate that these are the later candidates for search processes in the following translation process. Interestingly enough, it is not a syntactic problem but lexico-semantic problems we may expect.

The first translation problem, "movement", immediately before identified, is reintroduced. An interrupted introspective comment "one could that now, uh", obviously a metaprocedural statement, reflects the search process itself. It is interesting to note that the translation process after the scanning and recognition of the problem areas during the first reading is decomposed into the units that need particular attention and treatment.

The following statement, "now I must find an equivalent German word for it, for" — a translation equivalent of "movement", of course — is the explicit mention of the goal of the search process that has been initiated.

This search process begins with a second reintroduction of the problem expression "movement". The expressions "that is something like", "indeed", "perhaps", all evidently reveal hesitation and uncertainty, that is, search, just as the pauses do. The genitive suffix *s* in the German word for population and the following word for change disclose a compounding sub-process being developed, which, however, is not completely activated before the next run. The following long explanatory statement, "that people move away and other people move in probably", is an attempt to correct the anticipated false compound "population change" by connecting "movement" with the notion "to move" through which a clear distinction between the agent of the movement — the population — and the direction of the movement — from one place to the other — is sustained. Moreover, this line of thinking adds a good deal of realism to the extremely abstract kind of reasoning before. It also evokes elements of imagery. The concluding remark "wahrscheinlich" ("probably") from a semantic point of view expresses prevailing uncertainty and doubt; as a closing marker (x 'x x — with falling intonation contour) it signals the end of the first run and the anticipation of a second attempt to follow.

The second run starts with a complete reintroduction of the original L2 clause, "where there is less movement of the local population". It is then translated step by step, as the pauses clearly show. The compounding of "population" and "change" to "population change", announced in the preceding run, is almost realized but finally given up again in favour of the prepositional construction "change of population". This phrase, of course, is ambiguous as to the role of agent. It is connected with the — wrong — adjective, "little", in place of the English comparative, "less", in the original, which is a reference to "towns and cities" in the preceding main clause. But since the unit of translation is the subordinate clause, this referential problem is not even noticed.

The second translation which is found for "less" is quite interesting — "geringer" ("minor") may be understood as the comparative of "gering". In this function it would solve the referential problem just mentioned. Or it may be understood as the inflected form of the positive "gering" plus the suffix -er marking the masculine adjective preceding the masculine noun "Wechsel" ("change"). Thus the form, "gering-er", is a sort of transitional approach to the correct form, "gering-er-er". It seems to contribute to the subject's decision to stick to this translation even in cases where a different case marker — "gering-en" — is necessary.

The false start, "pf", in the same passage, lacking any semantic relation to anything uttered before or after, is an indication of an alternative plan being processed and the high processing load which inhibits the clear development of this plan. Unfortunately no other hint is given what this plan may be like.

The passage we have just been discussing which began with the reintroduction of the L2 version of the whole clause and aimed at the complete translation of the whole clause — different from the decomposition approach initiated in the first run — ends up in a complete mess: none of the translation problems identified before is solved. The translation found for "less" is incorrect. It is, thus, not surprising that the second run is suddenly broken off and a third run is initiated with the presentation of a new topic: the translation of the second problem expression, "local population", which is reintroduced for the first time.

The following statement, "let us write", signals the subject's dissatisfaction with the result of the preceding processing and her readiness to finish the search. Writing, to be sure, in the sequence of steps beginning with the first reading of the L2 version, is the concluding step throughout the whole translation process.

The passage begins with the translation of "local", but the unsolved translation problem, "movement", from the preceding runs is so active that at once the beginning of the clause is taken up and processed again, "wo ... es einen ... geringen ... äh ... Wechsel ... hm" ("where there is a minor change"). But once again the hesitations and the premature interruption, the unexpected introduction of an entirely new word for "movement" ("Bewegung"), which again is completely out of context, the use of fillers, etc. announce another failure of the translation process. The following false start, "Be-", reintroducing the wrong term "Bewegung" ("movement") again, reinforces the decision to write down the translated text and, therefore, come to an end with the search. Consequently the version, "minor change", is reactivated, and — after the parenthetical remark, "what have I just said", which explicitly refers to the suggested solutions — the second translation problem, "local population", is reintroduced for the third time in its original L2 gestalt.

The last run, taking up an earlier translation of "local", "dort ansässig" ("there residing"), is interrupted before the whole noun phrase is translated, since the metaprocedural remark, "perhaps later on something better will occur to me", again reflects a strong dissatisfaction with the equivalent suggested for "local". Nevertheless the same word is repeated, connected with the L1 equivalent for "population" and then inserted into the final translation of the whole clause at the end, "where there is a minor change of the there re ... siding population, indeed". There are, however, two distinct signals that this final version of the translation process is not fully agreed with, the breaking apart of "re ... siding" and the addition of "halt", which expresses doubt and dissatisfaction as an ironic English "indeed" would do.

To conclude, language processing in general, and second-language processing in particular, in so far as it is not proceduralized, is not a smooth linear sequence of events regulated by a rule but rather a multidirectional top-down/bottom-up reconstructive search for meaning. What the preceding analysis of the thinking-aloud data has shown, I hope, is that translating a text from one language into another is more than mapping words and collocational strings of words — the translational equivalents — and inserting them in an appropriate syntactic frame, but is rather activating and reorganizing a common underlying knowledge base.

It is the ambiguous nature of the given passage, of course, which in a very obvious way has initiated this complicated and unsuccessful search, as the meaning of the clause, "where there is less movement of the local population", is, by no means, perfectly clear. Does it mean that the local population in the country does not move as much as people in the towns and cities of England do, in the sense that they stay at home much more over the week-ends, during their vacations, if they have any? Or does it mean that they do not move house or change from one place to the other; as it were, change their place of residence as much as is the case in towns and cities? That they show less mobility, and consequently, metaphorically speaking, flexibility, physically and intellectually? Or was the author of this text not careful enough and should he have chosen the word "mobility" or "flexibility" instead?

The search for the equivalent German expression for "movement of the local population" in the clause, "where there is less movement of the local population", makes evident that second language processing is a struggle for meaning through a steady spread of activation and reorganization of the respective L1 and L2 knowledge sources.

Conclusion

Translation is not simply mapping translation equivalents stored in two corresponding lexical drawers, but activating and reorganizing equivalent areas of a common cognitive data base. If this activation is proceduralized, as shown in the first excerpt, "trans-lating" two areas does not cause overt conscious search, i.e. hesitation, interruption, decision making, etc.; it works smoothly. If it is not proceduralized, as in the third excerpt, finding translation equivalents in the common data base is a declarative activity that takes effort and time. Verbal protocols in connection with a careful study of temporal variables and speech errors, as we have attempted to demonstrate, may open up our view into the inner workings of speech production. The mind, after all, is much less clouded than some people, for a long time, have been inclined to think.

In the discussion of their model of human information processing to aid them in explaining the scope and function of thinking-aloud data, Ericsson & Simon take the traditional view that information is stored in different memories which are characterized by different access and different capacity. Short Term Memory has a limited capacity and accessibility and Long Term Memory a large capacity and permanent accessibility. According to this memory model, only information held and processed in STM is open to verbalization. Information in LTM must be transposed into STM in order to be reported.

In their article "The Metaphorical Structure of the Human Conceptual System" (1981) George Lakoff & Mark Johnson have made us aware that, in principle, we cannot understand the world without the use of metaphorical concepts and that, consequently, Cognitive Science, to a large extent, depends on the use of metaphors to describe and explain cognition. One of the basic metaphors frequently used in Cognitive Science is the so-called conduit metaphor (Reddy, 1979: 284–324) which models the mind as a container.

The memory model mentioned before rests heavily on the conduit metaphor as it insists that information must be taken out of one store and transferred to another store in order to be processed and reported. If one agrees with Lakoff & Johnson that "Cognitive Science needs to be aware of its metaphors", and needs "to be open to alternative metaphors — even if they are inconsistent with the current favorites" (ibid: 206) those metaphors which help achieve a deeper and more inclusive understanding of experiential phenomena must be favoured.

The notion of spreading activity and of memory organization packaging discussed by Schneider & Shiffrin, Shiffrin & Schneider, John Anderson and Roger Schank seem to enable us to better understand the processing of language in lexical search as revealed through concurrent thinking-aloud data. The expansion and analysis of the verbal protocol data I have attempted to present were implicitly based on these metaphors.

Notes to Chapter 5

1. There is no linguistic theory that can claim to describe the processes that are actually taking place when language is processed.
2. "Duncker kept a record of what his subjects said as they attempted to solve this problem. When he compared tentative solutions in the protocols one with another, they fell into certain groups. (...) Duncker characterizes a typical subject as moving down a particular branch 'in a family tree of such solutions', i.e. reformulating the problem into a subproblem, and so on until he can make no further progress. At this point the subject is likely to try another branch of the tree in a similar fashion, until ultimately he either gives up the problem or comes up with a practical solution (e.g. directing a number of weak rays from different directions through the tumour). In solving such a problem, past experience is invoked by what Duncker calls the principle of 'resonance'" (Johnson-Laird & Wason, 1977: 15–17).
3. cf. Key to Symbols of Translation Protocol on p. 110.
4. In Dechert (1983) we have transferred the "island" metaphor from computerized speech simulation to the discussion of natural language processing. It simply means that such processing depends on well-established proceduralized units of speech, "islands", in our case made accessible through an interaction of L1 and L2.

References

ANDERSON, J. R. 1983, *The Architecture of Cognition*. Cambridge, MA: Harvard University Press.
DECHERT, H. W. 1983, How a story is done in a second language. In C. FÆRCH & G. KASPER (eds), *Strategies in Interlanguage Communication*. London and New York: Longman, 175–95.
DECHERT, H. W. & SANDROCK, U. 1986, Thinking-aloud protocols: the decomposition of language processing. In V. COOK (ed.), *Experimental Approaches to Second Language Learning*. Oxford Pergamon, 111–26.
DEESE, J. 1984, *Thought into Speech: The Psychology of Language*. Englewood Cliffs, NJ: Prentice-Hall.
DUNCKER, K. 1945, On problem solving. *Psychological Monographs* 58 (Whole 270).

ERICSSON, K. A. & SIMON, H. A. 1980, Verbal reports as data. *Psychological Review* 87, 215–51.
— 1984, *Protocol Analysis: Verbal Reports as Data*. Cambridge, MA: MIT Press.
GICK, M. L. & HOLYOAK, K. J. 1980, Analogical problem solving. *Cognitive Psychology* 12, 306–55.
JOHNSON-LAIRD, P. N. & WASON, P. C. (eds) 1977, *Thinking: Readings in Cognitive Science*. Cambridge: Cambridge University Press.
LAKOFF, G. & JOHNSON, M. 1981, The metaphorical structure of the human conceptual system. In D. A. NORMAN, (ed.), *Perspectives on Cognitive Science*. Norwood, NJ: Ablex, 193–206.
REDDY, M. J. 1979, The conduit metaphor: A case of frame conflict in our language about language. In A. ORTONY (ed.), *Metaphor and Thought*. Cambridge: Cambridge University Press, 284–324.
SCHANK, R. 1981, Language and memory. In D. A. Norman (ed.), *Perspectives on Cognitive Science*. Norwood, NJ: Ablex, 105–46.
— 1982, Reminding and memory organization: An introduction to MOPS. In W. LEHNERT & M. H. RINGLE (eds), *Strategies for Natural Language Processing*. Hillsdale, NJ: Erlbaum, 455–93.
SCHNEIDER, W. & SHIFFRIN, R. M. 1977, Controlled and automatic human information processing. I. Detection, search, and attention. *Psychological Review* 84, 1–66.
SHIFFRIN, R. M. & SCHNEIDER, W. 1977, Controlled and automatic human information processing. II. Perceptual learning, automatic attending, and a general theory. *Psychological Review* 84, 127–90.
SIMON, H. A. 1979, *Models of Thought*. New Haven and London: Yale University Press.

Appendix

Key to Symbols of Translation Protocol

Today regional accents *can*	Italicized segments of text which are discussed.
Reading L2	Reading of the L2 source text segments, introducing a unit of translation.
ein Wort finden für/	End of a unit of translation or introspective remark, preceding the following L2 reading
ein Wort finden für/ a word find for	English word-by-word translation, disclosing search process as nearly as possible
Protocol	Thinking-aloud Protocol (TAP) of the translation process
(1.70)	Unfilled (silent) pause during verbalization process of TAP in sec. (cut-off point 100 msec.)
äh	Filled pause during verbalization process of TAP
(...)	Pause used to write down translated passage
Be po	False start

Thinking-aloud-protocol

Context: *Moreover, some people speak a dialect.* — *Today* regional accents *can* be
heard in all the big towns and cities of England; dialects, on the other
hand, are spoken mainly in the country, *where there is less movement of
the local population.* But less and less people are speaking dialect now.

First protocol excerpt

Reading L2:   *moreover some people speak a dialect*

Protocol: außerdem   sprechen   einige   Leute   einen   Dialekt (. . . .)
             besides   (0.90)   some   people   a   dialect
                         speak

Second protocol excerpt

Reading L2:   *today* regional accents *can* be heard in all the big towns and cities of
               England
Protocol:

heutzutage   können (...)   können (0.16)   äh   nee   heutzutage   kann   man
nowadays   can (P1)   can (p1)   uhm   no   nowadays   can   one

Third protocol excerpt

Reading L2: *where there is less* (0.30) *movement* (0.24) *of the* (0.12) *local population*

Protocol: movement   das   könnte   man   jetzt   äh   (1.13)   jetzt   muß   ich   da   mal   ein   adäquates
          movement   that   could   one   now   uhm   now   must   I   (there)   an   adequate

Wort   für   finden   für/
word   for   find   for

movement   das   ist   so   (0.60)   Bevölkerungs (0.34)   ja   Wechsel
movement   that   is   something like   population   yes   change

vielleicht (1.27)   also   daß (0.29)   da (1.33)   Leute (0.30)   wegziehen
perhaps   consequently that   (there)   people   move away

und andere   Leute   hinzu (0.16)   ziehen   wahrscheinlich (0.73)/
and other   people   to here   move   probably

Reading L2: where there is less movement of the local population

Protocol: wo   es   (0.68)   wenig (0.42)   pf (0.70)   Bev (1.11)   völkerungswechsel (1.5?
          where   (there) is   little   pf   pop   ulation   change

äh (0.10)   wo   ein   geringer (0.42)   Bev (0.90)   Wechsel   der   Bev (0.31)
uhm   where   a   minor   pop   change   of the   pop

der lo   (0.30)/
the lo

Reading L2: local population

Protocol: (0.59) der   dort (0.24) schreiben wir der   dort ansässigen (0.42)
          of the   there   let us write of the there residing

          wo   (...) es   einen (...) geringen (...) äh (0.10) Wechsel (0.28)
          where   (there is) a   minor   uhm   change

          hm (0.54) Bewegung (0.78) hä   Be (0.62) schreiben wir Wechsel geringen
          uhm   movement   uhm mo   let us write change minor

          Wechsel der   (...) was hab' ich jetzt gesagt/
          change of the   what have I just said

Reading L2: local population

Protocol: der   (0.57) dort   (...) dort   ansässigen (...) sässigen   vielleicht fällt
          of the   there   there   residing   siding   perhaps   occurs

          mir   da   später noch was   besseres für   ein (0.40) der   dort
          (to) me (there) later still something better   for it   of the there

          ansässli ansässigen (0.13) Bevölkerung (...) wo   es   einen geringen
          resil   residing   population   where there is a   minor

          Wechsel der   dort an (0.17) sässigen Bevölkerung halt   gibt/
          change of the there re   siding   population   indeed

6   Cognitive Plans in Translation

ANKE HÖLSCHER AND DOROTHEA MÖHLE

Introduction

In recent years scholarly research on language has undergone an important change. From the sophisticated description of linguistic systems, attention has shifted to the research of processes underlying the production as well as the reception of speech. This change is due to the increasing importance of investigations in human information processing which have entailed the view of natural language as a problem solving task, determined by consecutive planning processes (Wilensky, 1981: 298).

An important question within this area is how to get insight into the nature of planning processes involved in speech production. As pointed out in other contributions to this volume, as well as in Dechert & Sandrock (1984) and in Lörscher (forthcoming), one promising method for observing these normally invisible as well as unconscious processes is to make them accessible by means of thinking-aloud protocols, i.e. by making a person tell us what he is doing while performing a demanded task. Unfortunately, we cannot expect him to verbalize things he is not aware of. That means verbal reports generally cannot give us direct access to the processes we are looking for. They can, however, provide information about consecutive steps executed in the performance of the task. These steps could not be recognized in a finished translation because the procedures would not be evident in the resulting text. Therefore, the kind of information gained in the thinking-aloud protocols can help us to infer underlying processes.

Due to the special character of task environment, translation is a form of speech production that lends itself to this kind of investigation for several reasons. First of all, the content of the utterances to be produced is given and need not be planned by the speaker. What is given, furthermore, is the linguistic expression of this content in the source language. Since the task of translating, by definition, demands a version as close to the original as possible, the number of choices among available linguistic devices is restricted. For that reason, translation entails a considerable reduction of planning complexity compared to normal, active free speech planning.[1]

Beyond this, the above-mentioned task-specific constraints may increase the awareness of planning processes and thus facilitate the additional task of verbal report. Finally, the predetermined character of content and expression of utterances is most helpful to the observer because it increases the transparence of individual planning for him.

In spite of all this, the task of observing speech planning remains extremely difficult. It could be helpful, however, to make use of the results obtained in other areas of research on planning activity. We have chosen, therefore, the "Cognitive Model of Planning" worked out by Barbara and Frederic Hayes-Roth (1979) as a framework for our own observations. Our goal in this paper is to attempt an application of the categories of this model to the analysis of translation planning processes. It should be emphasized that in pursuing this goal, the use of thinking-aloud protocols as a central methodological device is in the focus of interest.

A Theoretical Framework for the Analysis of Planning

The opportunistic model of cognitive planning by Hayes-Roth & Hayes-Roth (1979) offers a new view to the investigation of human problem-solving processes. It refers to the first stage, i.e. planning, of a two-stage problem-solving process, comprising "planning" and "control". The authors define "planning" as the "predetermination of a course of action aimed at achieving some goal" (Hayes-Roth & Hayes-Roth, 1979: 275). Control, the second stage of problem-solving, is defined as the way a subject executes a plan to an acceptable conclusion. The most important trait of this model is its opportunistic character. The authors maintain that planning on many occasions is not a successive refinement process. Rather

"the planner's current decisions and observations suggest various opportunities for plan development. The planner's subsequent

decisions follow up on selected opportunities. Sometimes these de-
cision-sequences follow an orderly path and produce a neat top-
down expansion. However, some decisions and observations might
also suggest less orderly opportunities for plan development. For
example, a decision about how to conduct initial planned activities
might illuminate certain constraints on the planning of later activities
and cause the planner to refocus attention on that phase of the plan.
Similarly, certain low-level refinements of a previous, abstract plan
might suggest an alternative abstract plan to replace the original
one" (Hayes-Roth & Hayes-Roth, 1979: 276).

Planning, thus, is neither completely hierarchical nor chaotic but rather
a multi-directional process.

The concept of this planning model is based on the evaluation of
thinking-aloud protocols from 30 subjects. They were instructed to plan
a day's errands with the help of a town map and to comment aloud on
their planning activities. The complex task, thus, consisted in organizing
the performance of a considerable number of single activities in a way
that might save time and energy. Developing a suitable plan to reach this
goal demanded a number of decisions. Some of these decisions, as Hayes-
Roth & Hayes-Roth point out, reflect the best way of performing errands
and should be considered a direct contribution to the demanded plan.
Another group of decisions, however, is concerned with the best way of
planning errand performance and thus constitutes a meta-plan.

A detailed analysis of the thinking-aloud protocols leads the authors
to discern within the first group three different categories of planning
processes which can be attributed to three different planes of planning:
the *plan plane*, the *plan-abstractions plane* and the *knowledge base plane*.
Decisions produced on the plan plane are those which the planner would
like to carry out in the world.

"Decisions on the *plan-abstraction* plane characterize desired attributes of potential plan decisions. Thus, these decisions indicate the
kinds of actions the planner would like to take without specifying
the actions themselves" (Hayes-Roth & Hayes-Roth, 1979: 286).
The knowledge base plane contains information about facts and relationships in the world that can be helpful for planning.

Within the second group of decisions the authors discern two different categories which can be attributed to the *executive plane* and the *meta-
plan plane*. The executive plane consists of decisions about the aspects of

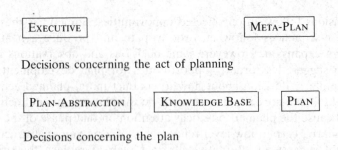

FIGURE 1

the plan that are to be developed by the planner. The meta-plan plane, finally, consists of decisions about how a planning problem is approached by the planner.

As the authors point out, each of the five planes is characterized in itself by different levels of abstraction. Thus, it becomes clear that the number of different planes and levels lends itself as a framework for investigation of extremely complex processes such as speech planning which, comparable to errands planning, includes a considerable number of different mental activities.

The plan plane

If we carry over this concept from errands planning to the cognitive processes underlying translation, *the plan plane* records all those decisions which are directly involved in the planning of the text to be produced.

The most abstract level, referred to as the level of *outcomes*, can be regarded as a store for decisions concerning the content of what is to be said. The level of *designs* refers to the choice of linguistic material as well as rhetorical strategies, such as emphasizing, relationship of grammatical against logical case structure, etc. Next, the choice of rules for combining linguistic elements belonging to the phonetical, lexical or syntactical domain of a language is a matter of the level of *procedures*. We think, however, that other kinds of procedures should be incorporated into this level as well, decisions about the way in which text production is going on, e.g. decisions about the scope of processing. In the case of translation, procedures such as translating word by word, syntagm by syntagm, etc. should be incorporated in this level of planning. On the last and most concrete level, the level of *operations*, planning must create the concrete linguistic form which derives from the whole of prior decisions. It is at this point that we produce the surface forms which result from the application of an abstract rule to a given linguistic element belonging to a specific and well-defined class of elements.

If, for example, on the level of designs we have chosen the French verb "chercher" and on the level of procedures we have recognized the third person singular present tense as the appropriate form, it is on the level of operations that our choice for the suffix -*e*, excluding corresponding suffixes of other classes of verbs, takes place.

The plan-abstractions plane

Decisions on this plane concern, as pointed out, the kinds of actions to be performed without specifying the actions themselves. On the highest level of this plane, the level of *intentions*, decisions concern the topic to be treated by the intended utterance without specifying in detail the precise content, which will be done on the corresponding level of the plan plane. The *scheme* level forming an abstract background for the choice of material in the corresponding design level of the plan plane contains general categories which characterize the desired attributes of the material such as precision, appropriateness of expression, semantic closeness and — in the case of the translation to be dealt with later on — germanization of loans. The notion of *tactics*, representing an abstract form of performing concrete operations in the plan plane, should be used to designate a certain type of instruction which is triggered by such phenomena as gender, case, temporality, agreement, and which result in the application of specific rules.

The knowledge base plane

This plane in our case contains all the information which must be considered as a necessary base for decision making in the described areas, that is, knowledge about the subject to be treated and the language to be used, e.g. knowledge about registers and about rule systems concerning linguistic as well as pragmatic and rhetorical areas.

We have so far described some of the most important decisions implied in the act of developing speech, that is, utterances or texts. The remaining two planes, as we have shown above, refer to the planning process itself, that is, to the act of planning speech production, in our case of planning translation.

The executive plane

As pointed out above, in this plane the planner takes decisions about the aspects of the plan that are to be developed. *Priority* decisions, for example, concern alternative possibilities of dealing with the task: to get ready within a given time at the expense of quality, or to do as well as possible at the expense of the demanded quantity. Other alternatives might include emphasis on meaning rather than literal translation or, vice versa, correctness might be regarded as superior to aesthetic style. Decisions taken on the level of *focus* refer to alternative possibilities of organizing work. That means, in the case of translation, to begin with a reading of the whole text before translating sentence by sentence, or to retrieve an appropriate expression for the main concepts before looking for details, etc.

The meta-plan plane

The next and final plane, referred to as the meta-plan plane, consists of decisions about how a planning problem, in our case the translation of a text, is approached by the planner. On the highest level of this plane *problem definition* reflects the planner's own understanding of the task. On the following level *problem-solving models* imply choices such as derivation in order to construct unknown words, retrieval of words by means of repeated reading of the context, use of dictionaries, and restructuring of syntagms, etc. *Policies*, finally, specify desirable features of the developing plan, for example efficiency, avoidance of unnecessary steps, etc.

This concludes our description of the Hayes-Roth Model in its original form and in an adapted version that might serve our goals. As pointed out above, the model is not regarded by the authors as a hierarchical order which has to be followed step by step. It rather serves as a framework for the description of opportunistic planning decisions switching from plane to plane in a sometimes unexpected order. Using this model for the description of speech planning we are compelled to dissect processes which in natural behaviour form an entity. Thus, the concrete act of employing a certain grammatical form, or of using an idiomatic expression, will be reflected in its different aspects at several points of the model. It is by the constraints of this differentiated view that we may understand what planning processes really are. We are quite aware that the application of this view to the interpretation of real speech acts, raises considerable difficulties. It is at this point that thinking-aloud protocols will be a most helpful methodological device.

Application of the Model to the Analysis of Translations

General considerations

The application of this model to the area of verbal behaviour raises difficulties as well as advantages that will be briefly discussed. An important objection that could be advanced is that the experimental research underlying the model of Hayes-Roth & Hayes-Roth was based on a problem-solving task in the area of daily life activities. Due to the specific structure of the task environment, the result of the planning processes consists of an oral or written document, the plan, which is clearly discernible as being separate from the act of executing the planned activity. Verbal planning, on the other hand, results in the execution of utterances without yielding a discernible plan. Investigation of planning processes, therefore, must be based in this case on information inferred from the result of a performed activity instead of being inferred from an available plan.

Another difference to be pointed out is that planning errands is a singular activity which is probably never repeated in exactly the same way. Yet certain levels of speech production, such as articulation or the application of lexical and syntactical rules, are frequently repeated in the same way, so that investigation of planning processes may be partly concerned with processing of procedural knowledge and with automated plans.

There are, nevertheless, some aspects which have encouraged us to attempt an application of the Hayes-Roth Model to verbal planning. First of all, this model is based on natural planning performed by human beings in information-rich situations such as those described by Simon (1979: 142). Furthermore, it is sufficiently complex to serve our goals. Finally, we are concerned here with what the authors call "an opportunistic model of planning", suitable to account for incremental planning processes which take place at various points without necessarily following a strict hierarchical order (Hayes-Roth & Hayes-Roth, 1979: 284). This is most important because, as we will show in the following analysis, speech production, especially if performed by non-native speakers, is highly determined by this kind of opportunistic planning.

Task and data

The texts we analyse in this paper are excerpts from thinking-aloud protocols of a translation from French L2 to German L1. These protocols are transcriptions obtained from a video-tape taken of the subjects with their permission. The source text (cf. text 1) was presented to seven intermediate-level students of French who worked on it consecutively in the university video studio. The subjects were informally instructed to give a written translation and to verbalize aloud as much as possible of what was going on in their minds while performing the task. They were allowed to use a monolingual dictionary. The subjects were given half-an-hour but they were told that we did not expect them to finish the task within this time.

Text 1

Guide de Paris mystérieux

Paris est une ville mystérieuse. Rien n'est plus mystérieux que Paris. Il n'y a qu'à voir la Tour Eiffel promener ses gros yeux sur la ville pour sentir qu'il se passe des choses. Lesquelles? On ne sait pas trop, mais c'est très inquiétant. La Seine est noire et roule une eau sale. La lune est pompeuse ou fugitive, au hasard des arrondissements. Elle étale sa lueur glacée sur l'Esplanade des Invalides; ailleurs, elle passe en 15 secondes tant le ciel est étroit. Elle éclaire d'un rayon oblique le tombeau des poètes, Baudelaire, Henri Heine, ceux d'Abélard et d'Héloïse, qui furent si malheureux et si intelligents (je tiens la chose de ma femme de ménage). Autant de fantômes, autant de mystères. Encore faut-il vouloir les voir. Wilde assurait qu' "un gentleman ne regarde jamais par la fenêtre". Il habitait alors Quai Voltaire. Moins de préjugé aristocratique lui aurait permis de s'étonner. Il eût été surpris de voir les arrondissements se succéder en escargot, et la Seine couler d'est en ouest, ce qui la met à deux pas de l'Océan, et fait de Paris l'un des plus grands de nos ports de mer. Caprices de la nature et hasards de l'Histoire semblent s'être ainsi donné le mot pour faire éclore et conserver mystérieusement l'originalité de Paris.

(Lallemand-Rietkötter, Annette, La langue française par la presse: textes d'exercices. Hueber Hochschulreihe 14, München, Hueber 1972.)

Before analysing in detail our first sample, a general problem must be mentioned. We have argued above that translation, for several reasons, lends itself well to the investigation of planning processes. One of these reasons is the reduction of planning complexity due to the fact that there is no content planning. We have to bear in mind, now, that this reduction refers to the productive part of the task only. The full task of translating, however, implies a receptive part, the understanding of the source text.

At this point the question arises how to interpret understanding in terms of problem solving. Wilensky (1981: 199) points out that understanding, though concerned with the use of plans, is quite an opposite task, compared to problem solving:

"Rather than actually create a plan, an understander must be able to use knowledge about plans to understand the plan under which someone else is operating."

We must note, however, that he is concerned with story understanding in a native language and not with problems arising from the task of understanding a foreign language. A second language learner, performing a translation task from L2 to L1 may find himself in the same situation as described here. If however, because of a poor command of the L2, he is confronted with linguistic problems of text comprehension, his situation, according to our observations, seems rather to be one of re-creating a given plan. In these cases, then, understanding becomes a problem-solving task in itself and translating even one sentence turns out to be a complex task consisting of a hierarchy of goals and subgoals. This gradual re-creation of sense sometimes requires a word-by-word re-coding in L1 which should not be confused with translation.

In the following sample (cf. text 2) we analyse an excerpt of the thinking-aloud protocol of speaker 1, consisting of his translation of the title and the first three sentences of text 1. Indications such as (2:5) refer to the number of the text and the respective line.

Text 2

Product	Planning

Guide de Paris mystérieux[2]

    "Guide de Paris mystérieux" das ist ein Füh-
                           that is a guide
    rer (100/360/) des (400/240/) mysteriösen
              of the   mysterious
    (680/200/) oder des (1640/–/) geheimnisvollen
           or   the   hidden

5   Paris brauche ich gar nicht so lang überle-
               Paris need I at all not so long to re-
               gen mystère ja geheimnisvoll würde ich sagen
               flect   yes mysterious should I say
               also ein Plan ein Führer ja
               well a plan   guide yes

Führer des   FÜHRER DES GEHEIMNISVOLLEN PARIS
geheimnis-   *guide of the   mysterious   Paris*
vollen Paris

10 *Paris est une ville mystérieuse.*
               "Paris est une ville mystérieuse" (–/400/)
               Paris ist eine (940/280/) geheimnisvolle Stadt
               Paris is a   mysterious   town
Paris ist eine ge- PARIS IST EINE GEHEIMNISVOLLE STADT
               Paris is a   mysterious   town
heimnisvolle Stadt.

15 *Rien n'est plus mystérieux que Paris.*
               "Rien n'est plus mystérieux que Paris" (–/240)
               nichts ist (1360/160/) mehr mysteriös oder
               nothing is   more mysterious or
               mehr geheimnisvoll (2500/120/) als Paris nichts
               more hidden   than Paris nothing
               da brauche ich gar nicht lang zu überlegen
               there need I at all not long to reflect
20   mystérieux ist klar que Paris n'est pas nichts
                    is clear   nothing
Nichts ist geheim- nichts ist geheimnisvoller als Paris GEHEIM-
               nothing is more mysterious than Paris more myste-
nisvoller als Paris. NISVOLLER ALS PARIS
               rious   than Paris
Il n'y a qu'à voir la Tour Eiffel promener ses gros yeux sur la

Product	Planning

25 *ville pour sentir qu'il se passe des choses.*

"Il n'y a qu'à voir la Tour Eiffel promener
ses gros yeux sur la ville pour sentir qu'il
se passe des choses" "il n'y a qu'à voir"
(1360/400/) il n'y a que nur ne que nur es
        only   only there

30   gibt (2680/1200/) also man muß (800/1020/)
       is   well one must
wahrscheinlich nur (1120/640/) den Tour
probably   only   the tower
Eiffel (1120/240/) sich anschauen oder sehen
Eiffel   look at   or view
(1760/720/) wenn er (420/300/) se promener
      when it
also s.. sich (1840/1480/) spazierengehen
well himself   to go for a walk

35   (1000/1160/) wandern (720/680/) promener ses
       to wander
gros yeux also wenn er seine großen Augen
       well when it its   big   eyes
(2960/720/) seine großen Augen (1400/880/)
        its   big   eyes
über die Stadt (900/680/) wandern läßt (880
over the town   wander lets
/640/) ja (440/440/) kann man das sagen über
      yes   can one that say   over

40   die Stadt wandern läßt (1640/1800/) um zu
the town wander lets   in order to
fü.. um zu fühlen pour sentir (2280/1120/)
fe..   to feel
daß (400/1200/) sich des choses daß sich
that   that
(1220/500/) puh (420/780/) einige Geschichten
        some stories
oder (1400/360/) einige Sachen viele Sachen
or   some things many things
passieren (1700/–/) viele kommt nicht drin vor
happen   many is   not contained
daß sich einige Sachen einige Sachen ereig-
that some things some things happen

Product	Planning
	nen "il se passe des choses" daß sich /et–
	that some–
	was / daß sich etwas ereignet etwas nee das
	thing that something happens something no that
	ist ein bißchen wenig daß sich viele Sachen
	is too little that many things
50	daß sich viele Sachen ereignen würde ich
	that many things happen would I
	sagen also man il il n'y a qu'à voir man muß
	say well one one must
	nur man muß nur den / Tour Eiffel beobachten
	only one must only the tower Eiffel watch
man	nee man muß nur den Tour Eiffel sehen man
	no one must only the tower Eiffel see one
muß	muß den Eiffelturm sehen man muß nur
	must only the Eiffeltower see one must only
55 nur den Eiffel-	"il n'y a qu'à voir la Tour Eiffel" NUR NUR
	only only
turm sehen,	DEN EIFFELTURM SEHEN der seine DER SEINE
der seine	*the Eiffeltower see which its which its*
	großen Augen ses gros yeux GROSSEN AUGEN
	big eyes big eyes
großen Augen	über die Bl.. über die Stadt schweifen läßt
über die	*over the over the city travel lets*
Stadt	ÜBER DIE STADT großen Augen wandern schwei-
	over the town big eyes wander travel
60	fen Blick schweifen Augen über die Stadt se
	glance travel eyes over the city
	promener WANDERN wandern ist besser für se
	wander wander is better for
	promener der seine großen Augen über die
	which its big eyes over the
wandern läßt,	Stadt wandern LÄSST pour sentir UM ZU FÜH-
	city wander lets in order to
um zu fühlen	LEN um zu fühlen daß sich viele / Dinge daß
	feel to feel that many things that

Product	Planning
65 daß sich viele Dinge ereignen.	sich viele Dinge ereignen DASS SICH VIELE *many things happen that many* DINGE EREIGNEN *things happen*

After reading the whole text, exhibited in a way that does not suggest any assumption about the degree of text comprehension, our subject reads aloud the title (2:2) which can be interpreted as a first *task definition*[3] such as "understand and translate this sentence". Planning begins, thus, on the META-PLAN PLANE.

To put it exactly, the goal to be located on the highest level of a goal hierarchy is to translate the whole text. The subject does not mention any reflection concerning a plan for this task. We can infer, however, the existence of a fragmental general plan: as he continually proceeds, translating phrase by phrase throughout the whole text, he seems to have decided — unconsciously perhaps — on this kind of processing on the META-PLAN PLANE of a general plan. For reasons of simplicity, we shall not mention this superordinate goal in the goal hierarchies to be described, but we shall place in a top position the respective goals explicitly given by the subject's task definition.

Let us return, then, to the first task definition already mentioned above. The thinking-aloud transcript informs us that with the next step, without any transitional stages and without the least measurable pause,[4] the subject passes to the most concrete, *the operations level* of the PLAN PLANE referring to the production part of the task, i.e. to a complete translation of the title. That means that understanding has occurred automatically, possibly already during the first complete text reading, without switching back and forth between fields of possible plans. This assumption is supported not only by his comment "brauche ich gar nicht so lang überlegen", (need I not at all long to reflect = I don't have to think about that very much) but also by the speed of production and the complete absence of even the least trace of a pause between reading and translating. The transmission into the L1 code has occurred automatically, too, with one exception. It has been interrupted by a shift to the PLAN-ABSTRACTIONS

PLANE on the level of intentions: "germanize the loan word 'mysteriös'" which leads on the PLAN PLANE to the insertion of "geheimnisvollen". A temporal reflection of this can be seen in the slight reduction of speech rate, resulting from two — nevertheless minimal — pauses and a certain reduced articulation rate of the word "des" (400 msec for one syllable v. 1000 msec for five syllables in the preceding sequences). The obligatory *operation*, the choice of the appropriate German case form, seems to be automatically combined with the choice of the retrieved lexeme. (Though the production part occurs in the subject's L1, this kind of processing is not self-evident, as we shall see in other examples.) The actual planning process is finished here. The revision, hereafter, concentrates on the appropriateness of two words and thus leads back to the PLAN-ABSTRACTIONS PLANE. An execution of the complete plan can be seen in the act of writing down the result. The one thing that obviously has not been revised, either before or after the execution, is the correctness of the result as compared to the task sentence.

Summarizing our observations we can say that the translation of this sentence has largely been done on the basis of procedural knowledge.

The first sentence of the text (2:10) is basically dealt with in the same way. The *task definition* on the META-PLAN PLANE is followed by a complete translation exhibited in one step with a very brief pause between reading and translating — 400 msec — and a rather high speech rate in which the translated sentence is uttered. This translation includes all *operations* required on the PLAN PLANE of the production part, i.e. a shift of the adjective from post-nominal to pre-nominal position. This fact is worth mentioning because the next sentence includes an example of planning which does not attain the operational level of L1 expression in the first step (2:17).

Once more comprehension is proceduralized here as we can see from the temporal values indicated for the second sentence. The production part of the whole sentence is áccomplished in one step up to the level of *procedures*. What has not been automatically included in this first step is the *operation* of passing from the abstract choice of a comparative to the respective German surface form of the adjective. This operation is performed only in the following planning step without being explicitly commented on (2:19).

In the last sentence of our sample we are confronted with a wide range of planning problems, located in different fields of production. The thinking-aloud protocol is rather detailed in this case and provides rich

information about the character of difficulties and about different problem-solving strategies.

Our subject first reads the complete sentence, i.e. he begins his
work on the META-PLAN PLANE by giving a task definition: "understand
and translate the following sentence". As translation is not induced this
time by an automatic comprehension of the task sentence, a *priority*
decision is made on the EXECUTIVE PLANE: "first try to understand the
sentence". Our subject does not explicitly mention that he is initiating a
sub-plan, but his reading of the first part of the task sentence, "il n'y a
qu'à voir" (2:26) can easily be recognized as being a *sub-task definition*
on the META-PLAN PLANE of a sub-plan 1: "understand this part of the
sentence". This sub-task obviously requires the choice of a *problem-
solving model* — segmentation into still smaller parts — a decision which
in our data structure has to be located on the second level of the META-
PLAN PLANE. As indicated by the short pause time — 400 msec — it is a
very prompt decision. It is displayed on the *procedural* level of the PLAN
PLANE in three consecutive steps. Procedure 1: "il n'y qu'à voir"→" il n'y
a que" (2:28/29), which implies a temporary shift to the *operational level*
in order to restore the surface form "que" (from "qu'" given in the text).
Procedure 2: "il n'y a que "→" ne que" (2:29) which now is immediately
understood. Procedure 3: identification of the remaining part "il y a" can
only be inferred by the uttered German form "es gibt" (2:29/30). As this
form is, in fact, an equivalent to "il y a", which, however, does not fit in
this case, we can see that up to this moment there is no real text comprehension but only comprehension of isolated elements. Therefore, the
retrieval of German equivalents for "ne que" and "il y a" can be regarded
as being a legitimate component of sub-plan 1 — understanding — and
does not yet indicate a temporary transition to a translation sub-plan.

Attention should be paid to the fact that all this processing occurs
in an extremely short amount of time. The whole chain of signs, "il n'ya
que nur ne que es gibt", is very quickly pronounced in 2680 msec without
any pause being instrumentally registered. At this point, a pause of 1200
msec is inserted in which real understanding of the sequence in question
seems to occur. This is indicated by the following shift to the level of
operations, leading to the substitution of "es gibt" by "man muß", which
may be called appropriate. Possibly the subject wants to express the
lacking nuance by "wahrscheinlich", which actually is not in the text. If
this assumption is true a shift to the *scheme level* of the PLAN-ABSTRACTIONS
PLANE is implied here.

It is important to notice that we are concerned here with an expression problem; that means our subject — without being aware of it — has passed over to the second sub-plan, 'translation', resulting from his main plan. There is at this point no elaborated construction of a sub-plan, consisting of *task definition*, choice of *problem-solving* models, etc. but rather an unsystematic passing over. We should refer here to Wilensky's theory of meta-planning. Dealing with complex tasks which require the construction of several plans, he points out that the individual's interest of avoiding unnecessary steps frequently leads to plan combining (Wilensky, 1981: 205). That is just what seems to have taken place in our case. Within the framework of Hayes-Roth (1979) this *policy* is to be located on the META-PLAN PLANE belonging in our case to the subject's main plan. In the course of the analysed planning process, this shift seems to have occurred simultaneously with real understanding of the task sequence in the above mentioned pause of 1200 msec.

Our subject finally returns to the remaining part of his sub-task, i.e. "à voir", adding after a pause of 640 msec the object "la Tour Eiffel". With this step he goes beyond the task definition of sub-plan 1. This decision concerning the META-PLAN PLANE of his main plan is taken because understanding in this case obviously has occurred automatically and is combined with a translation plan, which is accomplished by including the level of *operation*. We can recognize this phenomenon because the change from post-verbal position of the French object to pre-verbal position of the German object occurs only at this level. There is one exception, however: "Tour Eiffel" remains in its French form (*level of outcomes*) while processing of the respective article has been accomplished including choice of the appropriate German case for "den" (i.e. at the level of *operation*).

At this point — "sich anschauen" (2:32) — the construction of sub-plan 1, "to understand the first part of the whole sentence", is finished in the middle of a speech unit, i.e. the transition to other sub-goals follows without any registrable pause. We regard the next part of this speech unit as belonging to another sub-plan because the substitution of "anschauen" by "sehen" is obviously caused by the syntactic structure of the following clause.

An attempt to present, in a schematic way, the planning planes implicated in processing this first part of the given sentence, results in the following overview.

Without pursuing in detail our analysis of this very complex plan construction we shall for the following part of the sentence briefly comment on some important aspects.

Though there is no explicit task definition for a further sub-plan we can clearly determine the next sequence treated by our subject as marked by an intersection after "über die Stadt wandern läßt" (2:38).

What should be mentioned here is the spontaneous choice of "wenn er" (2:36) which indicates not only an automated recognition of the syntactic structure of the French sentence, but also a proceduralized access to the respective German structure requiring an entire dependent clause

Main Plan

META-PLAN PLANE
  task definition (understand and translate the sentence)
EXECUTIVE PLANE
  priority (first try to understand)
    Sub-Plan 1
      META-PLAN PLANE
        task definition (understand: il n'y a qu'à voir)
        problem-solving model (segmentation)
      PLAN PLANE
        $procedure_1$ (il n'y a qu')
        operation   (il n'y a que)
        $procedure_2$ (ne que)
        $procedure_3$ (il y a)
META-PLAN PLANE
  policy: combine Sub-Plan 1 with Sub-Plan 2
                    PLAN PLANE
                    operation (man muß)
META-PLAN PLANE
  policy: return to Sub-Plan 1
      PLAN-ABSTRACTIONS PLANE
        scheme
      PLAN PLANE
        operation (wahrscheinlich nur)
META-PLAN PLANE
  $policy_1$: go beyond $subtask_1$
  $policy_2$: combine Sub-Plan 1 with Sub-Plan 2
                    PLAN PLANE
                    $operation_1$ choice of case form: den
                    outcomes   (Tour Eiffel)
                    $operation_2$ change of noun position

FIGURE 2   *Planning planes overview:* IL N'Y A QU'À VOIR

instead of just an infinitive structure. Here, once more, comprehension and translation plans are combined, and planning is exhibited without transitional steps at the most concrete level of the PLAN PLANE.

A difficulty seems to arise when our subject is looking for an appropriate verb to continue the dependent clause introduced by "wenn er". What first comes into his mind after a very short hesitation (300 msec) is the reflexive French form "se promener" which obviously is not in the text but which probably is deeply anchored in his KNOWLEDGE BASE as a relic of vocabulary drills from secondary school. Thus, activities on the PLAN PLANE are misguided by automatized but, in this case, inappropriate knowledge. This influence can further be identified when, after a pause of 1480 msec, our subject cannot prevent himself from uttering the second part of this typical classroom equation "spazierengehen", though as his further behaviour shows he is quite aware of its inappropriateness.

After a short revision, "ja kann man sagen über die Stadt wandern läßt", the last part of the sentence, "pour sentir qu'il se passe des choses", is processed before our subject passes to the execution of his plan, i.e. writing down his translation (2:53). Incidentally, he revises certain expressions once more, which then finally remain unchanged.

A first summary of our analysis results in the following considerations: we are concerned here with an example of extensive planning of a rather complex translation task. By the way in which our subject starts his work the following META-PLAN can be inferred:

Main Plan:	understand and translate the whole sentence	
sub-plan$_1$: understand	the first part
sub-plan$_2$: translate	it
sub-plan$_3$: understand	the second part
sub-plan$_4$: translate	it
sub-plan$_5$: understand	the last part
sub-plan$_6$: translate	it

What happens, really, before even the first sub-plan is finished is an interrelated processing, combining partly three sub-plan pairs with prospective accesses to the following pair.

Mapped on the model of Hayes-Roth & Hayes-Roth (1979) the procedure, made observable by thinking aloud, turns out to be an unsystematic switching between different planes and levels rather than a systematic passing through a continually refined plan. We can, thus, ascertain that, at least in our sample, translation must be regarded as based on opportunistic multi-dimensional planning.

For reasons of comparison, we shall now present a transcribed exerpt of a second thinking-aloud protocol, recording the translation of the same sentence but performed by another subject.

Text 3

Product	*Planning*
Il n'y a qu'à voir la Tour Eiffel promener ses gros yeux sur la ville pour sentir qu'il se passe des choses.	
	"Il n'y a qu'à voir la Tour Eiffel promener ses gros yeux sur la ville pour sentir
5 Man muß nur	qu'il se passe des choses" MAN MUSS NUR
	one must only
	(840/4600/) muß nur (760/1920/) zusehen
	must only *watch*
zusehen,	(880/2200/) NUR (480/1120/) ZUSEHEN (800/2060/)
	only *watch*
wie der Eiffel-	WIE (400/740/) DER (360/1280/) EIFFEL (720
	how *the* *Eiffel*
turm seine	/800/) TURM (400/1200/) SEINE (680/1400/)
	tower *its*
10 großen Augen über	GROSSEN (720/2320/) AUGEN (560/2920/) ÜBER
	big *eyes* *over*
die Stadt	(560/1200/) DIE (280/1360/) STADT (600/3360/)
	the *city*
gleiten läßt,	GLEITEN (800/1300/) LÄSST (560/5100/) um (400
	glide *lets* *in order to*
um zu	/960/) Scheiße (600/320/) UM (400/960/) ZU
	shit *in order to* *to*
spüren, daß	(400/920/) SPÜREN (1360/3000/) DASS (600
	feel *that*
15 hier etwas ge-	/1560/) HIER (480/1480/) ETWAS (880/960/) GE-
	here *something*
schieht	SCHIEHT
	happens

We are informed by the transcript that — with the exception of one word — this subject does not perform any isolated planning before writing down her translation. We can assume, therefore, that complete understanding had occurred automatically during her first reading of the whole text or while she was reading aloud this sentence, i.e. during her *task definition* at the META-PLAN PLANE. As she did not find any problem in re-coding the sentence in her native language she passed on to the task execution — writing down her translation — without transitional stages. This assumption is confirmed by the video recording as well as by the indicated rate of speech and length of pauses. It must be noted that pause length in this case only marks the time lag between pronouncing and writing. There are no real pauses utilized for reflection. On the whole, it takes her 61.44 sec to work on this sentence (reading time excluded) while our first subject performs the same task in 310.52.

That does not mean, of course, that there is no planning in her task performance. Rather, we are concerned here with automated plans, or put differently, with procedural knowledge. What seems important to us when comparing the two samples is the insight we have gained, by the thinking-aloud protocol of our first subject, into the enormous amount of planning steps and processes on different planes and levels which have to be performed when comprehension and expression do not occur automatically. All this must be contained in some kind of frozen form in the proceduralized performance of our second subject, and there is still more if we consider that besides observable processing the translation of our first subject, too, is based partly on proceduralized knowledge containing further frozen processes.

At the same time, the thinking-aloud procedure has revealed a considerable difference in the degree of language command which could not have been inferred alone from the L1 sentences written down by the two subjects as their task result.

Summary

Based on thinking-aloud protocols we have attempted an analysis of planning processes occurring in translations from L2 to L1. As a theoretical framework for this analysis we have made use of the "Cognitive Model of Planning" as proposed by Hayes-Roth & Hayes-Roth. Our analysis has shown that differentiated processes can be observed as well as inferred by means of thinking aloud. Thus, we get insights into normally unobservable processing and, at the same time, into the proficiency level of learners, insights which could not have been obtained by analysing task results and ignoring underlying procedures.

Key to Symbols

Guide de Paris	Italics are used for sentences belonging to the original text
Führer durch das mysteriöse Paris	Normal typing in the left column is used for sequences written down as a task product
Führer durch das mysteriöse Paris	Normal typing in the right column is used for thinking aloud sequences representing planning processes
FÜHRER DURCH DAS MYSTERIÖSE PARIS	Small capitals indicate reading aloud what has been written or what is written simultaneously
"Il n'y a qu'à voir"	Quotation marks indicate a sequence read aloud from the original text
[mys..]	Incomplete word
(840/4600/)	The first figure indicates in msec speech time employed to pronounce the preceding sequence; the second figure indicates pause length after this sequence; the sequence between two pauses is called speech unit. Temporal variables are indicated only when they are relevant for considerations within this paper.

Notes to Chapter 6

1. It should be emphasized that this reduction of complexity refers to the productive part of the translation task only. However, additional complexity is generated by the comprehension part implied in translation. This problem will be dealt with later on in our paper.
2. Cf. Key to Symbols
   We have added English word-by-word equivalents of the German text including the speaker's comments.
3. We replace the term "problem-definition" employed throughout the model of Hayes-Roth & Hayes-Roth (1979) with "task-definition" in order to differentiate between the task as a whole, which in terms of problem-solving theory is regarded as a "problem", and specific "problems" in the sense of difficulties in the course of task performance.
4. In accordance with other investigations based on temporal variables we have decided on a cut-off-point of 200 msec. This means that any interruption longer than 200 msec is regarded as a pause.

References

DECHERT, H. W. & SANDROCK, U. 1984, Thinking-aloud protocols: the decomposition of language processing. Paper presented at the Third Colchester Second Language Acquisition Workshop. University of Essex, Colchester, England, Jan. 27–29.

HAYES-ROTH, B. & HAYES-ROTH, F. 1979, A cognitive model of planning. *Cognitive Science* 3, 275–310.

LÖRSCHER, W. forthcoming, On analysing translation performance. In W. LÖRSCHER & R. SCHULZE (eds), *Language in Performance*. Tübingen: Narr (forthcoming).

SIMON, H. A. 1979, *Models of Thought.* New Haven and London: Yale University Press.

WILENSKY, R. 1981, Meta-planning: Representing and using knowledge about planning in problem solving and natural understanding. *Cognitive Science* 5, 197–233.

7 Identifying the Unit of Analysis in Translation: Some Uses of Think-Aloud Protocol Data

PAMELA GERLOFF

"The problem" of interlingual translation has long been recognized. For centuries, the difficulty of rendering a portion of text written in one language into its precisely equivalent expression in another has been publicly acknowledged and deplored. In the thirteenth century, Dante poetically observed, "Nothing which is harmonized by the bond of the Muses can be changed from its own to another language without destroying all its sweetness" (Morgan, 1959). More recently, in our own era, Belloc (1930) flatly declared: "One should abandon the effort to translate the untranslatable".

Yet despite this long-standing interest in the problematic nature of translation, and a now vast body of literature on the subject, we know surprisingly little about what people actually *do* moment by moment when they translate. What kind of cognitive processing operations do people engage in when they translate a text from one language to another? What commonalities in processing exist across translators? Are individual differences identifiable? Is the use of particular text processing strategies related to quality of the final translation? What size units do people work with when translating a written text? Do they work in words, in clauses, in sentences, or in larger discourse chunks?

Such questions, yet to be answered, loom large. Thus far, the literature on translation has dealt with wide-ranging and important issues, including, for example, *questions of definition*: what is translation and how might it be characterized? (cf. Levy, 1967; Steiner, 1975; Lörscher,

1986); *prescriptive issues*, regarding how translation should be done and the skills and characteristics required of translators (e.g. Postgate, 1972; Weber, 1984); *issues of evaluation and training*: what constitutes "good" translation? Can good translation be taught? (e.g. Wilss, 1976; Carroll, 1977; House, 1977; Tirkkonen-Condit, 1986); and *descriptive attempts* to explicate the process of translation and/or identify the characteristics of language which make translation possible (e.g. Savory, 1957; Walmsley, 1970; Seleskovitch, 1976; Folkart, 1984).

In recent years, the view of translation as linguistic science has led to the creation of formal models of the translation process (e.g. Quine, 1960; Catford, 1965; Katz, 1978; Keenan, 1978) and to more practical considerations of theoretical application. Work in the development of machine translation (cf. Hutchins, 1984) and efforts at contrastive analysis of languages, performed with the intention of assisting the professional translator in his work (e.g. Vinay & Darbelnet, 1958), exemplify this interest in the intersection of linguistic theory with practice.

Nonetheless, despite this large body of varied and informative literature, our ability to understand translation *processing, per se,* remains negligible. To be sure, much of the limitation of our knowledge about translation derives simply from a restricted research methodology, both in the specialized domain of translation research and in the more general study of language processing. Until recently, regardless of the approach taken or the methodology used, translation and language researchers have generally relied for their data upon external measures of internal phenomena or upon second person observation of language outcomes. They have therefore *inferred* the underlying processes producing a given language outcome. With specific regard to translation, Steiner (1975: 273) alluded to the problem of an inadequate investigative methodology when he wrote:

> "... In the overwhelming majority of cases, the material for study is a finished product. We have in front of us an original text and one or more putative translations. Our analysis and judgement work from outside, they come after the fact. We know next to nothing of the genetic process which has gone into the translator's practice, of the prescriptive or purely empirical principles, devices, routines which have controlled his choice of this equivalent rather than that, of one stylistic level in preference to another, of word 'x' before 'y'. We cannot dissect, or only rarely...."

Because of the lack of available information about actual translation *processes*, it has been difficult to develop a viable *theory* of translation.

Consequently, "translation theory... remains a phantasm; there is at present no systematic way of talking about the transition from one...message to another" (Frawley, 1984: 159). In the words of Wilss (1982), "stagnation in theory has made it necessary to expand the methodological perspective" (ibid. 14).

Some steps toward an expanded methodology are beginning to be taken; as evidenced recently, for example, by Krings (1986), Lörscher (1986), and by a number of contributions to this volume. Their work, using think-aloud protocols to examine *translation processing as it occurs* clearly demonstrates that by expanding our methodology in such a way as to allow a focus on *process*, we can obtain very rich and useful data about on-line translation processing. Much more of this work, however, needs to be done.

Purposes and Intent

My intent in this chapter is to present some of the results of a pilot study which explored the use of think-aloud protocols for identifying and analysing processes of translation. The primary focus of the pilot work was methodological, with emphasis on development of methods for data analysis.

During piloting, language processing data in the form of concurrent think-aloud protocols were collected during participants' performance of a written translation task. A think-aloud protocol is a moment-by-moment description which an individual gives of his or her own thoughts and behaviours during the performance of a particular task. A translation task was chosen because of the need for process data in translation research; and because the act of translation provides an ideal "window" on to both comprehension and production components of language use — both of which, historically, have captured the interest of language researchers (cf. Clark & Clark, 1977). Anyone translating a text is obliged both to understand what is written (the comprehension component to the process) and to subsequently reproduce it into their own words (the production component). Since it is these two complementary phenomena which underlie all language activity, native or foreign, written or spoken, what we learn from translation protocol research should help us to unravel elusive questions about the nature of the cognitive operations that lie behind comprehension and production, and the relationships that exist between these two processes.

Specific purposes of the pilot work were to:
- identify the kinds of questions and issues which may be addressed through the use of think-aloud protocol data as applied to a translation task;
- develop a system for coding the data which would be usable in a larger study of translation, examining differences in the text processing operations of professional translators, bilingual speakers; and second language learners.

Design

The pilot study collected data from six participants: five native-English-speaking students studying French at the intermediate college level; and one competent bilingual speaker of French, whose native language was also English. Each participant was individually presented the French text and asked to translate it into English. They were instructed to "say aloud" everything they were doing and thinking while translating. All protocols were tape-recorded and later transcribed verbatim. (See Appendix for source text, sample participant translations, and sample protocol excerpts.)

To provide some indication of translation quality, each participant's translation was given an overall ranking, relative to the others in the study. Criteria for ranking were the overall degree of accuracy and completeness of the translation. According to the ratings, "Anna" produced the "least good" translation, "Bruce" the "best of the student translations", and "Fran" the "best overall translation".

This study differs from most other translation protocol research in the following ways:
- participants received no prior training in producing concurrent protocols. This was in order to determine whether significant differences existed in individuals' capacities to verbalize their thoughts while translating, and because I thought that prior training might cause participants to look more alike in their processing. The larger study does, however, provide for prior training;
- no dictionary use was allowed, on the assumption that the absence of a dictionary would elicit more of the participants' available text processing strategies, thus maximizing the number of operations identifiable for coding;
- except for the competent bilingual, included for purposes of comparison, participants were not particularly advanced in their knowledge

of the second language, having undergone no more than the equivalent of two years' study, taught at the pace of a U.S. college level course.

Data Coding Systems

Two coding systems were, in fact, developed from the pilot work: one for identifying the unit of analysis individuals used when translating; the other for identifying their problem-solving strategies and behaviours. For a full analysis of the participants' text processing operations, both codings should be used together, since they are designed to be complementary (cf. Gerloff, 1984, 1986). When used in complementary fashion, they illuminate considerably more aspects of language processing than either is able to separately. In this chapter, however, I discuss the Unit of Analysis coding only — showing the kinds of data analyses and comparisons which it may be used for; and offering some preliminary findings of the study.

Usefulness

Historically, one area of language research which has received considerable attention is the effort to identify units of planning and execution in language processing. By combining experimental data with observations of naturalistic phenomena (e.g. hesitations, pauses, and slips of the tongue), researchers have acquired valuable information regarding global and local levels of planning and execution, "fluent" and "hesitant" phases of speech production, chunking patterns, and the like (for example, Butterworth, 1980; Clark & Clark, 1977; Fromkin, 1973; Garrett, 1975; Goldman-Eisler, 1968). However, the relationship between written translation processing and the processing of other types of discourse is not well explored. We know very little, for example, about the extent to which processes of comprehension and production, as they occur in translation, resemble comprehension and production processes in other discourse activities — be they in the native, second, or foreign language. Might those processes, as evidenced in translation, vary, for example, according to such factors as language fluency, training in translation, or number of languages mastered?

One way to begin to assess the resemblance of written translation processing to the processing of other kinds of discourse is to examine the size of the linguistic units which people work with when they translate.

By examining units of text analysis, we can begin to identify the various levels of planning and execution that people use when translating; allowing us to subsequently progress to more specific questions. For example: are these units of analysis consonant with what researchers already know about the comprehension and production units used to process other types of language tasks? Do trained translators work with larger chunks of discourse than do untrained translators? To what extent do good versus poor translators work in syntactic or semantically meaningful units? Do editing styles vary predictably according to competence in the foreign language; or perhaps, according to translating skill? Which language do translators most commonly work in — the target or source language? Under what conditions is each most likely to be used?

Such questions, of course, carry theoretical implications not only for translation theory, but also for theories of language comprehension and production, second language acquisition, and bilingualism as well. In a more practical vein, as more is learned from this kind of research, understanding the units of analysis used in translation may enable us to know better how and what to teach in order to help learners develop their translation competence; and it may increase our understanding of the role that translation may play in foreign language learning.

Unit of Analysis Coding

It was with these kinds of issues in mind that the Unit of Analysis coding was developed. As shown in Table 1, the coding identifies seven levels of analysis: analysis carried out at the level of the syllable or morpheme; at the word-, phrase-, clause-, sentence- and discourse-levels; and a separate "group unit" coding for any unit which could not be identified as representing a complete and coherent syntactic unit. Theoretically, group units may be of any length. Empirically, they ranged from two to 15 words.

All units at all levels were coded according to language used; that is, as having been carried out in either French (the source language) or English (the target language). Since participants spoke aloud all portions of the text which they were reading, analysing, or reproducing into the target language, it is assumed that the coding results in a reasonably accurate representation of the units with which subjects were actually working.[1]

TABLE 1   *Unit of analysis coding showing the criteria used for coding participants' units of text analysis.*

Level 1 — morphemic or syllabic analysis (M)

Breakdown or expansion of a word into syllables or morpheme units, e.g. *re*, *reportent*, *porter*, or *reporter*; or treating *ne* and *pas* as separate units;

Level 2 — word unit analysis (W)

Treatment of a word as a complete unit. Articles with their associated nouns are coded as one unit, e.g. *Les Américains*, *Américains*, *mauvaise*, and *est* would each be coded as single word-units

Level 3 — phrase unit analysis (P)

Processing of a group of words constituting a grammatical phrase, e.g. noun phrase, verb phrase, adjectival phrase, prepositional phrase... Examples: *ne la reportent pas sur les autres*, *sur les autres*, *ne la reportent pas*, *que les Français*, *vivent mieux*.

Level 4 — clause unit analysis (C)

Processing of words in units containing a subject and verb alone; or subject and verb, plus complements. Examples: *s'ils sont de mauvaise humeur*, *Les Américains ne la reportent pas*, *Les Américains ne la reportent pas sur les autres*.

Level 5 — sentence unit analysis (S)

Processing a complete sentence as an entire unit, without breaking it down into smaller units of analysis, e.g. *Les Américains, s'ils sont de mauvaise humeur ne la reportent pas sur les autres*.

Level 6 — discourse level analysis (D)

Clearly processing two or more sentences together, either by referring back to something read previously in the text while decoding another unit; by skipping ahead to another sentence or paragraph in order to decode the unit being processed; or by reading two or more sentences consecutively, without significant pausing. Examples: A subject says *"Ils ont des formules de courtoisie. Oh. Back there I put forms, which is wrong. It must be they have formulas of courtesy"*; or *"Ils ont des formules de courtoisie. I better go on and see what they say. En France, il n'est pas inhabituel qu'un marchand soit désagreable avec ses clients"*; or *"Ils ont plus de formules de courtoisie. En France, il n'est pas inhabituel qu'un marchand soit désagreable avec ses clients"*.

Level 7 — group level analysis (G)

Breakdown of text portions into clusters of words which cannot be identified as constituting a complete and coherent syntactic unit. Examples: *humeur ne la reportent*, *vivent mieux en s'ils sont de mauvaise humeur*, *ne la*.

Data Coding

The units of analysis may be coded directly from the protocols (as shown in the protocol excerpts in the Appendix). However, by writing out the units as shown in Table 2, participants' characteristic patterns of analysis may be compared more quickly and easily.

From this display, showing three of the participants' processing of the first sentence of the source text, differences across individuals are immediately apparent.

Anna both begins and continues her processing in English. She starts with a clause-unit, then moves directly on to the full sentence. She does not stop for further analysis or immediate editing; and she never returns later for an edit check. In contrast, Bruce does considerably more processing, alternating back and forth from French- to English-language analysis. He begins with moderate sized clause-units, then moves to smaller group- and phrase-units, alternately expanding and reducing the size of the unit of analysis throughout. In this way, he builds up gradually to a translation of the whole sentence. Although most of his analysis is done at the phrase-unit level, he also engages in word-, clause-, group-, and sentence-level analysis; and, later on, in discourse-level analysis. His later editing tends to be done in larger chunks, except for those difficult areas of text which require small-unit work for comprehension. Also characteristic of Bruce is the way he frequently retraces and repeats portions of each previously analysed unit. This creates an accordion-like effect, as he makes numerous short backtrackings and expansions which move him in a somewhat repetitious and circuitous route — but which nonetheless afford a steady progression through the text.

Unlike Bruce, Fran begins with larger units — in this case, complete sentences, processed in French, not English. She then breaks these down into smaller units, working largely in English. Unlike the students in the study, this competent bilingual expends her efforts at analysis not primarily for comprehension purposes, but in the service of high-level "production" goals, that is, for determining the best way to express the original source text in English. Most of her processing is, therefore, done in English; and most of it occurs during her second time through the text, after she has already scanned the source text to find out what it says, and before she reads through the entire text again for final editing. Fran is the only participant in this study who proceeded through the text more than twice.

TABLE 2   *Unit of analysis coding, showing Anna, Bruce, and Fran's units of analysis, while working with the first sentence of the text.*

		French text: Les Américains vivent mieux en societé que les Français.
Anna:	1st time:	The Americans live better (Clause/English)
		The American society lives better than the French (Sentence/English)

Bruce:	1st time:	Des Américains vivent mieux en societé (Clause/French)
		they have a better (Group/English)
		a better society (Phrase/English)
		en societé (Phrase/French)
		standard of living (Phrase/English)
		que les Français. (Phrase/French)
	2nd time:	Américains (Word/French)
		Americans live better in society (Clause/English)
		live better in society than French (Phrase/English)
		I mean the French (Word/English)
		they live better in society than the French (Sentence/English)
	3rd time:	Americans live better (Clause/English)
		vivent mieux en societé que les Français (Phrase/French)
		in society (Phrase/English)

Fran:	1st time:	Les Américains vivent mieux en societé que les Français (Sentence/French)
		Les Américains vivent mieux en societé que les Français (Sentence/French)
		Americans live better (Clause/English)
		en societé (Phrase/French)
		socially (Word/English)
		sociable (Word/English)
		than the French (Phrase/English)
	2nd time:	Americans live better in society (Clause/English)
		live better (Phrase/English)
		en societé (Phrase/French)
		live better in (Group/English)
		it's not in society (Phrase/English)
		in high society (Phrase/English)
		in company (Phrase/English)
		in company (Phrase/English)
		in company (Phrase/English)
		live better in company (Phrase/English)
		live better in company (Phrase/English)
		act better (Phrase/English)
		act better in company than the French people do (Phrase/English)
		Americans act better than the French do (Sentence/English)
	3rd time:	Americans act better in company than the French do (Sentence/English)

Alternate Display Modes

An immediate visual representation of these various patterns of analysis may be obtained by displaying the individuals' movement patterns in diagram fashion, as shown in Figures 1 and 2.

This form of display affords us an immediate impressionistic view of an individual's total amount of processing activity, the language in which it is carried out, and his or her general patterns of movement through the text; it shows, as well, which text portions elicited changes or increases in processing activity, thus giving some indication of the effect of text on the participants' units of analysis.

Figure 1 shows what we have seen before: Anna's progression through the text in a fairly continuous line of forward movement, with few backtrackings, and very little editing throughout. She processes almost entirely in English, with French-language analysis occurring only when she has difficulty translating a specific unit.

Figure 2 reveals the pattern already noted in Bruce: he progresses steadily through the text, but with relatively short and frequent backtrackings in the process. Although most of his analysis is done in English, he alternates between the two available languages, resorting to repetition of French-language units when a text portion proves particularly difficult to comprehend.

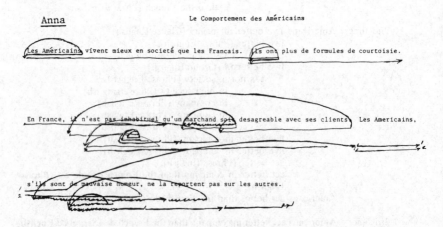

FIGURE 1 *Diagram of Anna's units of analysis, showing her pattern of movement through this portion of the text.* ——————— *= English language processing,* ∿∿∿∿ *= French language processing.*

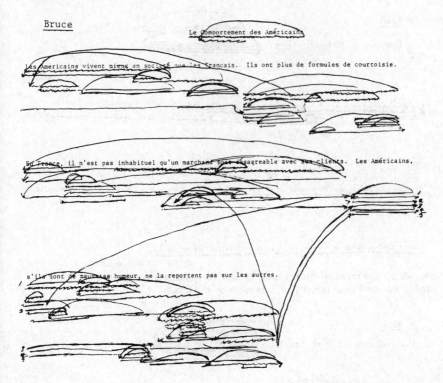

FIGURE 2   *Diagram of Bruce's units of analysis, showing his pattern of movement through this portion of the text.*

Figures 3 and 4 illustrate individual variation in the participants' patterns of analysis during repeated times through the text. By separating subjects' patterns of analysis into first, second, and subsequent times through the text, we see that Fran's first time through closely resembles Anna's "combined" pattern, as shown previously in Figure 1. (In fact, Anna proceeded through the entire text only once.)

In contrast, Figure 4, showing Fran's second time through the text, more closely resembles Bruce's "combined" diagram, in terms of the total amount of processing activity and the frequency of skips forward and backward in the text. The other student subjects in this study revealed movement patterns similar to either Anna or Bruce, showing little deviation from these two overall patterns; only the bilingual seemed to combine both patterns of movement.

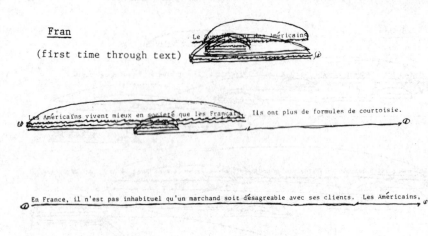

FIGURE 3   *Diagram of Fran's units of analysis, showing her pattern of movement during her first time through this portion of the text.*

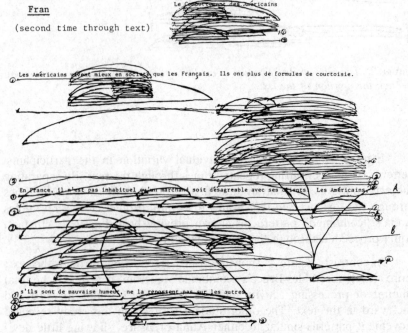

FIGURE 4   *Diagram of Fran's pattern of movement during her second time through this portion of the text.*

Numerical Displays

For more specific information about the amount of processing at each level of analysis, numerical profiles may be constructed. Table 3 shows the percentage of activity done by each of these three participants at the various unit levels. Noteworthy here is the high percentage of processing by all participants at the clause-, phrase-, and word-unit levels, indicating a strong preference for naturally occurring syntactic units, corresponding to what are commonly called "sentence constituents". Also of interest is the high percentage of sentence- and discourse-level analysis done by Fran, the bilingual, as compared with the student participants. Note, as well, Anna's high reliance on much smaller, morphemic and syllabic analysis (21% of her activity was done at this level, as compared with Bruce and Fran, who focused on this unit level only 2 % and 0% of the time, respectively.)

A surprising finding of this study was the relative frequency of analysis which occurred at the group-unit level. Although most of the participants' total activity in fact occurred in complete syntactic units, approximately 10% on the average occurred in syntactically incomplete clusters. In Bruce's case, a full 14% of his activity occurred at this "nonsyntactic" group-unit level. This seems a high percentage, given the fact that the group units represent neither syntactically nor semantically

TABLE 3 *Percentage of participants' total processing at each unit of analysis level.*

Anna	Bruce	Fran
CLAUSE...27% (20)	WORD 30% (95)	PHRASE...33% (68)
PHRASE...22% (16)	PHRASE...25% (78)	WORD 19% (40)
MORPHEME 21% (15)	CLAUSE...23% (72)	SENTENCE...................18% (38)
WORD 18% (13)	GROUP....14% (44)	CLAUSE...14% (29)
SENTENCE 7% (5)	DISCOURSE...................3% (10)	GROUP....10% (21)
GROUP.....4% (3)	MORPHEME 2% (7)	DISCOURSE...................6% (12)
DISCOURSE...................1% (1)	SENTENCE 2% (6)	MORPHEME 0% (0)

complete units, nor do they represent what would be considered to be natural comprehension or production units (cf. Clark & Clark, 1977).

Additionally, this high percentage of work in nonsyntactic fragments seemed to be connected to another finding: in the other coding system developed for the study — the coding for problem solving strategies and behaviours — a separate category was included for what was called "text repetition strategies" (Gerloff, 1985). This category consisted primarily of such verbal behaviours as repetitions and retracings of text portions. From the protocols, these activities appeared to be strategic devices used to solve particular problems comprehending the original text or producing the translation (i.e. they did *not* appear to be a kind of mindless repetition or stalling behaviour intended, for example, to keep the experimenter from asking what participants were doing during a silence).

As seen in Table 4, participants varied in the degree to which they engaged in these kinds of text repetition strategies; and they differed in the extent to which their analysis focused on the nonsyntactic group level units. *Higher levels of text repetition activity were associated with higher levels of group-unit processing.* Thus, a significant portion of the apparently strategic repetition of text segments seemed to be done not in whole syntactic units, but in nonsyntactic constituent fragments.

An additional finding was that over half (56%) of all group-unit work occurred in units containing only two or three words, with the remaining 44% distributed among units four to 15 words in length (Figure 5).

Morever, individuals who evidenced *more* text repetition as a problem-solving strategy tended to repeat text portions in the smaller two-to-three-word group units; whereas those who used this strategy *less* frequently tended to produce fewer but larger group units. Thus, *not only was more*

TABLE 4 *Increases in problem solving strategies of text repetition associated with increases in the percentage of text processing activity at the group unit level.*

Participant	Text Repetition Strategies	Group Unit Analysis
Anna	24%	4%
E	27%	8%
C	35%	11%
Fran	37%	10%
D	45%	13%
Bruce	61%	14%

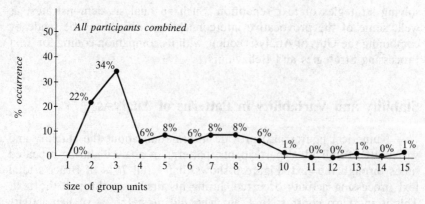

FIGURE 5   *Percentage of group unit processing done by all participants combined, at each of the group unit sizes (2-word, 3-word units, etc.)*

text repetition activity associated with more group unit processing, but it was associated as well with smaller sized group units. These associations suggest that repetition of small group units in partial constituents may be a strategic device used to hold the text in active memory while higher level problem solving is going on; the predominance of group units occurring in two-to-three-word clusters may simply reflect some sort of production or articulatory constraint. This hypothesis is consistent with a model of working memory proposed by Baddeley and various associates (cf. Baddeley, Scott, Drynan & Smith, 1969; Baddeley & Patterson, 1971; Baddeley & Hitch, 1974; Baddeley, Thomson & Buchanan, 1975). The model postulates the existence of an "articulatory rehearsal loop" which helps keep information accessible in active memory. Essentially, it suggests that by pumping information into the working memory's central processing mechanism, by means of verbal articulation, a person can hold information alive in working memory (Potter, 1985). As long as the pumped-in information does not exceed the memory capacity of the "phonemic response buffer" — a component of the system which is "able to store a limited amount of speech-like material in the appropriate serial order" (Baddeley & Hitch, 1974: 77) — little demand is placed on the system's "central executive" component, leaving that mechanism free to handle other storage and processing tasks. The capacity of the phonemic buffer appears to be limited to approximately two to three words (Baddeley, Thomson & Buchanan, 1975) — exactly the size of most of the group units observed in this study. This hypothesis provides a reasonable explanation for the relatively common occurrence in the protocols of group-unit processing in two-to-three-word groupings, as associated with the use of problem solving strategies of text repetition. Such an analysis demonstrates, as well, some of the provocative interconnections which may be made by combining the Unit of Analysis coding with its companion coding for Text Processing Strategies and Behaviours.

Stability and Variability in Patterns of Analysis

Numerical figures also provide information about the stability and variability of individual participants' patterns of analysis during repeated times through the text. Figure 6 shows that a full 76% of Bruce's total text processing activity occurred during his first time through the text. This is in sharp contrast to Fran, who did most (56%) of her activity during her *second* time through. It appears that the bilingual subject used her first and last times through the text to scan the source text for its meaning, and to check over her translation during her final editing.

This same pattern of activity at a more specific level is in evidence in Figures 7 and 8, showing the percentage of processing carried out at various individual levels of analysis, during repeated times through the

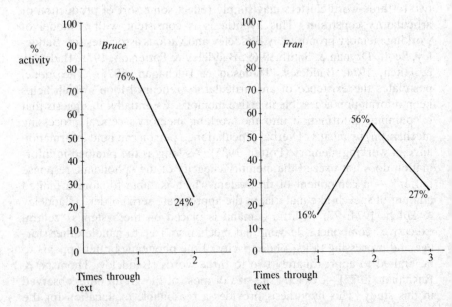

FIGURE 6 *Percentage of Bruce's and Fran's total processing activity occurring during each new time through the text.*

text. Fran's word-, phrase-, sentence- and group-level analysis changed significantly from one time to another; whereas her analysis at the morpheme-, clause-, and discourse-levels remained relatively stable from one time to the next.

The drop in processing at the word- and sentence-unit levels during her second time through the text (the time when most of her processing

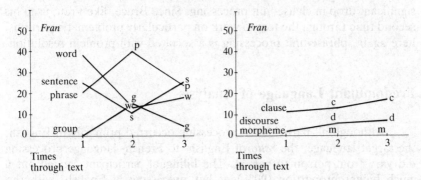

FIGURE 7   *The dramatic changes in Fran's processing activity during repeated times through the text occurred at the word-, phrase-, group-, and sentence-levels of analysis (left graph). Clause-, discourse-, and morphemic/syllabic-level analysis remained relatively constant all three times through the text (right graph).*

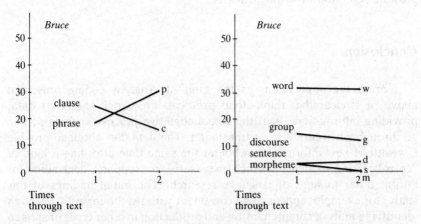

FIGURE 8   *The dramatic changes in Bruce's processing activity during repeated times through the text occurred at the clause- and phrase-levels of analysis (left graph). Word-, group-, discourse-, sentence-, and morphemic/syllabic- level analysis remained relatively constant both times through the text (right graph).*

activity actually occurred), accompanied by a dramatic rise in her level of phrase- and group-unit processing, reflects the fact that, for Fran, problems in translation were generally dealt with at the phrase level, accompanied by a great deal of repetition of nonsyntactic group units.

In contrast, Bruce's processing activity remained relatively stable across most unit levels during both his first and second times through the text. The only dramatic changes were a sharp increase in phrase-unit analysis during his second time through the text, accompanied by a significant drop in clause-unit processing. Since Bruce, like Fran, used his second time through the text to work on particularly problematic portions, here again, phrase-unit processing is associated with problem resolution.

Predominant Language of Analysis

Although all participants' processing occurred primarily in English, the target language, the *ratio* of English- to French- language processing did vary from person to person. The bilingual participant carried out a much higher proportion (90%) of her processing in English, with the students' ratio of English- to French-language processing more closely approximating a 50/50 proportion. This difference undoubtedly reflects the students' need to comprehend the source text and the bilingual's concern not with comprehending the source text but with crafting the best possible rendition of it into English.

Conclusion

From the applications of the Unit of Analysis coding presented above, it is clear that think-aloud protocols are a rich source of data, providing information about the actual cognitive processes which people go through when producing a translation. The data thus obtained provide a wealth of new information, while at the same time affording a kind of "corroborating evidence" which may serve to support, contradict, or inform other findings of language research. The initial findings of this study, for example, appear to be consonant with psycholinguistic research identifying units of comprehension and production in other types of spoken and written discourse. This is seen in the participants' strong preference for working with sentence constituent units at the phrase and clause levels, as well as the fact that they clearly used several levels of analysis, sometimes even at the same time.

The study suggests, as well, that clearly identifiable differences may exist between good and poor translators, as well as among less competent speakers and learners, in such areas as preferred language of analysis, size of units dealt with, editing styles, and characteristic patterns of movement through the text. In the larger study, we should be able to determine to what degree such differences may be associated with level of skill in the language, degree of training in translation, or with the number of languages a person has mastered. The knowledge acquired from this inquiry promises to move us toward a better theoretical understanding of translation, as it provides information which might well be given practical application in the fields of language learning and translator training. Certainly this method of data collection and analysis does not provide all we need to know. However, this coupling of an introspective data collection technique with a translation task does provide a good methodological start toward identifying what have, in the past, been rather elusive issues in language and translation research.

Notes to Chapter 7

1. Unfortunately, in this pilot study, accurate records were not kept as to when subjects' verbalizations represented their processing of the source text, their reading of their own translations of it, or other verbalizations made while they were writing out their translations. In the larger study, a video camera is being used to facilitate a more detailed analysis of these various stages of the translation process.

References

BADDELEY, A. D. & HITCH, G. 1974, Working memory. In G. H. BOWER (ed.), *The Psychology of Learning and Motivation*. New York: Academic Press.

BADDELEY, A. D. & PATTERSON, K. 1971, The relationship between long-term and short-term memory. *British Medical Bulletin* 27, 237–42.

BADDELEY, A. D., SCOTT, D., DRYNAN, R. & SMITH, J. C. 1969, Short-term memory and the limited capacity hypothesis. *British Journal of Psychology*, 60, 51–5.

BADDELEY, A. D., THOMSON, N. & BUCHANAN, M. 1975, Word length and the structure of short-term memory. *Journal of Verbal Learning and Verbal Behavior* 14, 575–89.

BELLOC, H. 1930, *On Translation*, Oxford: Clarendon Press.

BUTTERWORTH, B. 1980, Evidence from pauses in speech. In B. BUTTERWORTH, (ed.), *Language Production*. London: Academic Press, Vol. I, 154–76.

CARROLL, J. B. 1977, Linguistic abilities in translators and interpreters. Paper presented at the NATO Symposium on Language Intepretation and Communication, Venice, Italy, September 26–October 1.

CATFORD, J. 1965, *A Linguistic Theory of Translation: An Essay in Applied Linguistics*. London: Oxford University Press.

CLARK, H. & CLARK, E. V. 1977, *Psychology and Language*. New York: Harcourt Brace Jovanovich.

FOLKART, B. 1984, A thing-bound approach to the practice and teaching of technical translation. *META* 29, 3.

FRAWLEY, W. 1984, Prolegomenon to a theory of translation. In W. FRAWLEY (ed.), *Translation: Literary, Linguistic, and Philosophical Perspectives*. New Jersey: Associated University Press, 159–78.

FROMKIN, V. (ed.) 1973, *Speech Errors as Linguistic Evidence*. The Hague: Mouton.

GARRETT, M. E. 1975, The analysis of sentence production. In G. H. BOWER, (ed.), *The Psychology of Learning and Motivation*. New York: Academic Press, Vol. IX, 133–77.

GERLOFF, P. 1984, From the inside out: Using talk-aloud protocols to assess second language learner translation processing. Unpublished Doctoral Qualifying Paper, Cambridge, Mass.: Harvard Graduate School of Education.

— 1985, From the inside out: using talk-aloud protocols to investigate L2 learner processes of translation. Paper presented at the Second Language Research Forum, University of California, Los Angeles, February 22–4.

— 1986, Second language learners' reports on the interpretative process: Talk-aloud protocols of translation. In J. HOUSE & S. BLUM-KULKA (eds), *Interlingual and Intercultural Communication*. Tubingen: Narr. 243–62.

GOLDMAN-EISLER, F. 1968, *Psycholinguistics: Experiments in Spontaneous Speech,* New York: Academic Press.

HOUSE, J. 1977, *A Model for Translation Quality Assessment*. Tübingen: Narr.

HUTCHINS, W. J. 1984, Machine translation and machine-aided translation. In W. FRAWLEY (ed.), *Translation: Literary, Linguistic and Philosophical Perspectives*. New Jersey: Associated University Press, 93–149.

KATZ, J. 1978, Effability and translation. In F. GUENTHNER & M. GUENTHNER-REUTTER (eds), *Meaning and Translation*. New York: NYU Press, 191–234.

KEENAN, E. 1978, Some logical problems in translation. In F. GUENTHNER & M. GUENTHNER-REUTTER (eds), *Meaning and Translation*. New York: NYU Press, 157–89.

KRINGS, H. 1986, The translation strategies of advanced German learners of French. In J. HOUSE & S. BLUM-KULKA (eds), *Interlingual and Intercultural Communication*. Tübingen: Narr. 263–76.

LEVY, J. 1967, Translation as a decision process. In *To Honor Roman Jakobson: Essays on the Occasion of his 70th Birthday*. The Hague: Mouton, Vol. II, 1171–82.

LÖRSCHER, W. 1986, Linguistic aspects of translation processes: towards an analysis of translation performance. In J. HOUSE & S. BLUM-KULKA (eds), *Interlingual and Intercultural Communication*. Tübingen: Narr.

MORGAN, B. W. 1959, A critical bibliography of works on translation. In R. A. BROWER (ed.), *On Translation*. Cambridge, Mass.: Harvard University Press, 271–93.

POTTER, M. 1985, Why is short-term memory so accurate? Talk presented at Harvard University, Cambridge, Mass , Nov. 3.

POSTGATE, J. P. 1922, *Translation and Translations: Theory and Practice*. London: G. Belland Sons, Ltd.

QUINE, W. V. O. 1960, *Word and Object*. Cambridge, Mass.: MIT Press.

SAVORY, T. 1957, *The Art of Translation*. London: Jonathan Cape.

SELESKOVITCH, D. 1976, Interpretation: A psychological approach to translation. In R. BRISLIN (ed.), *On Translation*. New York: Gardner Press, 92–116.

STEINER, G. 1975, *After Babel: Aspects of Language and Translation*. Oxford: Oxford University Press.

TIRKKONEN-CONDIT, S. 1986, Text type markers and translation equivalence. In J. HOUSE & S. BLUM-KULKA. (eds), *Interlingual and Intercultural Communication*. Tübingen: Narr. 95–113.

VINAY, J. P. & DARBELNET, J. 1958, *Stylistique Comparée du Français et de l'Anglais: Methode de Traduction*. Paris: Didier.

WALMSLEY, J. B. 1970, Transformation theory and translation. *IRAL*, 8, 185–99.

WEBER, W. 1984, Training translators and conference interpreters. In *Language in Education: Theory and Practice*. Orlando, Fla.: Harcourt Brace Jovanovich, 58–.

WILSS, W. 1976, Perspective and limitations of a didactic framework for the teaching of translation. In R. BRISLIN (ed.), *Translation: Applications and Research*. New York: Gardner Press, 117–38.

— 1982, *The Science of Translation: Problems and Methods*. Tübingen: Narr.

Appendix

A: Source text and participant translations

French language source text

Le Comportement des Américains

Les Américains vivent mieux en société que les Français. Ils ont plus de formules de courtoisie. En France, il n'est pas inhabituel qu'un marchand soit désagreable avec ses clients. Les Américains, s'ils sont de mauvaise humeur, ne la reportent pas sur les autres.

En revanche, il semble y avoir des contradictions dans le comportement des Américains. Ils ont les formules de courtoisie mais mettront les pieds sur la table — ce qui choque les Français.

Un exemple de différence de comportement entre Américains et Français a frappé Colette. Elle raconte qu'à une "party", les gens sont arrivés en smoking. Tous ces gens élègants se sont tout de suite mis à éplucher le maïs. En France, dit-elle, on serait venu en jeans, mais personne n'aurait aidé à préparer la nourriture.

from "Le Comportement des Américains"
by Marie Galanti, in *Le Journal Français d'Amérique*, septembre 1982

English translation as rendered by Fran, a bilingual speaker

Polite Behaviour of Americans

Americans act better in company than the French do. Courtesy is more a matter of course. In France, it is not unusual for a merchant to be unpleasant to his clients. If an American is out of sorts, he does not burden other people with it.

On the other hand, there seem to be contradictions in the polite behavior of Americans. They take courtesy for granted, but they put their feet on the table — a shocking sight to the French.

Colette was struck by one particular example of the differences. She describes a party at which everyone arrived in formal attire; and then, elegant as they were, they set about husking corn. In France, she says, people would have come in jeans, but no one would have helped prepare the food.

English translation as rendered by Anna, a student

The American society lives better than the French. There are more formulas of courtesy. A merchant isn't usually disagreeable with his clients. If Americans have a bad sense of humour _____ on the other.

In reflection it seems that there are contradictions in the behavior (manners) of Americans. There are formulas/rules of courtesy but putting feet on the table — this would shock the French.

An example of the difference of behavior between Americans and French hit Colette. She encountered this at a party when people were smoking. All the elegant people _____ . In France, she said, one can come in jeans, but no one helps to prepare the meal.

English translation as rendered by Bruce, a student

Deportement of Americans

Americans live better in society than the French. They have more courtesy. In France it is not unusual for a shopkeeper to be disagreeable w/ his customers. Americans, if they are in bad humour, they will not take it out on their customers.

In reflection, it seems there are some contradictions in the deportment of Americans. They have courtesy, but put their feet on the table — this shocks the French.

An example of difference between the deportement of Americans and French struck Colette. She recalls that at a party the people arrived while the meal was being prepared. All these elegant people quickly put themselves husking corn. In France, she says, people would come in jeans, but no one would help prepare the meal.

B: Protocol excerpt

I = Interviewer
... denotes pauses
??? denotes inaudible utterance

Bruce

B: Le Comportement des Américains (laughs). Maybe I'll find out what the title is... comportement...oh...des Américains...vivent mieux en société...like...uh...en société...standard of living, I guess... I've seen that word before... ... que les Franç... ... O.K...uhm... ... Américains... ...Americans...live (writes)...better...society..

I: Now what are you doing?

B: I'm tryin' to figure out...it doesn't really make sense... ... live better... (laugh) ...in society than French... I mean the French... it kinda means oh well, maybe let me just go on farther...and see... ...ils ont plus de form..de....courtesy Oh. This is the harder one, right? (laughs) Ils ont plus...de for.. formules...de...courts... ... they have more... ... they have more..of...oh...huh...yeah, so it must be they live better in society. That's what it says... ... ??? than the French... controversial statement... uh...they have... ...de...they have greater, they have more... ... have more... I was wondering uh...maniere...for...have courtesy, courtesy.–.courtesy?... form...no..uh... ... don't laugh if I'm way off... In France... ... ... in France... boy I wish I could just look there... (referring to vocabulary list on side of page folded over).

I: There are hardly any words there anyway (laughing)

B: Oh, sure (laughs)... ... They uh... inhabituel...qu'un marchand...dés...soit désagreable avec ses clients... ... uhm... In France there is... ... they...have...they...are not inhabitual...

I: Now what are you doing?

B: qu'un... I'm just trying...that one...merchant...is disagreeable, is...disagreeable...with his clients... ... it is not...it is not unusual... ...that a merchant...is disagreeable...In France...oh, *I* see what they're saying! ...In France...see...they there...now these make a little more sense.

I: Oh.

B: I hope (laughs) Let's see... ... ... unusual...see, that's a little, that's what I'm using now...that... ... a...merchant...shop ...disagreeable...it is not unusual *for* ... ... a shopkeeper...to be... ...disagreeable... ...

Anna

A: The Americans live...better...the American society...lives better than the French... ... ... (writing)... There were...uhm... there are...more...formulas...of... ... ... courtesy... ... ...

I: Now what are you doing?

A: Tryin' to figure out what...inhabituel means...uhm...tryin' to use context clues...........

I: Like what?

A: Marchand is a ...merchant...is...is disagreeable with his clients...uhm...

I: What are you thinking about...while you're doing this?

A: Uhm...I'm thinking...maybe it has to do with habit but........ ....

I: Now what? ... Just keep saying out loud what you're doing...as if you were thinking it to yourself and I weren't even here. I only have to be here so I can keep prompting you. (both laugh)

A: O.K....uhm...hab...habit...inhabit...tryin' to ...maybe...the habit but this doesn't really make sense... ... uhm...guess it's not... ....a merchant doesn't usually, isn't usually... ... disagreeable with his clients... ... .

I: So what did you put for that one?

A: A merchant isn't usually disagreeable with his clients.

Fran

(first time through text)

F: O.K.! Le Comportement des Américains. Comportement is a word I always have trouble with. Comportement seems to be more ??? It's also...uhm...it's a technical word, translated as uh...behavior...Americans. The way Americans behave, le comportement des Américains...The way Americans conduct themselves. For now. Until I see what I say. Les Américains vivent mieux en société que les Français I'm supposed to write that down now, right? or...shall I write now? or write whenever I want to?

I: Whatever you want to do.

F: O.K. Les Américains vivent mieux en société que les Français..Americans live better...en société... ... socially...sociably...than the French. They have..more...formulas...of courtesy... ... In France, it is not unaccustomed... for a merchant to disagree with his clients....

8 The Use of Introspective Data in Translation

HANS P. KRINGS

Rationale

The object of my investigation was an inquiry into the structure of the translation process in advanced German learners of French as a foreign language. Although a vast bulk of literature exists on the problems of translating in general (sometimes referred to as the "science of translation" or "translatology") and on problems pertaining to the role of translation in foreign language teaching in particular, scarcely a mention has been made of the actual process whereby the final translation is obtained. It was not until very recently that several investigators independent of one another developed the idea of analysing the translation process by means of thinking-aloud data (see Gerloff, this volume, Chapter 7; Hölscher & Möhle, this volume, Chapter 6; Dechert & Sandrock, in press; Lörscher, 1986). The starting points for these investigations were similar. There seemed to be a shared belief among the investigators that nothing much can be said about the relationship between foreign language learning and translation until there is at least some knowledge of the cognitive processes taking place in the heads of learners while translating.

There are several good reasons why such knowledge is assumed to be of importance for a theory of foreign language learning and teaching and for a theory of translation:

1. The role of translation in foreign language teaching has always been a matter of controversy. It seems that the value attached to translation as a teaching device has so far been determined largely by "ideological" preconceptions (based on simplistic theories of the role of the mother tongue in foreign language learning) rather than by empirically substantiated knowledge about the effect that

translation exercises may have upon the learning of a foreign language.

2. In recent times, ever more frequent demands have been made for the introduction of translation skills ("translational competence") as a separate goal into the foreign language curriculum. These demands are substantiated by reference to the multiplicity of applications of such skills in professional and private contexts: "Translation, itself, is a valuable skill, and an important means of refining one's knowledge of a foreign language at an advanced stage of learning" (Catford, 1981: 17; compare the similar statements by Tinsley, 1974: 12; Wilkins, 1974: 82). Note the number of language learners who seek a job in commerce and industry, where translation skills are required (e.g. as a bilingual secretary) or even become technical, scientific or literary translators. Even private life situations in which one has to translate or interpret are not uncommon. When translation skills become an object of foreign language teaching, the need for a theory of the best way of teaching such skills arises. Despite the confusion caused by the theories of Brian Harris (1977; 1978; Harris & Sherwood, 1978), who assumes that translational competence is automatically attained by all bilinguals (for a criticism of Harris' theory see Newmark, 1981: 97; Toury, 1984a; Krings, 1985), most researchers seem to agree that translational competence is more than bilingual competence (especially when considered as a *text*-bound skill). For it includes the ability to create equivalent texts or, to put it in Nida & Taber's words, to find the "closest natural equivalent of the source-language message, first in terms of meaning and secondly in terms of style" (Nida & Taber, 1969: 12). In addition, translational competence also implies the ability to make use of compensatory strategies in all those cases where no proper equivalent is extant. On the other hand, it is evident that bilingual competence and translational competence overlap at least to some degree or, to put it another way, that translational competence is at least partially enhanced by second language acquisition and (probably even more) by foreign language learning in formal classroom settings, right from the beginning of the learning/acquisition process even, as Toury (1984b) has pointed out. The particular aspects, however, in which bilingual competence and translational competence coincide, have still not been precisely determined. I assumed that introspective data on the translation process of advanced learners could contribute significantly to the answering of these questions.

3. Whereas the two goals mentioned above refer to foreign language learning and teaching, a third goal is directly related to translation

studies proper (that is to say, to the "science of translation" or "translatology"). Although this field of research has so far produced a vast bulk of literature (see, for example, the bibliographies by Bausch, Klegraf & Wilss, 1971; Lehmann, 1982; van Hoof, 1973), it has been almost exclusively concerned with the *linguistic* features of the finished *product* and not with the *psycholinguistic* features of the translation *process*, features that have hitherto been completely neglected. Although a psycholinguistic account of the translation process should be undertaken predominantly on the basis of data taken from professional translators, corresponding data from second language learners might be equally significant because in learners, translation skills can still be studied in *statu nascendi*, i.e. many processes automated in highly proficient professional translators still take place on a conscious level in learners, and are therefore more accessible for verbalization (see, also, pp. 163–67 of the chapter). I, therefore, consider my investigation a groundwork for a psycholinguistic theory of translation; a theory that will be necessary to overcome that notorious deficiency of traditional translatology mentioned above.

Design

The subjects of my study were eight native speakers of German, all studying to become secondary school teachers of French. All of them were approaching their exams in their last year at Bochum University. All had some experience of translating because translation exercises as a teaching and test device are compulsory for language students at German universities. None of the subjects, however, had experience as a professional translator. Four of them, randomly picked, translated a German text into French (i.e. from L1 into L2), the remainder translated a French text into German (i.e. from L2 into L1). Both types of translation (from and into the mother tongue) were deliberately included because the processes were assumed to differ, at least partially. The two texts chosen for the experiment were both fairly difficult. The French text selected was an article from the satirical journal "Le Canard Enchaîné". The text is concerned with the reshuffling of the French cabinet. It ridicules the idiosyncrasies of certain French ministers. The German text to be translated into French was an article from Düsseldorf's main newspaper "Rheinische Post" and describes in a humorous fashion the odyssey of a fieldmouse which happened to bring the restaurant service in a German Intercity train to a complete standstill. My reason for choosing these two articles was the great variety of translation problems the texts posed: In addition to "ordinary" grammatical, semantic and stylistic translation problems found in almost every type of text, these texts included puns, metaphorical expressions and other instances of literary finesse. I wanted these to be included because I assumed that the structure of the translation process would depend on the type of translation problem. Due to the pilot nature of the study I preferred to include a wide range of translational phenomena rather than a large number of subjects.

For the elicitation of the process data a thinking-aloud technique was used, i.e. the subjects were asked to verbalize whatever came to their minds while translating. The choice of the thinking-aloud technique was determined by theoretical considerations (see pp. 163–67 of the chapter). Before the collection of data began, I subjected myself to the experiment to acquaint myself with the task the subjects would have to face (on the idea of self-observation see, also, Cavalcanti, 1982). One result of this self-experiment was the observation that during those phases when thinking was most intensive (e.g. strenuous retrieval phases), my verbalization stopped automatically for a few seconds and did not continue until the problem had been solved (e.g. after the item in question had been retrieved). This observation coincides with the predictions made by Ericsson & Simon (1980; 1984) in terms of their model (see pp. 163–67 of this chapter). From this observation I concluded that it was advisable to allow the subjects to pause at their own discretion so as not to press them into verbalizing, because frequent intervention on the part of the experimenter might distort the cognitive processes of the subjects.

After the texts and the subjects had been chosen, a trial run with an additional subject was undertaken (these data were discarded later on). The trial run showed that the chosen texts were as difficult as they were supposed to be and that the translations into the foreign language (as opposed to the translation into the mother tongue) required *two* experimental sessions of two to three hours each.

The last step consisted in preparing an informal questionnaire to obtain information about subjects' personal history of language learning (how many years of French had been taught at school; at what kinds of school; what teaching materials were used; were the teachers native speakers or non-native speakers of French; what was the role of translation exercises during lessons, etc?).

During the experiment, great care was taken to create a relaxed atmosphere. After the task had been explained the subjects were given the opportunity to practise the thinking-aloud technique on a single sentence (not taken from the texts to be translated). The subjects were permitted to use all the reference books they were accustomed to use at home, such as monolingual and bilingual dictionaries, grammars, etc. My role during the translation experiments was basically that of an active listener. I frequently uttered gambits like "ja" and "hm" to encourage the subjects to go on with thinking aloud. All sessions were recorded and transcriptions made (thinking-aloud protocols: TAPs). The transcriptional system could afford to be very simple (i.e. without phonetic transcription and without indication of intonation patterns) because it was not the features of speech production that were the subject of the study. The length of unfilled pauses, repetitions and false starts were, however, systematically indicated in the thinking-aloud protocols because it soon became apparent that the concept of "temporal variables" as indicators of mental processes, hitherto applied successfully to the analysis of speech production (see, for example, the Kassel project: Dechert & Raupach, 1980; Dechert, Raupach & Möhle, 1984), was equally applicable to the investigation of the translation process (see, also, the contributions by Dechert and by Hölscher & Möhle to this volume). When the subjects made use of dictionaries or other types of reference books, this was noted in the transcriptions because strategies also became apparent in the way dictionaries and reference books were applied. Figure 1 gives a synoptical view of the design of the study.

Some Theoretical Problems Involved in the Use of the Thinking-Aloud Technique in Translation

The use of so-called "introspective data" in psychology, which I would prefer to call "verbal report data" because the term "introspection" is tainted by its variable and contradictory applications throughout its history, is as old as it is controversial. The main objections to this type of data (see, for example, Nisbett & Wilson, 1977) are:

- that the subjects have little or no access to their cognitive processes because most of these are unconscious and, therefore, not accessible to verbalization;
- that the subjects produce verbalizations that are inconsistent with their actual behaviour;
- that the verbalization task alters the normal course of the task performance;
- that the verbalizations are necessarily incomplete even for the conscious part of the processes.

Such objections have recently been extended to the domain of second language acquisition by Herbert Seliger, who has referred to every type of research based on verbal report data as the "psychoanalytic school" of second language acquisition research (1983: 185). I would like to argue that most of the above-mentioned objections are not applicable to the study of the translation process by means of thinking-aloud data and that, therefore, I see no need to consider myself a "psychoanalyst" and the subjects my "patients". The reasons can be summarized as follows:

1. The thinking-aloud technique is a type of *concurrent* probing as opposed to different types of *retrospective* probing. Even if one accepts the assumption that processes and verbalizations cannot be perfectly simultaneous, there remains one basic difference between these two types of probing which can be explained in terms of Ericsson & Simon's information processing model: concurrent verbalizations are made while the relevant information is still available

    I. Preparations for the data collection:

        thinking-aloud as method for data collection chosen
        ↓
        self-experiment
        ↓
        choice of subjects
        ↓
        choice of texts
        ↓
        trial run with additional subject
        ↓
        improvement of the design
        ↓
        drafting of the informal questionnaire

    II. Collection of data:

        creation of a relaxed atmosphere
        ↓
        explanation of task
        ↓
        opportunity to practise the thinking-aloud technique
        ↓
        the translation experiment proper

    III. Preparations for data analysis:

        establishment of the transcriptional rules
        ↓
        transcriptions of the tape-recordings (production of the TAPs)

FIGURE 1   *Synopsis of the design of the study*

from short-term memory. Retrospective verbalizations, by contrast, refer to information processed at an earlier point in time; information that must be retrieved from long-term memory before being verbalized. Since the two memory types have different modes of access, one would expect the information retrieved from long-term memory not to be recalled in its original form but in a form altered by elaboration, abstraction, reduction or evaluation (cf. Norman & Rumelhart, 1975). Sometimes the information retrieved from long-term memory may not even be the original information at all but similar to it, processed at a different point in time. It is, therefore, not surprising that most previous criticism of verbal report data was made with the retrospective type of probing in mind, i.e. where the subjects had to verbalize their mental processes after completing the task. Taking these differences into account one would expect few, and quite unreliable, verbalizations from a retrospective type of probing (in the study of the translation process) where questions like "What did you think when you translated the word ×?" might be asked half-an-hour after the event. Whereas one might expect much more, and more reliable, information from verbalizations immediately preceding or following the translation or made while searching for a possible equivalent.

2. A second characteristic of the thinking-aloud technique is that it does not demand abstraction, selection or inference processes on the part of the subjects. As opposed to types of verbal data collected by "requests for general reports", "probing general states", or even "probing hypothetical states" (cf. Ericsson & Simon, 1980: 224), the subjects were not asked how they *usually* tackle a translation task or how they *would* try to solve a specific kind of translation problem, but were simply encouraged to verbalize whatever came to their minds while translating. Here, again, one must be aware of the fact that most criticism levelled at verbal report data does not relate to thinking-aloud but to other types of probing. Ericsson & Simon have convincingly shown that the validity of verbal report data decreases with the degree of selectivity and abstractness of the verbalization task. It appears particularly important to avoid a type of probing that *forces* the subjects to verbalize. For, in this case, we would blur the clear-cut distinction between automated and non-automated parts of the translation process, which became apparent in the thinking-aloud protocols, in a very natural way: verbalizations spontaneously uttered by the subjects referred almost exclusively to non-automated processes, because automated processes take place on an unconscious level and are not accessible to verbalizations. This is perfectly in line with what Seliger maintains.

But what, to Seliger, looks like a serious drawback is in reality an essential advantage of the thinking-aloud technique, when applied to the study of the translation process. The identification of automated and non-automated parts of the translation process is an important step towards a psycholinguistic model of translation. It also makes an essential contribution to the explanation of differences in the translation performance of trained and non-trained translators.

3. The third and perhaps most important argument justifying the use of the thinking-aloud technique for the investigation of the translation process is the nature of the information to be verbalized. Since translating is, by its very nature, a linguistic process, the verbalizations externalize linguistically-structured information and can normally do without an *additional* process of verbal encoding. Ericsson & Simon refer to this type of verbalization, involving the articulation of information stored in a verbal code, as "Level 1 verbalization" as opposed to "Level 2 verbalization" where the task is predominantly a non-verbal one, e.g. in a problem-solving task with geometrical figures or in putting together a puzzle, and to "Level 3 verbalizations" where additional scanning, filtering, inference or generative processes are involved (Ericsson & Simon, 1984: 16). On the basis of these differentiations Ericsson & Simon come to the conclusion that thinking aloud as a type of Level 1 verbalization "will not change the structure and course of the task processes, although it may slightly decrease the speed of task performance" (Ericsson & Simon, 1980: 226). Even if one does not fully agree with the assumption that the processes remain completely unchanged in the case of concurrent verbalizations of the Level 1 type, one can, nevertheless, say that the thinking-aloud technique produces the verbal data with the least degree of distortion compared with all other types of probing.

Summing up these three main arguments, one might say that thinking aloud while translating is an almost natural type of activity to which most of the criticism levelled at verbal report data does not apply. This conclusion is strengthened by the observation that translating is often accompanied by "inner speech" as one can easily verify by self-observation or by observing the lips of a translating person when he or she is not "speaking". One should, therefore, expect a high degree of validity for such data.

At this point, I would like to remark briefly on another problem that is frequently debated in connection with the validity of thinking-aloud data, namely the problem of the "completeness" of the verbalizations. When the argument is put forward that thinking-aloud data are incomplete, the question arises: incomplete in relation to what? If it is argued that concurrent verbalizations are incomplete in the sense that unconscious processes are not verbalized, then this is no drawback where verbal report data are concerned; it is even a desirable effect. For Ericsson & Simon have shown that the validity of the thinking-aloud data would decrease significantly if the subjects were compelled to verbalize automated processes (see above). The question of completeness should rather be put in the following way: are the verbalizations complete in relation to the information processed in short-term memory in the normal course of the task? This is a fundamental question which could not be treated within the framework of my study. I would, however, like to report an observation based on my data that shows that individual differences between subjects with regard to their willingness to verbalize might be greater than Ericsson & Simon seem to assume. It was one and the same subject who:

- made the greatest number of uncommented alterations to the first draft of her translation;
- made the greatest number of uncommented choices between competing potential equivalents;
- verbalized the least number of translation problems explicitly;
- verbalized the least number of interlingual word-associations.

Since this subject was also the subject with the greatest number of unfilled pauses, calculated relative to the complete length of the experiment, it is doubtful that the degree of automatization in the subject would have been high and therefore responsible for the above-mentioned phenomena. Further studies especially designed to investigate such individual differences are called for to shed more light on these problems.

Analysis of the Data

Since thinking-aloud data have a low degree of structuring, it is necessary to develop analytical categories step by step and to refine them gradually. In accordance with the criterion of openness as a typical feature of qualitative methods (see Grotjahn, this volume, Chapter 3), one has to begin the analysis by searching for such structures as are inherent in the data. One such structure that became immediately apparent was the presence of translation problems and of systematic strategies to solve these. For various reasons (explained in more detail in Krings, 1985), the concepts of translation problem and translation strategy were chosen as fundamental categories for the description of the translation process data, and all further categories were based on these. The data were analysed with respect to a total of 117 features. 19 of these refer to the identification, classification and distribution among the subjects, of different problem types, e.g. comprehension problems v. production problems. 20 features refer to what I have named "macro-strategies", i.e. to the organization of the single steps in which the translation task as a whole is carried out (e.g. are unknown vocabulary items looked up in the dictionary before, or during, translating?). 25 features refer to comprehension strategies, e.g. the use of reference books. Comprehension problems and comprehension strategies were not restricted to the translation from L2 into L1 but were also found when the source-language text was in the mother tongue, e.g. "Miese machen" (a popular term for "to incur debts") or "Oberzugleitung" (name of the section of the German railway company responsible for the co-ordination of the time schedules of the trains). 38 features refer to equivalent retrieval strategies, e.g. the number of competing potential equivalents that are compared for the rendering of a given source-language text item; the order in which they were found; the role of the mother tongue in finding equivalents, etc. 15 features refer to evaluation and decision-making strategies, e.g. monitoring L2-segments by means of "implicit" or "explicit" linguistic knowledge, use of morphosyntactic, lexicosemantic, pragmatic knowledge, the role of native language intuitions, etc. All features can be sorted into four types according to the amount of information provided by the thinking-aloud protocols. Since it is impossible to comment on all the features analysed, I shall restrict myself to a few of these and only mention some of the others in passing.

The first type comprises all those features of the translation process which can be counted, for example, the number of translation problems encountered by each subject in a given text. The first step in analysing the thinking-aloud protocols consisted in identifying the problems one by one for each subject and relating them to those source-language text items that were initially responsible for the problem in question. Then the problems were listed and counted. All together 454 single translation problems could be identified in the thinking-aloud protocols. The identification of the translation problems was an essential step towards a further analysis of the data because this allowed the activities of the subjects to be interpreted as a set of systematic moves directed towards the solving of these problems. In addition the counting of translation problems permitted quantitative comparisons to be made. Among other things the number of problems for each individual could be compared and an average number could be calculated. I could determine the extent to which the type of text influences the number of problems created, and comparisons could be made between translations from, and into, the foreign language. I also determined the degree to which the subjects had problems in common when translating the same text. By doing this I was able to build a hierarchy of problems, beginning with problems common to all the subjects and ending with those which were unique to a single individual.

Table 1 shows that only a fifth of the translation problems (19.0% in translations into L1, 20.9% in translations into L2) were common to *all* four subjects. These problems can be considered typical for the given text and the given group of subjects. The table also shows that half the problems (50.0% in translations into L1, 48.5% in translations into L2) were restricted to one subject only. These problems can be considered idiosyncratic. It is apparent that the distinction between typical and idiosyncratic translation problems is a valuable aid for designing translation exercises and for choosing texts with an adequate degree of difficulty for a given group of learners. It is interesting to note that there was almost no difference between translations from, and into, the foreign language. The problems were further categorized linguistically, e.g. according to the rank of the source-language text item that created the problems in question. About 90% of the problems were on the word-rank. Finally, problems the subjects deal with successfully were compared with problems that could not be solved, and both types were related to the strategies used. All-in-all one may say that the translation problems proved to be the most important single feature of the translation process.

The second category comprises those features of the translation process for which the information contained in the thinking-aloud protocols is abundant but not quantifiable. As an example I will treat a complex of features that I have named "potential equivalent retrieval strategies". Normally, the subjects search for several potential equivalents when they are faced with a translation problem, compare these and choose the one they deem most suitable for the target language text. To make transparent

TABLE 1 *Distribution of problems according to the number of subjects that had them in common*

	L2→L1		L1→L2	
4 subjects	16	19.0%	28	20.9%
3 subjects	14	16.7%	19	14.2%
2 subjects	12	14.3%	22	16.4%
1 subject	42	50.0%	65	48.5%

the network structure of this search for equivalents, I have developed a special instrument I will refer to as "the equivalent retrieval diagram". Figure 2 shows the structure of the search for equivalents undertaken by the subject Manfred in the case of the source-language text item "Miese machen". The horizontal axis represents the interlingual and the vertical axis the intralingual dimension of the equivalent retrieval network. The diagram shows 12 steps in all, taken by the subject to find an adequate equivalent for the text item in question. The most important equivalent retrieval strategy is the one called "rephrasing", i.e. the exchange of a source-language text item for a synonym, near-synonym or an expression at least semantically similar. Thus the subject in this case tries to find a suitable translation by replacing the item "Miese machen" in turn by "ein Defizit machen" ("to make a deficit") (step 2), "Schulden machen" ("to incur debts") (step 5), "kein Geld haben" ("to be without money") (step 6) and "rote Zahlen" ("to be in the red") (step 9). In addition the subject makes use of dictionaries: three times he uses a bilingual and once a monolingual dictionary (see the encircled Ds in the diagram). All together four different potential equivalents were found in this case (see the squares marked PE for "potential equivalent" in the diagram). After a detailed analysis of these four potential equivalents, involving yet another set of strategies, the subject finally decides upon the third equivalent as the best suited and chooses this one as the translation of the text item.

An equivalent retrieval diagram of this kind was produced for each of the 454 translation problems, which allowed systematic comparisons to be made of the ways in which the subjects tried to find equivalents, as can be seen from the equivalent retrieval diagrams of the three other subjects for the same problem (Figures 3 to 5). This undertaking was made possible by the abundance of information contained in the thinking-aloud protocols. An investigation entirely based on the product of the translation process, i.e. the final translation, would be singularly ill-equipped to describe what happened between the first and the last step in the diagram.

The third and fourth categories comprise those features of the translation process for which the information in the thinking-aloud protocols is incomplete or scarce. One example of a feature for which the information is incomplete is the choice between different translation equivalents suggested by a bilingual dictionary for the translation of German source-language text items into the foreign language. To check which of the equivalents is the most suitable translation, the subjects use a strategy that can be referred to as "back-translation". That is to say, they translate the L2-item in the bilingual dictionary "back" into German and check if

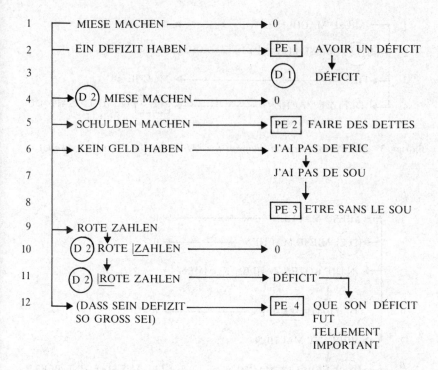

FIGURE 2   *Equivalent retrieval diagram for "Miese machen" (subject: Manfred)*

the German equivalent fits into the context of the German source-language text. They then choose the foreign language equivalent according to their German native speaker's competence because their lexicosemantic knowledge of the second language is insufficient. Two other strategies consist in avoiding items suggested by the bilingual dictionary with which they are unfamiliar or choosing the item with the greatest range of application. Both strategies might be referred to as playing-it-safe strategies. In about 50% of the cases it could be established that the choice of the equivalents from the bilingual dictionary was managed by one of these strategies. In the other cases the verbalizations in the thinking-aloud protocols were insufficient to establish what strategies the subjects made use of. There is even less information to be obtained from the thinking-aloud protocols for some of the other features of the translation process. For instance, there is a lack of indication regarding the subjects' belief in the likelihood of the correctness of their final choices. In less than 5% of the cases the subjects expressed approval or disapproval of their choices.

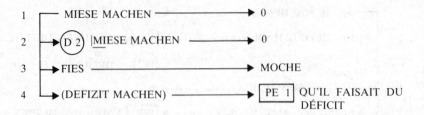

FIGURE 3 *Equivalent retrieval diagram for "Miese machen" (subject: Anne)*

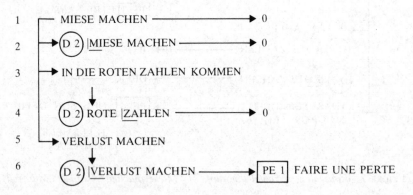

FIGURE 4 *Equivalent retrieval diagram for "Miese machen" (subject: Heidi)*

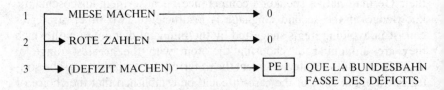

FIGURE 5 *Equivalent retrieval diagram for "Miese machen" (subject: Stefanie)*

Adding all features together, it was possible to develop a tentative psycholinguistic process model of translation in advanced learners (see Krings, 1986a: 263 and 1986b: 479–82). This model has several consequences for second-language learning and teaching which, unfortunately, I cannot discuss here.

Summary

I would like to conclude with a summary of my experiences with the thinking-aloud technique in the framework of my study:

1. The thinking-aloud technique seems especially suited for the investigation of the cognitive processes involved in translating because it constitutes the most direct means of getting access to these processes and it provides more process information than any other procedure (especially when compared to retrospective types of probing).

2. The validity of the thinking-aloud data must be considered high when minimal intervention on the part of the experimenter takes place and no pressure to verbalize is exerted in any way.

3. Thinking-aloud data cannot be analysed adequately on the basis of pre-established categories. Instead, the analytical categories need to be developed and refined gradually, taking into account the internal structure of the data.

4. Thinking-aloud data are especially suited to uncover individual differences in the translation procedure of the subjects, thereby avoiding the wash-out effect of large samples.

5. Thinking-aloud data of translations reveal processes of language comprehension as well as processes of language production (either in the mother tongue or in the foreign language, depending on the direction of the translation). They therefore permit valuable insights into:

   (a) the cognitive organization of the learner's linguistic knowledge of the mother tongue;
   (b) the cognitive organization of the learner's linguistic knowledge of the foreign language;
   (c) differences between (a) and (b);
   (d) differences in the cognitive organization of the linguistic knowledge of different foreign languages (see Færch & Kasper, 1986).

6. The information provided by the thinking-aloud data is not equally abundant for all features of the translation process. Wherever the information is scarce (e.g. because the subjects do not focus on these aspects in their verbalizations) the thinking-aloud data can be complemented by other kinds of data that provide the missing information (e.g. data from word-association tests or "judgemental tasks", see, for example, Arthur, 1980; Bialystok, 1979; Kellerman, 1978; Kohn, 1982).

The investigation of the translation process by means of introspective data has only just begun. What has to be done next is to extend the investigation to make it cover other subjects, other types of texts and other pairs of languages. Especially interesting insights might be expected once data from second language learners and bilingual professional translators are compared. I believe that if this research programme is put into practice successfully, it will give a substantial boost to both translatology and to second language acquisition research.

References

ARTHUR, B. 1980, Gauging the boundaries of second language competence: a study of learner judgements. *Language Learning* 30, 177–94.

BAUSCH, K. R., KLEGRAF, J. & WILSS, W. 1970/1972, *The Science of Translation: An Analytical Bibliography*. Vol I and Vol II. Tübingen: Narr.

BAUSCH, K. R. & WELLER, F. R. (eds) 1981, *Übersetzen und Fremdsprachenunterricht*. Frankfurt: Diesterweg.

BIALYSTOK, E. 1979, Explicit and implicit judgements of L2 grammaticality. *Language Learning* 29, 81–103.

CATFORD, J. C. 1981, Translation and language teaching. In BAUSCH & WELLER, 122–26.

CAVALCANTI, M. 1982, Using the unorthodox, unreasonable verbal protocol technique: qualitative data in foreign language reading research. In S. DINGWALL, S. MANN & F. KATAMBA (eds), *Methods and Problems in Doing Applied Linguistic Research*. Lancaster: Department of Linguistics and Modern English Language, University of Lancaster, 72–85.

DECHERT, H. W., MÖHLE, D. & RAUPACH, M. (eds) 1984, *Second Language Productions*. Tübingen: Narr.

DECHERT, H. W. & RAUPACH, W. (eds) 1980, *Towards a Cross-Linguistic Assessment of Speech Production*. Frankfurt: Lang.

DECHERT, H. W. & SANDROCK, U. in press, Thinking-aloud protocols: the decomposition of language processing. In *Proceedings of the Third Coleslaw Workshop*, University of Essex.

ERICSSON, K. A. & SIMON, H. A. 1980, Verbal reports as data. *Psychological Review* 87, 215–51.

— 1984, *Protocol Analysis. Verbal Reports as Data.* BRADFORD: MIT Press.
FÆRCH, C., HAASTRUP, K. & PHILLIPSON, R. 1984, *Learner Language and Language Learning.* Clevedon: Multilingual Matters.
FÆRCH, C. & KASPER, G. 1980, Processes and strategies in foreign language learning and communication. *Interlanguage Studies Bulletin* 5, 47–118.
— (eds) 1983, *Strategies in Interlanguage Communication.* London: Longman.
— 1986, One learner—two languages. Investigating types of interlanguage knowledge. In HOUSE & BLUM-KULKA.
GERVER, D. & SINAIKO, W. (eds) 1978, *Language Interpretation and Communication.* New York: Plenum.
HARRIS, B. 1977, The importance of natural translation. *Working Papers on Bilingualism* 12, 96–114.
— 1978, The difference between natural and professional translation. *Canadian Modern Language Review* 34, 417–27.
HARRIS, B. & SHERWOOD, B. 1978, Translating as an innate skill. In GERVER & SINAIKO, 155–70.
HOUSE, J. & BLUM-KULKA, S. (eds) 1986, *Interlingual and Intercultural Communication. Discourse and Cognition in Translation.* Tübingen: Narr.
KELLERMAN, E. 1978, Giving learners a break: native language intuitions as a source of predictions about transferability. *Working Papers on Bilingualism* 15, 59–92.
KOHN, K. 1982, Beyond output: the analysis of interlanguage development. *Studies in Second Language Acquisition* 4, 137–52.
KRINGS, H. P. 1986a, Translation problems and translation strategies of advanced German learners of French (L2). In HOUSE & BLUM-KULKA, 257–69.
— 1986b, *Was in den Köpfen von Übersetzern vorgeht. Eine empirische Untersuchung zur Struktur des Übersetzungsprozesses an fortgeschrittenen Französischlernern.* Tübingen: Narr.
LEHMANN, D. 1982, *Arbeitsbibliographie Übersetzen: Interdisziplinäre Aspekte der Sprach- und Übersetzungswissenschaft sowie der Übersetzungspraxis.* Trier: LAUT-Paper No. 83, Series B.
LÖRSCHER, W. 1986, Linguistic aspects of translation processes: towards an analysis of translation performance. In HOUSE & BLUM-KULKA.
NEWMARK, P. 1981, *Approaches to Translation.* Oxford 1981.
NIDA, E. A. & TABER, CH. R. 1969. *The Theory and Practice of Translation.* Leiden: Brill.
NISBETT, R. E. & WILSON, T. D. 1977, Telling more than you can know: verbal reports on mental processes. *Psychological Review* 84, 231–59.
NORMAN, D. A. & RUMELHART, D. E. 1975, *Explorations in Cognition.* San Francisco: Freeman.
SELIGER, H. W. 1983, The language learner as linguist: of metaphors and realities. *Applied Linguistics* 4, 179–91.
TINSLEY, R. L. 1974, An alternate major in German. *Die Unterrichtspraxis—For the Teaching of German* 7, 10–17.
TOURY, G. 1984a, Natural translation and the making of a native translator. Paper read at the 7th World Congress of Applied Linguistics, Brussels, 1984.
— 1984b, The notion of "native translator" and translation teaching. In WILSS & THOME, 186–95.

VAN HOOF, H. 1973, *Internationale Bibliographie der Übersetzung*. Pullach: Verlag Dokumentation.

WILKINS, D. A. 1974, *Second-Language Learning and Teaching*. London: Arnold.

WILSS, W. & THOME, G. (eds) 1984, *Translation Theory and its Implementation in the Teaching of Translating and Interpreting*. Tübingen: Narr.

9   The Collective Learner Tested: Retrospective Evidence for a Model of Lexical Search

RÜDIGER ZIMMERMANN AND KLAUS P. SCHNEIDER

"Introspection is a fickle mistress"
(Miller, Galanter & Pribram)

1.   Background

This is a report on our first attempt to make use of introspective methods for the analysis of advanced learners' approximations[1] in the framework of our ALE project.[2] It bears witness to our initial methodological innocence as beginners in this field. We started out with a traditional error analysis of L1 to L2 translations, then took into consideration unedited slips showing planning traces (blends, double forms), supplemented this by looking at drafts and deleted forms, and ended up with what might be called a "delayed retrospective" analysis (cf. Færch & Kasper, 1987).

2.   Methodological Considerations

2.1.   Translations as data

Despite the well-known fact that translating is in many ways an artificial form of L2 communication, at least as compared to everyday conversation, it seems to be the safest source of information about processes of lexical search, more so than reproductive exercises: the original intended meaning is mostly given for the analyst (except for misinterpretations of the source text); therefore (some aspects of) learners' strategies can be pinned down with higher certainty.

We hypothesize that lexical search in oral communication shares major aspects of the better-monitored search in translation, particularly so where the subject-matter of L2 conversation is non-trivial and lexical deficits become more or less conscious.

2.2. Introspection and retrospection

We share the view on the advantage of immediately consecutive retrospection as outlined in Færch & Kasper (1987), particularly so with respect to the accessibility of short-term memory: whereas, in introspective and immediate retrospective tests we can expect to learn (part of) what L2 users really did while planning their utterances, delayed tests will give information about what learners think they did, the more so the more delayed they are (cf. Figure 1).[3] Immediate retrospection results in an interruption and fragmentation of the process of translating connected texts: the wider context is lost for processes of lexical search and appropriateness checks. Therefore, if we want to observe the process of translating longer texts as more natural units, delayed retrospective interviews following the translation of a complete text (passage) seem justifiable if they are not over-interpreted:

- they can be a basis of hypothesis formation for in-depth introspection and interviews;
- if they are not reliable in telling us what learners actually did in trying to solve particular lexical problems, they will, at least, give

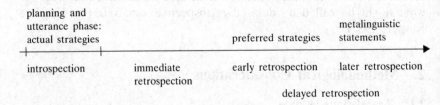

FIGURE 1 *Types of information obtained through the use of different introspective and retrospective techniques*

us indications on the learners' preferred strategies, i.e. strategies which learners think they used or might have used.

From a technical point of view, it is not a minor point that delayed retrospective commenting is easiest to administer.

2.3. Combined analysis

Our current approach is a combined one, in unison with some of the related present research (cf. for example, Poulisse, Bongaerts & Kellerman, this volume, Chapter 11; Haastrup, this volume, Chapter 10). We are considering four variants:

a. thinking-aloud protocol of individual translation of connected texts, audio-taped, followed by retrospective comments on problems of lexical choice; no interview;
b. dialogical translation of connected texts, audio-taped, subsequent (delayed) interview;
c. thinking-aloud protocol of individual translation of (lexical problems in) short passages, audio-taped; immediate interview;
d. dialogical translation of (lexical problems in) short passages; immediate interview.

In agreement with Juliane House (personal communication) we think that lexical search in dialogical translation is a more natural situation than thinking aloud during individual translation (cf. also, Haastrup, 1985, and in this volume, Chapter 10, for the "dialogical method". This raises the question of how much of their inner planning dialogical translators will communicate to each other (and the tape).

We expect the following kinds of evidence to be derivable from the different tasks:

– actually employed strategies: thinking aloud (individual) and dialogical phases (less individual), immediate interviews;
– preferred strategies: delayed comments and delayed interviews;
– declarative knowledge: as above.[4]

2.4. Training of subjects

We are insecure as to how training is possible without influencing subjects by researchers' hypotheses: even the choice of thinking-aloud models and examples seems to be problematic from this point of view.

At present we are considering tasks conducted by trained and untrained groups in parallel. Otherwise, training will be restricted to familiarization with equipment and general cautioning instructions for interviewers. Pairs of interviewers/interviewees will be self-selected to minimize inhibitions (but will have the same overall level of L2 competence). They will change roles for another round with a new text (cf. section 6).

3.   The Hypothesis Tested: A Partial Model of Lexical Search

Comparatively little is known about details of lexical search in L1 speech production and in L1 to L2 translations, beyond the generally accepted dichotomy between search in the semantic and the phonological lexicon (cf. Butterworth, 1980, 1983; Dechert, Möhle & Raupach, 1984, Reiss & Vermeer, 1984). But since there are recurrent identities and similarities in a learner group other than content- and form-orientation of errors and approximations (cf. Zimmerman, 1987b), we have proposed a partial model of lexical search which contains a sequential hypothesis (cf. Figure 2).

Our term "lexical search" is intended to cover both attempts at lexical retrieval of an L2 form previously known, as well as all approximative ("achievement") strategies, i.e. attempts to replace an adequate L2 form which is unfamiliar or inaccessible.

We suppose that if initial L1 synonym search fails, in at least one strategy of lexical search, learners decompose L1 lexical items into L1 paraphrases and translate them into the L2, or that they form L2 paraphrases right away. Whereas, for some learners, these paraphrases are the final approximations, others go on to condense such paraphrases into shorter lexical phrases and complex words, omitting irrelevant semantic aspects. This condensation process can go on and result in a simplex word, reducing the information further, often too far (cf. Zimmerman, 1987a).

In addition, it is assumed that what are approximative forms for some learners in a fairly homogeneous group, can be seen as transitory stages of lexical search in others. It is also in accordance with the model that correct forms can be "covert approximations" reached via longer search processes, i.e. re-creations of types (4) and (5).

By all this we do not wish to imply that these lexical derivational processes should be seen as strictly sequential: steps can be omitted, re-

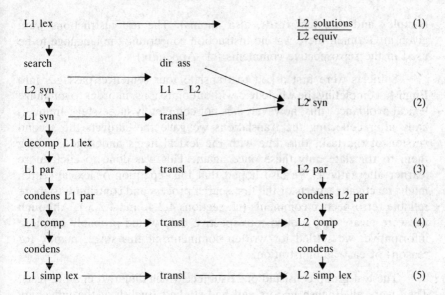

FIGURE 2 *A partial model of lexical search*[5]

runs are possible, but the process seems to occur in its entirety, too (cf. Zimmerman, 1987a, part 2).

The "collective learner" hypothesis can be seen to supply additional comparative data, so that we obtain four kinds of supplementary and introspective data in addition to the final output:

1. Draft and crossed-out versions: traces of individual planning;
2. Parallel versions in group output: potential traces of planning in other learners of the group;
3. Learners' retrospective comments;
4. Thinking aloud and dialogical protocols.
(5. In addition, interview data).

Type 2 data can be useful in interpreting other unclear data, and in preparing interviews.[6]

4. A First Retrospective "Test"[7]

4.1. Design and population

The translation task centred on lexical items of different complexity whose difficulty had been established in examinations and mock-exams (simplex and complex words, also idioms). The test instructions were given in German; there was no instruction concerning the language to be used in the retrospective comments (cf. Appendix).

Subjects were first asked to translate four sentences/passages into English, completing the whole text without omissions, in order to minimize lexical avoidance (this, however, was not completely successful). Immediately after collecting the translations we gave the subjects the second version of the task, this time with the lexical items underlined, asking them to translate only these once again. This was done to elicit more learner alternatives. We also hoped that the repetition of lexical search might reactivate aspects of the first search process and contribute to more reliable retrospective comments (cf. sections 4.2.4. and 4.2.5.). Although we were aware that spoken retrospective data would probably be more informative, we settled for written comments at this stage, mainly for reasons of easy administration.

The test group consisted of 22 subjects (including two in a pre-test). They were all English majors and had studied English at the university and abroad for between three and five years. (Nevertheless, there were wide differences in competence in the group). All knew Latin (at least three years in High School); a strong minority knew and/or studied French; a few had some command of other languages. There were 15 female and 7 male participants. The time for translation was such that it created a mild time pressure for the average subject (some were very hurried in the end; others, however, handed in early).

4.2. Methodological problems

The following is an attempt to mention recurrent observations, at least in summary.

4.2.1. Degree of co-operation

Since the subjects were participants in a seminar, who had been asked to take part (which they all did), problems in willingness to co-operate were expected. They were visible in the rate of completion and the number of items commented upon.[8] Seventeen subjects completed their comments, five did not (one of whom had arrived late for the task and did not finish). Six subjects commented on all items, four on more than 15, seven on 12 and more, five on 11 and less.

Comments on a few items only may indicate a reluctance to co-operate, but also a lack of familiarity with the task. The most evident lack of co-operation was found in the subject who did not finish the translation test, but handed it in earlier. Her comments were also sparse.

There were also some cases of subject inhibition against co-operation. Inhibition is shown most clearly in the fact that two subjects copied from each other during the test, and that some alternatives in the translation itself were crossed out so thoroughly as to make them illegible.

4.2.2. Value of the comments

The quality of the comments varies considerably: whereas three subjects gave almost no relevant comments at all ("vermutlich richtig" — "probably correct" and the like in half of the items; "nicht übersetzt" — "not translated" (indeed!) etc.), the majority gave a lot of evidence about their (potential) interior processes of search, and some were so detailed that their preferred strategies became quite obvious (cf. 4.4.3.).

unentbehrlich—indispensable[9]
(C 19)   unentbehrlich: unbekannt, also sich gefragt Was ist "unent-behrlich"? Antw.: etwas, dass man immer braucht. Also: strongly needed
         (unentbehrlich: unknown, therefore I asked myself What does "unentbehrlich" mean? Answer: something you always need. Therefore: strongly needed)
(C 18)   a muscle which you need most urgently — without it you can't cope in life
         --> ich habe die Übersetzung gehört, sogar gelernt, sie liegt mir auf der Zunge, aber ich komme nicht darauf --> vielleicht indeligible — bin mir zu unsicher und umschreibe lieber in 2 Varianten um möglichst genau an den eigentlichen Sinn heran-zukommen
         (I've heard of the translation, I've learned it, it's on the tip of my tongue, but I cannot think of it --> perhaps indeligible — I'm too uncertain and will paraphrase in 2 interpretations in order to approach the actual meaning as precisely as possible)
(T 18)   one of the most necessary muscles you can't cope without it

4.2.3. Lack of memory

Owing to the fairly long time-span between test and comments (about half-an-hour) some subjects expressed insecurity about the lexical

items chosen or they "remembered" other or similar items (particularly
so in details of paraphrases, cf. above, C/T 18). This became more or less
obvious in at least seven subjects. On the other hand, some of the same
subjects remembered other details very clearly, and some others had an
excellent overall memory of items chosen (which may also make their
comments more reliable).

4.2.4. Reconstructive attitude

Some comments suggest that subjects tried to find some explanation
for a form chosen when not remembering the process of search (exactly).
Subject 16 repeatedly seems to grope her way back from the item chosen
to the L1 form.

strahlend — dashing and *Darstellung — presentation*
(C 16) "gliming" erinnert mich an glimmern, scheinen, funkeln, strahlen
        ("gliming" reminds me of glimmern, scheinen, funkeln, strahlen)
        Komposition — Zusammenstellung — Darstellung
(T 16) gliming
        composement

Considering *strahlend* --> *gliming* and *Darstellung* --> *composement* the
search process might have occurred exactly the other way round (cf. also
4.4.2.).

4.2.5. Difficulties with L1 items

The comments also showed that the test contained some unfamiliar
German words. They were either misunderstood or learners expressed
lack of L1 knowledge. This was most frequent in *extrapoliert, Sanitätsrat*
and *Kurfürst*.

extrapoliert — extrapolated
(C 8)   Ist für mich ein Fremdwort, habe aus dem Sinnzusammenhang
        geschlossen, was der Sinn sein könnte und so ein annäherndes
        engl. Wort eingesetzt. "put forward", "presented"
        (It's a foreign word, from the context I decided what the meaning
        could be and used the approximate English word).
(T 8)   presented

4.3. Results related to the model of lexical search
4.3.1. Search via L1 synonyms

This was clearly one of the most popular (first) approaches to solve
lexical problems: 11 subjects reported on it, most of them repeatedly.

That this must be quite reliable information is borne out by many crossed-out alternatives in the text of the first translation (cf. (T 5), section 4.3.7. and (T 6) section 4.4.1. below). A few typical comments:

Schattierungen — colours
(C 17) Schattierungen --> Variationen, Tendenzen --> tendences, vaities [sic], --> Meinungen --> views
(T 17) views

strahlend — dashing
(C 19) strahlend: 1. Bedeutung: blendend — unbekannt 2. (unwahrscheinlichere) Bedeutung: lachend, fröhlich direkte Übersetzung ins Engl.: beaming
        (strahlend: 1st meaning: blendend — unknown 2nd (less probable) meaning: laughing, happy direct translation into English: beaming)

There are more than 20 comments of this kind out of the total number of about 250 (meaningful) comments.

4.3.2. Direct "association" with L2 synonym

Subjects report less frequently that an L2 form of similar meaning occurred to them spontaneously (five subjects).

schmächtig — frail
(C 2)   *Schmächtig* — "frail" — intuitiv eingesetzt (inserted intuitively)

strahlend — dashing
(C 3)   bright — spontaner Einfall; nach einigem Nachdenken viel [sic] mir auch kein besseres Wort ein (bright — spontaneous idea; after some thought no better word came to me)

4.3.3. Lexical "decomposition"[10]

There are several comments trying to express what happened before the production of a paraphrase or other form.

Hansdampf in allen Gassen — Jack of all trades
(C 18) ... *was bedeutet dieser Spruch* — also folgt die *Übersetzung* (*what does this saying mean* — so the *translation* follows)
(T 18) the man who takes part in everything

Cf. also (C 19) in 4.2.2., an even clearer instance.

4.3.4. *L1 paraphrase translated*

This is another frequent strategy: it was reported by 10 subjects, in several cases repeatedly, and it materialized in many solutions.

unentbehrlich — indispensable
(C 12) unentbehrlich: absolutely necessary
da ich das englische Wort dafür nicht wusste habe ich versucht darzustellen, was "unentbehrlich" eigentlich bedeutet
(because I didn't know the English word for it, I tried to express what "unentbehrlich" actually means)

Sanitätsrat — doctor
(C 13) *male nurse*
Ich dachte an Sanitäter so etwas ähnliches wie männliches [sic] Krankenschwester
(I thought of sanitarian, something similar to a male nurse)

Cf. also (C 18) in 4.3.3.

4.3.5. *Immediate L2 paraphrasing*

Several comments give paraphrases in the L2 without mentioning recourse to the L1. It is impossible to establish to what extent they were formed in the L2 right away or translated from unmentioned L1 paraphrases. Since all comments used German as "metalanguage", it can be assumed that there are many hidden cases of 4.3.4.

Hansdampf in allen Gassen — Jack of all trades
(C 6) "Hansdampf in allen Gassen" — idiom unbekannt;
Eigenschaften Wilsons aus der Gesamtbedeutung d. 2 Sätze = => decision, man of action
(idiom unknown; characteristics of Wilson from the global meaning of the two sentences)
(T 6) decisive man of action

Volkswirtschaftler — economist
(T 15) knowing a lot about economy
(C 15) lecturer of economy [preferred in second attempt]

4.3.6. *Condensation*

Several comments and/or a comparison of test solutions and second attempts show the way from paraphrasing to complex and simplex words.

unentbehrlich — indispensable
(C 4)   *essential*
          --> weder Vokabel für "entbehrlich" noch "unentbehrlich"
          gewusst, deshalb statt "unentbehrlich" "grundlegend wichtig"
          genommen ... [via G. "essentiell?"]
          (neither the vocabulary word for "entbehrlich" nor "unent-
          behrlich" was known. Therefore, instead of "unentbehrlich" used
          "fundamentally important")
(C 14) necessary
          erwogen: a muscle one cannot do without
          (considered)
(T 14) unre   muscle
Cf. also T/C (15) above (knowing a lot ==> lecturer).

4.3.7.   Word-formation avoidance

     A few subjects also discarded complex words (some of them "cor-
rect") for paraphrases or other forms.

Gedächtnis — memory
(C 4)   kein Wort für "Gedächtnis" gewußt, deshalb versucht das Ganze
          zu umschreiben ⤙ außer "memory", was ich unpassend fand in
          diesem Zusammenhang
          (didn't know the word for "Gedächtnis", therefore tried to para-
          phrase the whole thing; except "memory" which I found unsuit-
          able in this context)
(T 4)   ability to remember

Zauberer — magician/Volkswirtschaftler —' economist/Pragmatiker —
pragmatist
(T 5)   the small man with magic power, the expert in economy and
          pragmatismn [sic]
(C 5)   Ich wusste nicht, ob sich diese Begriffe direkt als Substantive
          übersetzen lassen, habe versucht zu umschreiben expert in ...
          (I didn't know whether these terms can be translated as nouns,
          tried to paraphrase them)

4.3.8.   Conscious formal transfer

     As could be expected between closely related languages there was
a lot of conscious formal transfer (cf. Ringbom, 1978, 1985), particularly
in complex words of Greco-Latin origin.

Pragmatiker — pragmatist
(C 21) Pragmatiker — pragmatician
        versuchte das Wort einfach zu "verenglischen"
        (simply tried to anglicize the word)
(C 7)   *Pragmatiker*: aus dem Dtsch. übernommen
        (taken from German) = => pragmatic

extrapoliert — extrapolated
(C 22) extrapolished Bedeutung des Fremdwortes nicht bekannt deshalb
        Probleme Wort für Wort übertragen (meaning of the foreign word
        not known as a result translated the problems word for word)

But the same learner forms are obviously also reached by intralingual
transfer:

(T 22) pragmatician
(C 22) abgeleitet von pragmatics ähnlich wie politics/politician
        (derived from pragmatics — similar to politics/politician)

Abtritt — resignation
(C 2)   *Abtritt*: bekannt ist mir nur das Verb "resign", ...
        Deshalb habe ich "resignation" gebraucht, ohne mir sicher zu sein
        ...
        (only the word "resign" is familiar to me.
        Therefore I used "resignation", without being certain)

4.3.9. Complex and simplex words

    There is almost no clear evidence in the comments for the last
putative stage in the model: a simplex word chosen after considering a
complex one.

Stück — play
(C 7)   *Stück*: zuerst dachte ich an "Theatre piece", aber dann beliess ich
        es mit "piece" weil das auch im Engl. verwendet wird
        (first I thought of 'Theatre piece', but then I left it with 'piece'
        because that is also used in English)

Gutshof-Politiker — grousemoor politican
(C 7)   Gutshof-Politiker
        "Gutshof" ... "Hof" = court, ...
        "court-politician"

4.3.10   Covert errors

The comments of about two-thirds of the subjects show the importance of covert lexical errors in this group. The words "recreated" or "guessed" include all kinds of forms except idioms: *doctor, dashing, extrapolated, weak, bent, colours, resignation, magician, economist, pragmatist*, some of them multiple.

strahlend — dashing
(C 1)   dashing — war das, was mir als erstes in den Sinn kam. Da ich nicht *wusste*, wie "strahlend" auf englisch genau heisst, hab' ich's bei dem ersten Einfall belassen, obwohl ich auch nicht sicher weiss, was "dashing" genau heisst.
(dashing — was what came to my mind first. Because I did not *know* exactly what "strahlend" means in English I kept the first solution although I didn't exactly know what "dashing" means)

Zauberer — magician
(C 7)   Zauberer: verwandtes Wort "Magie", daher magician
(related word "Magie", therefore magician)

Volkswirtschaftler — economist
(C 8)   "economic" geraten
(guessed)
(T 8)   economist

extrapoliert — extrapolated
(T 13)   extrapolated
(C 13)   wenn ich Glück habe stimmt's
(if I'm lucky, it's correct)

The range and frequency of such covert approximations suggest that there may be many more hidden instances.

To sum this part up, the evidence for our partial model of lexical search is not very impressive with regard to individual learners as far as complete processes are concerned, whereas certain parts of it, particularly L2 complex words as results of paraphrasing and/or formal transfer from L1 forms as well as L2 synonym search via L1 synonyms, find some validation.

4.4.   Additional results

There was more or less clear evidence of other factors influencing lexical search, which are not directly related to the model. For reasons of space we do not quote comments stating (assumed) knowledge or ignorance (very frequent), admitting guesses and the like, invoking "Sprachgefühl"/idiomaticity, and references to a third language as well as "etymological" analysis of L1 forms. But it is worth pointing out the relative importance of three other aspects.

4.4.1.   Content- and form-orientation

Although the majority of the learners in our group favour content-oriented L2 solutions over form-oriented ones, there is a strong minority who rather take recourse to form-driven strategies such as indicated in 4.3.8. As a rule, however, the comments show that content-orientation had form-oriented alternatives, whereas form-oriented solutions were normally not arrived at without considering content-oriented possibilities. We do not quote complete comments, but rather list T solutions and C alternatives for comparison (cf. Zimmerman, 1987b).

"Schattierungen"	(C1) shades	(T1) (political streams)
"Sanitätsrat"	(C5) sanitary committee	(T5) surgeon committee
"extrapoliert"	(C5) extracted	(T5) pointed out
"Kurfürst"		(T6) ~~eure~~-delegated duke
"Sanitätsrat"	(C13) sanitary council	(T13) male nurse

On the other hand:

"schief"	(C6) bent	(T6) crooked [via "krumm"]
"strahlend"	(C14) beaming	(T14) glamorous [via "glänzend"]
"Schattierungen"	(C15) shades in diesem Kontext auch: opinions, views, parties (also in this context...)	(T15) parties

4.4.2.   Metalinguistic statements

Some comments also contain learners' statements about what they regard as rules of English or good translation procedures.

Sanitätsrat — doctor
(C 2)   sanitary director ...
      Entsprechend der engl. Konvention bei zusammengesetzten Begriffen ist die grammatische Form des Adjektivs gewählt.

(according to English conventions when dealing with compounds
the grammatical form of the adjective is chosen)

Hansdampf in allen Gassen — Jack of all trades
(C 3)   Da wörtliche Übertragung ins Englische unmöglich ist ...
        (Because word-for-word translation into English is impossible)
(T 3)   energetical statesman

Erhellung — elucidation (clarification)
(C 9)   da (Verb-) Substantivierungen im Englischen nicht üblich, ...
        (because (deverbal) nominalizations not usual in E.)
(T 9)   to make the present more clearer [sic]

Cf. also 4.3.2.

4.4.3.   Preferred strategies

As we had expected, owing to the fairly long time-span, many
alternatives and comments are indicative of preferred rather than of
actually used strategies. This is quite often obvious implicitly, but some
learners are very explicit about it. Instead of quoting various statements
by different learners, we conclude with one learner's comments on one
of her principles of reaching lexical approximations.

Sanitätsrat — doctor
(C 18) da ich ... nicht weiss was ein Sanitätsrat ist, muss ich diese
        Umschreibung sehr allgemein halten
        (because I don't know what a "Sanitätsrat" is, I have to keep this
        paraphrase very general)
(T 18) doctor

Kurfürst — elector
(C 18) da mir der Unterschied zwischen Fürst und Kurfürst unklar ist ...
        behalte ich den allgemeinen *Überbegriff Fürst* bei
        (because I don't know the difference between "Fürst" and "Kur-
        fürst", I'll keep the general *supernym Fürst*)
(T 18) duke

extrapoliert — extrapolated
(C 18) ... erschliesse ... den etwaigen Sinn ... und versuche einen ganz
        allgemeinen Begriff zu finden (... determine ... the approximate
        meaning ... and try to find a very general term)
(T 18) stressed and pointed out

Zauberer — magician
(C 18) Kenne das Wort nicht, also Wahl des Überbegriffs
        (Don't know the word, so choice of supernym)
(T 18) artist

   Other preferred strategies include anchoring an approximation both in the L1 and L2.

5. Problems for In-depth Studies

   Apart from the necessity for methodological refinement, some empirical questions stand out from the preceding preliminary research. The possible interdependence between decomposition and paraphrase formation deserves further study. Do (some) learners first decompose the meaning of the L1 item into an unordered set of words/meaning components? Which information appears in the L1 paraphrase, which in the L2 paraphrase? Do some learners really form L2 paraphrases without recourse to their mother tongue? How do learners make the transition from a paraphrase to a (complex) word which contains other lexemes but is semantically related? Does repeated condensation from paraphrases via complex words to simplex words take place at all in individual learners? To what extent do learners apply preferred strategies (beyond their comments)? To what extent do their strategies vary in relation to the degree of difficulty experienced with a particular lexical item? Does form-orientation lose ground with rising overall competence? We hope to find some answers to questions like these in our current work.

6. Outlook

6.1. A second series of investigations

   Our second series of investigations along some of the lines outlined above (2.3. and 2.4.) was finished in January 1986. We worked with thinking-aloud protocols of connected translations (cf. 2.3.a, but without retrospective comments) and of passage-wise translations (cf. 2.3.c.) as well as dialogical translations (as in 2.3.b.) with groups of 10 and 12, respectively. In the second task, self-selected pairs of interviewers/interviewees switched roles after half the task (a connected text divided into short passages).

6.2. Preliminary methodological results

We were surprised by the extent to which thinking-aloud protocols contain information not only on actually used strategies of lexical search, but also on preferred ones and on declarative/metalinguistic knowledge, particularly so when subjects considered their search not to be successful.

As regards the training of subjects, a first global analysis is not conclusive: one or two subjects who had prior methodological and other relevant theoretical knowledge displayed a certain tendency to theorize along the lines of the "models". On the other hand, there were a few rather poor thinking-aloud protocols from untrained subjects who did not produce much except reading the L1 text, verbalizing their written-down solutions and re-reading them. It is unclear, as yet, whether this was the case owing to lack of training and/or inhibition and/or general short-comings in L2 competence.

Some advantages of the thinking-aloud protocols seem to stand out quite clearly as compared to the retrospective test reported on in the main part of this chapter; on the whole, there is much more relevant infor-mation. This includes a wider range of attempts and lines of search for individual lexical items. The strength of particular strategies also becomes visible much better through repeated attempts.

Although the retrospective comments proved quite useful in hypoth-esis formation and refinement (cf. section 5), some new evidence for lines of lexical search emerged in the thinking-aloud protocols, e.g. the importance of appeals to the episodic memory.

Without detailed analysis it is unclear whether the immediately consecutive interviews added relevant information to the thinking-aloud protocols themselves. We hope to report on these methodological issues and the material findings on lexical search in due course.

Notes to Chapter 9

1. "Approximations" is used here as a cover term for all learner forms (lexical replacement forms), i.e. in a much wider sense than in Færch & Kasper (1983).
2. Our Marburg project "Analysis of Lexical Errors" has so far concentrated on a linguistic classification of errors in terms of semantic deviation (cf. Zimmermann, 1986) and on attempts to gain insights into psychological processes in the learners, i.e. aspects of lexical search and achievement strategies (cf. Zimmermann, 1987a,b,c).
3. We are not sure whether the criticism of introspection in Seliger (1983) would be so relevant for our investigation, which is on performance and not learning. But since we

agree with the main line of argumentation in Cohen (1984 and in this volume), we can probably disregard this question.

4. "Declarative knowledge" refers to comments in which learners tell us what they think they did or even ought to have done in solving a lexical problem. If such statements come in a rule-like or terminological format, we call them "metalinguistic".

5. Abbreviations: lex = lexical item, equiv = equivalent, syn = (loose) synonym, dir ass = direct "association"/retrieval, transl = translation, decomp = decomposition, par = paraphrase (in the sense of what is generally called "circumlocution"; cf. Zimmermann, 1987c, section 2), condens = condensation, comp = complex lexical item (compound or derived form), simp lex = simplex lexical item.

6. As to evidence in relation to the collective learner hypothesis (cf. our final remark at the end of 4.3.10), this hypothesis, which is characterized in more detail in Zimmerman, 1987a, will appear the more valid the more of the overall sequential processes in a group are also found in the introspection of individual subjects.

7. For our second series of investigations cf. section 6.

8. We did not count sheer repetition of the items chosen as comments. Although it may show some willingness to co-operate, it does not provide any additional information.

9. This is the format of the examples in this paper. The L1-(source) lexeme and an adequate solution (target lexeme) are displayed in the first line, followed by the comment (C; numbers refer to the subjects). All comments are quoted unchanged, including underlining, arrows, crossed-out forms etc. The English translation of the comments is given in parentheses, authors' remarks in square brackets. Learners' solutions from the original translation test (T) are only presented when different from the solution in the comment.

10. This term is not used in any strict generative semantic sense (as resulting in "atomic" features or the like), but meant to characterize the subjects' attempts to become aware of the (most relevant) meaning components of a lexical item.

References

BUTTERWORTH, B. 1980/1983, *Language Production*. Vol. I and II. London: Academic Press.

COHEN, A. 1984, Studying second-language learning strategies: How do we get the information? *Applied Linguistics* 5, 101–12.

DECHERT, H. W., MÖHLE, D. & RAUPACH, M. (eds) 1984, *Second Language Productions*. Tübingen: Narr.

ERICSSON, K. A. & SIMON, H. A. 1984, *Protocol Analysis: Verbal Reports as Data*. Cambridge, Mass.: MIT Press.

FÆRCH, C. & KASPER, G. (eds) 1983, *Strategies in Interlanguage Communication*. London: Longman.

— 1987, Introspektive Methoden in der Lernersprachenanalyse. In S. BÖRSCH (ed.), *Die Rolle der Psychologie in der Sprachlehrforschung*. Tübingen: Narr.

HAASTRUP, K. 1985, Lexical inferencing — a study of procedures in reception. *Scandinavian Working Papers on Bilingualism* 5, 63–86.

HUBER, G. & MANDL, L. (eds) 1982, *Verbale Daten*. Weinheim and Basel: Beltz.

LÖRSCHER, W. 1986, On analysing translation performance. In J. HOUSE & S. BLUM-KULKA (eds), *Interlingual and Intercultural Communication*. Tübingen: Narr. 277–92.

REISS, K. & VERMEER, H. 1984, *Grundlegung einer allgemeinen Translationstheorie*. Tübingen: Niemeyer.

RINGBOM, H. 1978, The influence of the mother tongue on the translation of lexical items. *Interlanguage Studies Bulletin Utrecht* 3:1, 80–101.
— 1985, Transfer in relation to some other variables in L2 learning. In H. RINGBOM (ed.), *Foreign Language Learning and Bilingualism*. Åbo: Åbo Akademi, 9–21.
SELIGER, H. W. 1983, The language learner as a linguist: Of metaphors and realities. *Applied Linguistics* 4, 179–91.
ZIMMERMANN, R. 1986, Classification and distribution of lexical errors in the written work of German learners of English. *Papers and Studies in Contrastive Linguistics*, 21, 31–41.
— 1987a, A model of lexical search in L1 — L2 translation: the collective learner, covert and potential errors. In H. W. DECHERT (ed.), *Interlingual Processes*. Tübingen: Narr.
— 1987b, Form-oriented and content-oriented lexical errors in L2 learners. *IRAL* 25, 55–67.
— 1987c, Paraphrase errors and word-formation errors in advanced German Learners of English. In D. NEHLS & J. KLEGRAF (eds), *Contributions to English Linguistics Presented to Gerhard Nickel on the occasion of his 60th Birthday*. Heidelberg: Groos.
— 1987d, Retrospective and introspective methods in the study of L2 lexical strategies. In R. BÖHN & H. WODE (eds), *Anglistentag 1986: Vorträge*. Giessen: Hoffmann.

Appendix: Instruction sheets

subject number
number of semesters
sex

1. Translation task:
   Translate the following sentences/passages into English. Please complete the whole text, even where you may have difficulties. Do not copy from other students as that would defeat the purpose of the test. Your translation will be evaluated on an anonymous basis.

   You will have 25 to 30 minutes.

   ———————

2. Retrospective test:
   Please translate the italicized forms from the following sentences/passages once more. Please write down as much as possible about the translation process by which you arrived at your English version (especially with regard to your first version, but also regarding your second version). Mention the alternative solutions which you considered for the italicized words but finally did not choose.

   Please do not hesitate to indicate frankly cases in which you "took a guess at it".

   Your remarks can be completely informal short notes.

Please comment in the manner given above on any difficulties you had in translating words other than those italicized.

1. Der *Sanitätsrat* sagte, man werde die Wunden nähen müssen, denn die Zunge sei ein *unentbehrlicher* Muskel.

2. Der "Prinz von Homburg" war kein *strahlend* junger Held, sondern ein 42-jähriger Familienvater, der seit Jahren mit der Nichte des *Kurfürsten* verheiratet war.

3. Das *Stück* ist eine kritische *Darstellung* der Zeit durch eine "andere" zukünftige Welt: Politische Tendenzen der Zeit werden *extrapoliert*, um der *Erhellung* der Gegenwart zu dienen.

4. Mein *Gedächtnis* für Politik ist ziemlich schwach, und doch erinnere ich mich genau jener Zeit, da Harold Wilson auf seinen *schmächtigen*, *schiefen* Schultern die Nachkriegshoffnungen vieler Engländer meiner Generation und aller politischen *Schattierungen* trug. Mit dem *Abtritt* von Macmillan und Lord Home, so beschlossen wir, müsse die Ära der *Gutshof-Politiker* enden: Bühne frei für Harold Wilson, den kleinen *Zauberer*, für den *Pragmatiker* und *Volkswirtschaftler*, den Technokraten und *Hansdampf in aller Gassen*.

10 Using Thinking Aloud and Retrospection to Uncover Learners' Lexical Inferencing Procedures

KIRSTEN HAASTRUP

Introduction

This chapter discusses the use of introspective methods in connection with a study of inferencing procedures. These are considered to be the central procedures in language reception, covering language use as well as language learning. Inferencing involves making informed guesses as to the meaning of (part of) an utterance in the light of all available linguistic cues in combination with the hearer's general knowledge of the world, her awareness of the situation and her relevant linguistic knowledge (Carton, 1971; Færch, 1981; Færch, Haastrup & Phillipson, 1984). In the study, focus is on lexical inferencing, i.e. guessing the meaning of unknown words.

The text below gives a first impression of how lexical inferencing is elicited by means of one of the introspective methods employed, viz. pair thinking aloud. A pair of Danish learners of English (A and B) are confronted with an English text in which the word "affluence" appears in one sentence. They do not know this word, and it is their task to make guesses about its meaning, agreeing upon a Danish word as the most likely translation equivalent. Their discussion (in Danish) is recorded and transcribed as illustrated by Text 1 (in which the Danish original text has been translated into English).

TEXT 1

Test Word in Context: In the rich world many diseases are caused by *affluence*.
Think-aloud Protocol:

A   : affluence — do you think it is the opposite of influence? (A+B laugh) —
      non-influence
B   : what does fluence mean?
A   : I don't know — I know what influence means — fluence (A laughs)
B   : isn't the idea that in the rich world you don't catch diseases — they are not
      infectious — it's more mental problems, perhaps — mental influence more
      than in the poor world when it's simply infection — don't you think?
A   : well, yes
B   : shall we say external influence — that fits with influence too
A   : yes that's okay

The two main *research questions* addressed in this study concern the
knowledge sources that learners at different L2 proficiency levels make
use of, and the way they combine such knowledge. It is assumed that
inferencing procedures are of interest, first because they throw light on
learners' hypothesis formation and, secondly, because a study of such
procedures facilitates the proposal of a valid model of L2 reception.

As far as *research design* is concerned, the *informant population* and
the *inferencing task* will be described only in brief so as to allow for a
more thorough discussion of the introspective methods employed.[1] The
population, selected from Danish secondary schools, comprises two groups
of learners, 31 pairs with high and 31 pairs with low proficiency in English,
the individual pairs consisting of informants with the same level of proficiency. All 62 pairs were exposed to the same text with 25 unknown test
words in a comprehensible context. The text was adapted from an authentic text, but in order to make the context of the test words fully
comprehensible, even to low-proficiency informants, the text had to under-
go a radical simplification process. The inferencing text itself, exemplified
by Text 2, is therefore a somewhat artificial product comprising difficult
words in an easy-reader context.

TEXT 2: Extract from the text with test words italicized
At the beginning of the nineteenth century some of the Zulu clans were
ruled by a king called Chaka. He was a clever military leader with *insatiable*
political ambitions. He won most of south-eastern Africa and united all the
Zulu clans into one great empire, the Zulu nation. Soon afterwards, however, the downfall of the Zulu empire started by *dissension* among the
blacks themselves, and ended in conflicts with the whites.

The introspective data are analysed along two dimensions: what knowledge sources do learners make use of when they guess? and how do they (if at all) combine the knowledge gained from these sources? In this chapter, reference will be made to the first dimension only.

When informants guess at word meaning they use cues which are of three main types:[2]

Interlingual: cues based on L1, loanwords in L1 or knowledge of foreign languages other than English

Intralingual: cues based on knowledge of English

Contextual: cues based on the text or on informants' knowledge of the world.

A *taxonomy* was established on the basis of the data from this study. The overview presented in Table 1 contains the resulting main categories only (for a more detailed account, see Haastrup, 1985).
Texts 3 and 4 give an impression of the introspective data and of informants' cue use.[3] The column on the left contains the protocol from the session where A and B think aloud about word meaning. This is followed by a retrospection (column 2) in which the same two informants, individu-

TABLE 1   *Taxonomy of knowledge sources.*

Contextual	Intralingual	Interlingual
I. The text	I. The test word	I. L1 (Danish)
1. A single word from the immediate context	1. Phonology/ orthography	1. Phonology/orthography
	2. Morphology	2. Morphology
	a. prefix	3. Lexis
2. The immediate context	b. suffix	4. Collocations
	c. stem	5. Semantics
3. A specific part of the context beyond the sentence of the test word	3. Lexis	II. L_n (Latin, German, French, etc.)
	4. Word class	
	5. Collocations	1. General reflections
	6. Semantics	a. Reflecions about the origin of the word
4. Global use of the text	II. The syntax of the sentence	b. Test word pronounced in L_n
		2. Morphology
II Knowledge of the world		3. Lexis
		4. Semantics

ally, reflect on the thinking aloud, assisted by a researcher (R). The columns headed "Hypotheses" and "Cues" contain the informants' assumed hypotheses about word meaning and the analyst's interpretation of what cue(s) the informants have used. In Text 3 the discussion focuses on linguistic form, notably phonology/orthography, and neither of the informants seems to worry about the fact that their proposal is incompatible with context. In Text 4, however, the discussion is ruled by a combination of semantic and contextual considerations.

Introspective Methods

The aim of the present study is to get as close as possible to learner procedures in word processing, i.e. a special feature of procedural knowledge in reception.[5] It was assumed that introspective methods would

TEXT 3

Test Word in Context: Many factors serve as *contributory* causes to malnutrition.

Excerpts from Protocols: *Analysis:*

Thinking aloud	Retrospection	Cues	Hypotheses
A I can't really see what this is /kʌntrɪ/ – what does it say	A thought of country even if it isn't spelt like that	intralingual, lexis	"country"
B yes, that's it (They return to the item after having discussed other items)		intralingual, orthography/ phonology	
A this one has something to do with country I think — con- no it isn't spelt that way	R Lisa suggested something to do with country and then you said concerning the country?	intralingual, lexis + semantics	"concerning the country"
B no — concerning the country	B yes R why? B it looked like it	intralingual, orthography/ phonology	

Text 4

Test Word in Context: Doctors should analyse why people become ill rather than take such a keen interest in the *curative* effect of medicine.

Excerpts from Protocols: Analysis:

Thinking aloud	Retrospection	Cues	Hypotheses
A this is easy I think — it must be something with the therapeutic effect	A very easy — one knows cure and then it fits the context	intralingual, lexis + semantics	
B yes			
A of the medicine			
B yes it has to do with *kurere*[4]	B a bit of guessing — something to do with *kurere* — if one were to use something that resembles it	contextual, the immediate context of the test word interlingual, L1, lexis + semantics	"therapeutic"

be better suited for this aim than, for instance, performance analyses because informants' verbalization of their thoughts allows the researcher more direct access to learner processes.

The assumed validity of introspective methods rests on Ericsson & Simon's model (1984), which predicts that information recently attended by the central processor is kept in short term memory and is directly accessible for producing verbal reports.

An important issue is the extent to which introspection may influence informants' procedures. According to Ericsson & Simon (1984) there is no need to worry about the potential changes in the structure and course of the task processes when both the task and the introspection are verbally encoded. Færch & Kasper (1986), on the other hand, are not so optimistic and fear that the optimism rests on a one-dimensional view of language storage and activation.[6] As this study was not designed to investigate the possible effect of verbalization on cognitive processing, this issue will only be dealt with in passing.

As mentioned in the introduction, two methods are employed, thinking aloud and retrospection. The first method is considered ideal in order to find out how informants inference of their own accord, i.e. when undirected by detailed instructions or questioning. However, since thinking aloud has certain shortcomings, such as incomplete reporting and protocols that are difficult to interpret, this procedure was supplemented by a retrospective interview, the purpose of which was to probe into some of the statements made during the thinking aloud, thereby improving the reliability of the protocol analysis.

The combined method of thinking aloud and retrospection is used for approximately half of the informant pairs (32). For the rest (30 pairs) only thinking-aloud data were elicited, due to time and financial constraints. This makes it possible to evaluate thinking aloud as a method in its own right.

The discussion of thinking aloud is followed by a description and evaluation of the combined method (see pp. 203–11).

Pair Thinking Aloud

Pair thinking aloud was preferred to individual thinking aloud on the following grounds: by using pairs, one stimulates informants to verbalize all their conscious thought processes because they need to explain and justify their hypotheses about word meaning to their fellow informant. It is hard to imagine that a setting with one informant thinking aloud for the benefit of a tape-recorder would have elicited protocols that were as informative as the ones based on pair work.

Since the aim was to study informant-initiated inferencing procedures, informants were set a very open task. The instruction simply asked informants to guess at the meaning of the underlined words in the text, and to verbalize all their thoughts while doing so. According to Færch & Kasper's taxonomy of elicitation procedures (1987, and this volume), the thinking aloud in the present study is characterized by the following key-terms: task integrated, undirected, self-initiated and involving informant interaction.

Basically, pair thinking aloud has proved an adequate method for studying inferencing procedures, offering rich and highly informative data. However, not surprisingly, given an undirected task, there is enormous variability between the protocols, and the analyst is often faced with data that are either difficult to interpret or uninformative. In general, length of protocol and informative value show high correlation, but there may also be long stretches of protocol that are not at all helpful because the informants talk incoherently, jump from one problem to the next or immediately agree upon a solution without any argumentation.

Important issues relating to the use of introspective techniques concern the possible *incompleteness of verbal reports* and *the question whether incompleteness invalidates the data*. Incompleteness of verbal reports is discussed, among others, by Ericsson & Simon (1980) and by Weidle & Wagner (1982), who mention the problems of informant capacity (informants need to select what they verbalize because a complete verbalization would over-charge their processing capacity) and of informant consciousness (not all processes are conscious). In the present study, the incompleteness of reports is most evident with the weakest informants in the low-proficiency group. Thus one informant may say "prevalent means normal", and if the other informant agrees, that is it! But, also, item difficulty and item chronology affect the completeness of the obtained reports, "easy" items and items that come late in the text eliciting shorter protocols than items that are "difficult" and occur early.

Socio-psychological variables are particularly relevant both for the completeness and for the validity of data obtained through pair thinking aloud. Thus one informant may dominate the other, resulting in incompleteness relative to the dominated informant, or informants may withhold certain cues because they are afraid of their fellow informant's reaction. There is evidence that informants suppress hypotheses based on, for example, phonological similarity between the test word and an L1 term, for fear of laughter, a reaction they may have received in connection with previous items. In the light of such evidence, it is difficult to be as optimistic about the validity of (incomplete) verbal reports as Ericsson & Simon, who express the view that "Incompleteness of reports may make some information unavailable, but it does not invalidate the information that is present" (1980: 243).

In order to meet some of these shortcomings it was decided to supplement thinking-aloud procedure with retrospective sessions for as many informant pairs as possible, choosing informants whom their teachers described as relatively self-confident, outgoing and talkative.

The Combined Method of Thinking Aloud and Retrospection

In the research situation, while one pair of informants did their thinking aloud, two researchers monitored this from an adjoining room, each making notes about the informant that they immediately afterwards met individually for the retrospection.

With a view to retrospection and *elicitation techniques*, there is no doubt that interviewer control ensures a fair amount of informant input. Such advantages are, however, counterbalanced by the risk of only getting the expected answers. Naturally interviewers' questions reflect the categories they have established, and there is a risk of pressing the informants into the mould of a previously established framework.

The opposite approach, informant-initiated retrospection, meets the requirement that researchers must keep completely open minds if they want to learn something new. Drawbacks are that some informants do not spontaneously take an initiative and that a very open task is a difficult one, i.e. informants are insecure and passive because they are uncertain of what is expected of them.

The policy was followed of making the retrospective session researcher-controlled and informant-initiated. This was a compromise with the researcher being expected to strike a balance between exercising too much control and leaving all the initiative to the informant. For each test word the researcher started by saying, "What came into your mind first when you saw this word?" After this the initiative was left with the informant for as long as she had something to contribute. If necessary, she was asked supporting questions of the type:

– You made a long pause at this point. Do you remember what you were thinking of?
– What led you to suggest this meaning of the word?

Characterizing the retrospection by help of key-terms from Færch & Kasper (1987 and this volume), we can say that it is task-oriented and involves interaction between informant and researcher.

The approach adopted for combining the thinking-aloud and retrospection data is to *consider the thinking-aloud data as primary*. These are the most genuine since they are informant-initiated. The elicitation during retrospection serves the purpose of elaborating on what was said or hinted at during the thinking-aloud session.

It may seem appropriate to provide some argument in support of an approach that combines data that are (1) undirected as opposed to semi-directed and, (2) pair data as opposed to individual data.

As the aim of the study is to investigate learners' undirected use of lexical inferencing procedures, it may seem unwarranted to include the use of data obtained partly through direct questioning. However, we find it legitimate to combine informant-initiated and researcher-initiated data as long as the first set of data is regarded as the primary source. This is emphasized first by the questioning technique, where the researcher's point of departure is the informant's utterances during the thinking aloud, and secondly, during the data analysis phase where informant hypotheses that only appear during the retrospection are discarded from the analysis (see below).

Concerning the second point, it is legitimate to combine individual data and pair data when the result is worked out as a *pair* result. It is assumed that the present data give a valid description of the inferencing procedures of informant pairs. Whether the same data can be regarded as valid for the reconstruction of the inferencing procedures of the individual, is a moot point which is beyond the scope of this chapter.

Using the test word "dissension" as an example (cf. Text 5), the analytical method used when combining the two sets of data can be described as follows. In the thinking-aloud protocol the analyst spots the first informant hypothesis about word meaning, in this case "quarrels/a split". She finds that the informant builds her hypothesis on a contextual cue and indicates this in the cue column (context T; T for thinking aloud). Then the retrospective protocols are examined to find confirmation of the indicated cue use (cue marked T+R) or new cue types related to the same hypothesis (cue marked R). The relevant extract(s) of the retrospective protocol(s) are added to the thinking-aloud protocol to constitute the analysis sheet for this particular item. In Text 5 the three cues activated during the thinking aloud are elaborated on and confirmed by the retrospective protocols. Indeed, it would have been problematic to postulate the use of an intralingual cue without the retrospective data.

Thinking-aloud and retrospection often go hand-in-hand, as seen above. However, in a few cases completely new information appears during the retrospection. In this case, a distinction is made between new informant hypotheses and new cue activation. New hypotheses are discarded from the analysis, whereas new cues related to the thinking-aloud hypotheses are included. This reflects the decision of regarding the thinking-aloud data as the primary data.

Also investigated was the extent to which there are *qualitative differences between the two methods*, i.e. whether thinking aloud and retrospection elicit different cue types. Three test items out of the 25 were selected as being representative, namely "curative" (expected to elicit L1 + L2 cues), "insatiable" (expected to elicit L2 cues) and "affluence" (expected to elicit contextual cues, since there are no semantic cues). For each test item the following questions were asked about cue types (cf. Table 1):

Text 5

Test word in Context: Soon afterwards, however, the downfall of the Zulu empire started by *dissension* among the blacks themselves, and ended in conflicts with the whites.

Excerpts from Protocols: *Analysis:*

Thinking aloud	Retrospection	Cues	Hypotheses
B it must be something with quarrels or a split A yes, a split because it says (reads aloud: "among the blacks themselves")	A "among the blacks themselves" — then it has to be a split — because later it develops into conflicts with the whites — so it has to do with the context	contextual $^{T+R}$	
B yes — dissension — dissect — split A oh, yes B if one is to use logical reasoning	R something in the word? B if we were to come up with a subtle solution — something to do with dissect — something to do with splitting — and then I thought split fitted in	intralingual $^{(T)+R}$ contextual $^{T+R}$	quarrels/ a split

- how many cue types are used/referred to both in thinking aloud and retrospection?
- how many cue types are not used/referred to either in thinking aloud or in retrospection?
- how many cue types are used in thinking aloud but not referred to in retrospection?
- how many cue types are used in retrospection but not in thinking aloud?

These questions were asked in relation to 18 pairs with high proficiency and 14 pairs with low proficiency. Since differences are slight between the two groups, only one of these, the high-proficiency group, is discussed in the following.

For the test item "insatiable", for instance, the high-proficiency group used the following 11 cue types both in thinking aloud and retrospection (numbers refer to Table 1):

contextual: I 1, 2, 3, 4, II;
intralingual: I 2, 3, 4, 6;
interlingual: I 5, II 1.

Table 2 indicated the number of activated/non-activated cue types for the high-proficiency group, the total number of cue types being 21. The upper two categories indicate the shared features between the two methods, the lower two categories show the methods separately. The numbers are high for shared cue types, and low for types elicited by one of the methods only.

TABLE 2   *The high-proficiency Group (N = 18)*

| | Test items | | |
	Curative	Insatiable	Affluence
Number of cue types activated by both methods	11	11	9
Number of cue types not activated by either of the methods	6	5	4
Number of cue types activated by thinking aloud only	2	2	6
Number of cue types activated by retrospection only	2	3	2

The very low numbers found in the bottom column, i.e. cue types used in retrospection only, illustrate a point already made above: retrospection adds little new information compared to what is elicited through the use of thinking-aloud procedure on its own. Although the numbers found in the category, "cue types activated by thinking aloud only" (not used in retrospection) are also relatively low, it is interesting to ask why, at all, there are cues that informants used during thinking aloud but which they rejected on second thought. If one looks at what cue types tend to be discarded in the whole sample, one finds that, at least for the low-proficiency group, there is a loading towards interlingual cues, both L1 (Danish) and L_n (German, Latin etc.). This is what may be expected from intermediate students, who are often warned by their teachers about the risks of transferring from Danish to English, and who, therefore, may be unwilling to admit to the researcher that this in fact was what he or she had done. Furthermore, although I have not looked into this systematically, it is my distinct impression that there is a high percentage of phonological/ orthographic cues among the discarded ones.

Discussion

Returning to the problems experienced in this study, these are discussed on the basis of the overview below:

TABLE 3   *Overview of problems related to thinking-aloud procedure, retrospection and the combined procedure*

Thinking-aloud procedure	1. Informants' focus is on the product
	2. Informants do not know what the researcher wants
	3. Socio-psychological variables interfere with cognitive variables
Retrospection	4. Informants' awareness of inferencing procedures is low
	5. Informants cannot communicate their thoughts
	6. Informants' lack of confidence and extroversion influences the quantity and quality of the data
Thinking-aloud procedure + retrospection	The following problems are revealed during retrospection:
	7. Informants have forgotten what they were thinking of during the thinking-aloud session
	8. Informants do not retrospect but come up with new ideas
	9. Informants' lack of motivation influences the quantity and quality of the data
	10. Informants' utterances have been influenced by reactions from others, from the fellow informant as well as from the researcher
	11. Different informants assume different roles

Points 1, 2, 4 and 5 are closely interrelated. The problems stated are a direct result of *the nature of the task and of the instruction*: Informants were instructed to write down the result of their discussion, therefore they may tend to focus on the product (point 1), which has an adverse effect on their level of awareness with regard to processes (point 4), they are not sure what the researcher wants (point 2), and consequently cannot communicate their thoughts (point 5). These problems might be reduced if informants were told more about the purpose of the study and were offered a metalanguage in which to think aloud and reflect. This, however, involves the risk of influencing informants' inferencing procedures, and was therefore discarded.

Socio-psychological variables are at play in points *3, 6, 9, 10 and 11*, covering a broad range of aspects such as sex differences, motivation and group dynamics. That they are grouped together reflects the fact that, in the design of the study, the focus is on the cognitive variables, and the socio-psychological variables are left largely uncontrolled. The first point (3), "*Socio-psychological variables interfere with cognitive variables*" involves, for instance, sex differences, as may be illustrated by the processing of the test word "prevalent". In the context of "polygamy being prevalent among the Zulu people", more boys than girls propose "privileged" or "natural" and many girls "perverse" or "permitted"! Furthermore, in extreme cases discussions are so dominated by "power struggle" that it overrides the natural, spontaneous procedures. In my experience, the ideal thinking-aloud pair are equals with respect to status in their peer group and academic achievement, as well as congenial to one another.

Point 6, related to retrospection, mentions informants' *lack of confidence* as a problem. As mentioned above, the criterion in selecting informants for retrospection was that they were relatively self-confident, outgoing and talkative. However, not surprisingly, it was extremely difficult to find self-confidence in learners at the very bottom of the proficiency scale, so it is in this group that the problem is most acute.

Point 9 deals with informants' *lack of motivation to talk during retrospection*. This is a direct effect of the combination of methods in that some informants consider the retrospection a boring and superfluous activity because it follows directly on the thinking aloud. During retrospection utterances like the following are not unusual: "There is no more I can tell you" and "We said so before".

There is evidence that informants are influenced by *reactions from their fellow informants and the researcher (point 10)*. The expression "reactions from others" covers evaluative and affective reactions, which may be overt or covert. Overt reactions during thinking aloud such as derogatory laughter or comments like "Idiot!" or "You don't mean that seriously, do you?" are not unusual from fellow informants. Add to this the, hopefully, more covert reactions from the researcher during retrospection, which may, nonetheless, be decisive since most individuals are highly sensitive to, for instance, hints of doubt expressed through mimicry or intonation.

Point 11 claims that *"Different informants assume different roles"* such as "the good informant" who tries to find out what the researcher's hypotheses are and to co-operate to prove these, and "the self-promoting informant" whose behaviour is aimed at impressing both the researcher and the fellow informant. Ulich interprets the informants' "motives, roles and response sets" (1982) as being the product of the situational context and the interaction. Rather than considering it as a case of "permanent personality traits", Ulich argues that informants take refuge in roles when they are over-challenged, anxious or unmotivated. His viewpoints originate from a discussion of interaction between researcher and informants; however, such problems increase when, on top of this, one has the between-informant interaction of the present study.

Finally, *points 7 and 8* which both deal with *the time-lag between the task and the probe*. According to Ericsson & Simon (1980: 226) the time factor is crucial:

> "If the subject is asked immediately after performing the process, the model predicts that some previously heeded information will still be in short term memory, permitting direct reporting by the process described earlier, and facilitating retrieval of additional information."

Although the retrospection in this study takes place immediately after the thinking aloud, there is a considerable time-lag between event 1, where a pair discusses test word 1, and event 2, where they retrospect about the same word.[7] It is, however, possible that the absolute time span is less important than the kind of activity the informant is involved in (Zimmermann, personal communication). In our case, the informant did not do other things, but was engaged in the same kind of activity, i.e. word processing, although the test words differed. Nonetheless potential influence of these design factors on informants' mind set should not be underestimated. As Table 3 indicates, there are cases where informants state that they have *forgotten what they were thinking during the first session*, or when they come up with *new ideas during the retrospection* because they presumably experience the two sessions as separate exercises. Experience with media support during the pilot phase was not positive enough to justify the extra time required.[8]

Conclusion

The rationale behind combining the two methods is to try to overcome the problems connected with using each of them in isolation. The main problems with the method of thinking aloud are firstly, the varied quantity and informative value of the data, which makes identification of procedures difficult, and in the most unfortunate cases leaves the analyst to infer on the basis of products only (the written result of the inferencing task); secondly, for pair thinking aloud, socio-psychological variables are difficult to control. For retrospection, the problems are that the data are only partly informant-initiated, and that it is difficult for the researcher to strike a balance between the too-loose and too-controlled interview.

To some extent these shortcomings are overcome when the two methods are combined, so there are distinct advantages: first of all, the two sessions provide a larger quantity of data than either of them in isolation. Secondly, the quality of the data is improved in two ways: (1) by using informant-initiated data as the starting point and enriching them by eliciting additional information, (2) by using pair work that invites the verbalization of thought, supplemented by deeper probing into the individual's thought processes. By using the methods as complementary, one has the best of both worlds, although for this particular study retrospection did not add a great deal of information.

The increased quality of the data also influences the reliability of the identification procedure. When the two researchers listen in on the thinking aloud, they are able to diagnose where the problems lie for the analyst, and can consequently plan to probe into these particular areas during the retrospection. The fact that the interviewer/analyst is "present" during both sessions is a great advantage.

The last point highlights how the retrospection is not simply appended to the thinking aloud. Rather, the interviewer is already involved in the thinking-aloud in order to be able to use the retrospection as a complementary method.

Notes to Chapter 10

1. The research design is accounted for in Haastrup (1985).
2. The three main cue types are from Carton (1971).
3. The introspective sessions were conducted in Danish, which means that the quoted texts are translations. This is regrettable since it makes informants' cue use less transparent, e.g. *kurere* in Text 4.
4. *Kurere* in Danish means "cure" (verb in the infinitive). The Danish form is kept to explain that cue use is characterized as interlingual, L1.
5. Procedural knowledge is discussed by Færch & Kasper (1985).
6. Færch & Kasper refer to the difference between implicit and explicit knowledge, between varying degrees of automatization and control by which such knowledge can be activated, and to the shift between L1 and L2 in many introspective tasks.
7. Most informants work their way through the 25 test words chronologically.
8. In the pilot study we tried to play back the thinking-aloud audio-tape during the retrospection. On the whole, informants found it dull and not very helpful to listen to the recording, and as this was extremely time-consuming, it was abandoned. It seems likely that video-tapes are much more stimulating than audio-tapes.

References

CARTON, A. S. 1971, Inferencing: A process in using and learning language. In P. PIMSLEUR & T. QUINN (eds), *The Psychology of Second Language Learning*. Cambridge: University Press, 45–58.

ERICSSON, K. A. & SIMON, H. A. 1980, Verbal reports as data. *Psychological Review* 86, 215–51.

— 1984, *Protocol Analysis*. Cambridge, Mass.: MIT Press.

FÆRCH, C. 1981, Inferencing procedures and communication strategies in lexical comprehension. Paper read at the BAAL Seminar on Interpretive Strategies. University of Lancaster, September 1981.

FÆRCH, C., HAASTRUP, K. & PHILLIPSON, R. 1984. *Learner Language and Language Learning*. Clevedon: Multilingual Matters.

FÆRCH, C. & KASPER, G. 1985, Procedural knowledge as a component of foreign language learners' communicative competence. In H. BOLTE & W. HERRLITZ (eds), *Kommunikation im Sprachunterricht*. Utrecht: Rijksuniversiteit, 169–99.

— 1986, One learner — two languages: Investigating types of interlanguage knowledge. In J. HOUSE & S. BLUM-KULKA (eds), *Interlingual and Intercultural Communication*. Tübingen: Narr. 211–27.

— 1987, Introspektive Methoden in der Lernersprachenanalyse. In S. BÖRSCH (ed.), *Die Rolle der Psychologie in der Sprachlehrforschung*. Tübingen: Narr.

HAASTRUP, K. 1985, Lexical inferencing — a study of procedures in reception. *Scandinavian Working Papers on Bilingualism* 5, 63–86.

HUBER, G. L. & MANDL, H. 1982, *Verbale Daten*. Weinheim and Basel: Beltz.

ULICH, D. 1982, Interaktionsbedingungen von Verbalisation. In HUBER & MANDL, 43–60.

WEIDLE, R. & WAGNER, A. C. 1982, Die Methode des Lauten Denkens. In HUBER & MANDL, 81–103.

ZIMMERMANN, R. in press, A model of lexical search in L1 — L2 translation. In H. W. DECHERT (ed.), *Interlingual Processes*. Tübingen: Narr.

11 The Use of Retrospective Verbal Reports in the Analysis of Compensatory Strategies[1]

NANDA POULISSE, THEO BONGAERTS AND ERIC KELLERMAN

Introduction

Anyone who has attempted to communicate in a foreign language (FL) outside the classroom will recognize the annoying experience of wanting to say something, but lacking the appropriate vocabulary for it. The strategies which FL learners employ to overcome such problems are generally referred to as *communication strategies* (CmS). Færch & Kasper (1983b: 36) have defined these as "potentially conscious plans for solving what, to an individual, presents itself as a problem in reaching a particular communicative goal". They distinguish two types of CmS: *reduction strategies* and *achievement strategies*. In the case of reduction strategies the learner is prepared to give up part or all of his original communicative goal in order to avoid a problem. Examples of such strategies at the lexical level are *meaning replacement* and *message abandonment*, where the goals are respectively changed or fully abandoned.

Achievement strategies are adopted by learners who are determined to reach their goals via alternative speech plans. Besides *retrieval strategies*, which are used when the learner has difficulties in retrieving specific interlanguage items, this category includes *compensatory strategies* (CpS). Examples of compensatory strategies are strategies such as *language switch*, *foreignizing* and *literal translation*, which originate in the learner's L1 (or L3), as well as strategies like *approximation*, *description* and *word coinage*, which are available to both L1 and L2 speakers. Other classes of CpS are *co-operative strategies* (the learner asks the listener for help), and *non-linguistic strategies* such as the use of gestures. In general, one could say that with reduction strategies the solution is based on omission, while with achievement strategies the solution is based on commission.

In the present chapter we will be concerned with CpS as used by Dutch learners of English. Following the definition of CmS by Færch & Kasper quoted above, we set up a working definition of CpS. It reads:

"Compensatory strategies are strategies which a language user employs in order to achieve his intended meaning on becoming aware of problems arising during the planning phase of an utterance due to (his own) linguistic shortcomings."

(Poulisse, Bongaerts & Kellerman, 1984: 72)

There are three points which are of crucial importance to this definition:

1. the language user must be aware of a problem;
2. the problem must be linguistic in nature;
3. the language user must aim at the solution of this problem, that is to say, he must attempt to communicate his originally intended meaning.

In fact, we do not study all the CpS covered by this definition. We have restricted our research to the strategies used by *L2 learners* compensating for *lexical* shortcomings in the *oral production* of language.

So far, we have concentrated on the relationship between CpS choice and foreign language proficiency level. For this purpose we have collected data from three groups of 15 Dutch learners of English at three different proficiency levels. Two of these groups consisted of secondary school pupils who had been learning English for three and five years respectively. In the text they are referred to as 3 VWO and 5 VWO pupils.[2] The learners in the most proficient group were all second-year university students of English. They had done six years of English at secondary school and were now studying English full time. Each subject was confronted with four tasks.

Task I was a concrete picture description task. The subject was shown photographs of 40 objects. Pre-tests had revealed that even highly proficient learners of English did not know the conventional English names for 20 of these objects (e.g. *fly swat, abacus, stilts*). The other 20 objects were included as dummies (e.g. *door, socks*) to encourage the subjects. The photographs were presented in random order. The subject was asked to look at them one-by-one and to make clear in English what object he saw, either by naming it, or in any other way. He was asked to do this in such a way that an Englishman who would later listen to the recordings of it, would be able to identify the object.

Task II was an abstract picture description task. For this task 12 of the figures used in various experiments on referential communication in L1 by Krauss and his associates were selected (cf. Glucksberg, Krauss & Higgins, 1975; Krauss & Glucksberg, 1977, for overview articles). As these figures were so complex that native speakers, too, would have problems in describing them, this task was extremely suitable for obtaining comparable L1 data. For this reason, each subject was asked to conduct the task first in Dutch and then in English. The instructions were similar to those in task I.[3]

Task III was a story re-tell task. The subjects were asked to listen to recordings of five ten-line stories in Dutch. After each story they were asked to re-tell it in English. They were given pictures to accompany the stories to make sure they would not omit any essential details. The first of the stories served as a practice story and was later discarded from the analysis.

Task IV was a 20 minute interview on everyday topics such as school, holidays, cooking and sports, with a native speaker of English.[4] As the subjects and the interviewer needed some time to get used to each other and the task, the first five minutes of the interview were not analysed.

This combination of four tasks in which various degrees of control were established — ranging from strictly controlling for feedback and contents to resembling natural conversation — was felt to be necessary to obtain a fairly balanced, and hence reasonably generalizable, picture of CpS use. The four tasks were administered in two sessions of approximately one-and-a-half hours. Each subject was tested individually, which enabled us to record all the data on video.

Problems in the Identification of CpS

Early research relied heavily on the researcher's intuitions in deciding where CmS had been used. As a result many errors which were, in fact, manifestations of the learner's interlanguage system were interpreted as CmS (cf., for example, Tarone, Cohen & Dumas, 1976). Similarly, correct forms, which might well be CmS, were often disregarded (cf. Corder's 1967 notion of "covert error").

We think it is essential for the validity of CpS research to distinguish strategic from non-strategic behaviour. In order to do so we set up a method of identification with rigorous criteria to determine clear cases of CpS and we decided to restrict our subsequent analyses to these "clear cases". From the working definition presented above it is clear that this method should enable us to answer the following three questions:

1. was there a problem?
2. was this problem linguistic in nature?
3. what was the speaker's originally intended meaning?

In general, it is not too difficult to answer these questions with respect to the data collected in tasks I and II. After all, we ourselves determined the principal problems, and therefore the intended meanings, when we developed these tasks. Besides, temporal variables and hesitation phenomena have been shown to point to problems during the planning process (cf. for example, Raupach, 1983; Möhle, 1984; Wiese, 1984). Thus, pauses, repetitions and false starts, but also rising intonation, sighs, laughs and comments like "oh dear", "what's it called again?", function as problem indicators on the basis of which one can identify the CpS in these tasks with a reasonable degree of certainty.

The data from tasks III and IV are more problematic, however. In task III it is not always clear whether the problems are the result of lexical shortcomings, or whether the subject had simply forgotten some of the details of the story. In task IV the subjects were relatively free to determine the topic of the interview. This enabled them to avoid or hide problems whenever they felt like it. Therefore, problem indicators in the data no longer suffice to decide whether a CpS has been used. In particular, this is the case with very proficient L2 learners, who foresee possible problems at a relatively early stage in the planning of an utterance. As their L2 resources are fairly large, they are able to develop an alternative speech plan in good time. As a result, it is extremely hard to find evidence for their CpS use in the form of hesitations, restructurings, and the like.

In order to arrive at a reliable identification of the more obscure CpS in tasks III and IV it was decided to use a combination of two identification procedures. Firstly, two independent judges would identify CpS on the basis of problem indicators in the data themselves. Secondly, we would make use of retrospective data, i.e. of the comments which the subjects themselves had given on their performance immediately after having completed the task. Eventually, the criterion for a "clear case" in tasks III and IV was set up as "identified by both of the judges and/or by the researcher on the basis of the retrospective comments".[5]

The Reliability of Retrospective Data

In 1973, Corder called for the use of intuitive data in second language acquisition research. Since then there have been sporadic attempts to incorporate introspective techniques into the research methodology (cf. Kellerman, 1974; Cohen & Robbins, 1976; Schlue, 1977; Tarone, 1977; Glahn, 1980). However, it is only recently that such techniques have been applied systematically. One reason for this is that the use of introspective data, including retrospective data, is generally considered to be controversial (see, for example Nisbett & Wilson, 1977). Ericsson & Simon's (1984) survey of the literature in this field reveals that there are two main points of objection to the use of retrospective data:

1. retrospective data are not reliable; they are incomplete, inaccurate and affected by researcher bias;
2. the knowledge that one will be required to retrospect, influences the performance of the task.

In their discussion of these points of criticism Ericsson & Simon argue that retrospective data *can* be considered as a reliable source of information provided they are collected under certain conditions. They suggest the following:

1. the data should be collected immediately after task performance, when memory is still fresh;
2. the subjects should be provided with contextual information to activate their memories;
3. all the information asked for must be directly retrievable, i.e. must have been heeded during task performance, so that the subjects are not induced to generate responses based on inferencing and generalizations;
4. for the same reason the information asked for should relate to specific problems, or a specific situation;
5. no leading questions should be asked, to minimize the effects of "researcher bias";
6. the subjects should not be informed that they will be asked for retrospective comments until after task performance, so as not to affect their performance on the task.

We believe our procedure largely satisfies these six conditions. A detailed description of it will serve to illustrate this. In each of the two test sessions the subject was asked to perform two tasks. The first time he carried out tasks I and III and the second time tasks II and IV. Immediately after having finished task III, or task IV (condition 1), the subject, who had previously not received any instructions in this respect (condition 6), was asked to listen to, and watch, the video-recordings of his own task performance. He was instructed to stop the tape, using a remote control, whenever he wanted to comment on his performance. The video-recordings served as contextual information (condition 2). Pretests had revealed that when subjects recognized a particular situation, they usually remembered how they set about it. Only in cases where the subjects did not spontaneously comment at points where pauses and other performance characteristics clearly suggested that a CpS had been used, did the experimenter stop the tape. Sometimes this in itself was enough to trigger a comment. In other cases it was necessary to ask the subject a question. These questions always related to a specific problem (condition 4) and special care was taken that they did not suggest any "suitable" answer (condition 5), or force the subject to base his answer on more than the information directly available to him from his own memory (condition 3).

In order to familiarize the subject with this procedure each retrospective session was preceded by a five-minute practice session. For this purpose we used the recordings of the practice story and the first five minutes of the interview respectively. Most subjects were responsive in the practice session and commented spontaneously on their problems. Those who did not were urged to take the initiative more often. It was again emphasized that all the information they could provide was relevant, and they were assured that they should not worry about having had too many problems, nor about the time (and the tape!) they were taking. All the retrospective data were recorded on audio tape.

The Usefulness of Retrospective Data

Considering that the retrospective data which we collected largely satisfy Ericsson & Simon's requirements, we assume that we have created the conditions for maximum reliability in the data. We would now like to demonstrate in what ways these retrospective data can contribute to the solution of the problems related to the identification of CpS in tasks III and IV. We have already seen that to identify a CpS one must know 1) whether there is a problem, 2) whether this problem is linguistic in nature, and 3) what the originally intended meaning is.

In task III the second question turns out to be particularly prominent. In spite of the accompanying pictures some subjects still had problems remembering all the details of the story. It is of course essential that such memory problems are distinguished from linguistic problems. In extract 1 the subject, a 3 VWO pupil, is re-telling a story about a man who gets a job as a caretaker in an old people's home and who, on the day of his removal, receives a bunch of flowers with a card saying, "with our deepest sympathy". Of course he is very upset about this, so he rings the florist and finds out that two bunches of flowers have been mixed up and that his flowers have been sent to a funeral with a card saying, "congratulations on your new position".[6]

Extract 1

S: uh, a man 1 who 1 hadn't a job 1 uh, wanted to 1 have, a job 2 erm, to help 1 old people, in a house, where /auld/, old people lives 2

   1) S: "bejaardentehuis" (="old people's home") I didn't know either
      E: mm, do you remember what sort of job he wanted to have in that house?
      S: yes, "concierge" (="caretaker") *but I didn't know what that was either, so I thought, someone who helps there and so*

... 2 uh 4 the day after 1 that he, got the job 2 erm, he got 2 uh, some flowers 2 erm 1 with 1 standing on 1 uh 1 erm crazy thing,

   2) S: uh yes, I didn't know, *I didn't remember exactly what it said*
      E: mm, but it was something crazy?
      S: uh yes ⟨laughs⟩ yes something unusual in any case
      E: yeah

In the retrospective session it is made clear that the subject had indeed remembered that the story was about a caretaker. He clearly indicates that he had to make do with "someone who helps there" because he did not know the appropriate word, so this is a CpS. Later on, he explains that he did not remember exactly what the card said. Thus, his second problem is due to a memory lapse rather than a lexical short-coming. Hence, "crazy thing" is not a CpS, at least not in our sense.[7]

To identify the CpS in task IV, the answers to questions 1 and 3 are also of crucial importance. Due to the fact that the contents of the interview are frequently determined by the subject himself, it is not always clear to an outsider whether there was a problem, and whether what the subject says is, in fact, what he had originally intended to say. In this respect too, retrospective data proved to be most helpful, and many CpS that would otherwise have gone unnoticed could be identified on the basis of the subjects' comments. Thus, there was a boy who said that his family always ate a lot at Christmas. It was not until the retrospective session that we found out that what he had really wanted to say was that they ate "lekker" (= "good things"), but, he added, "I didn't know how to say that".

The importance of the retrospective comments for the identification of CpS in the data of our most proficient group of subjects is clearly illustrated in extract 2, which led to the identification of "organizations" as a CpS for "verenigingen" (= "societies"/"associations").

Extract 2

S: and uh, I'm a member of two organiza, uh two organizations

    S: is that correct, "verenigingen"? I don't know, uh it seems a big word, organizations
    E: erm, association 1 society, I don't know
    S: yeah, uh yeah I don't really know a word for "vereniging", but something like a yes, *organization seems to me such a such a big word for*
    E: yeah
    S: *for something like that*
    E: yeah

The subject, a nineteen-year-old student of English, tries to make clear that he is a member of two societies. He hesitantly refers to these societies as "organizations", but comments that this word is really "too big" for his purposes.

Besides enabling us to identify CpS which might otherwise have remained unidentified, retrospective data have frequently yielded confirmatory evidence with respect to CpS use exclusively identified on the basis of hesitation phenomena and the like. In this way, the reliability of the identification method was increased. An example is given in extract 3, where a 5 VWO pupil is talking about her father's garden.

Extract 3

S: 2 erm, there he erm 1 erm he teels

1) S: *that's not correct either* ⟨*laughs*⟩
   E: no, you knew didn't you?
   S: "verbouwen" (= "to grow"), yes I knew
   E: yes

S: 2 erm 3 o jee 3 boons?

2) S: "sla" (= "lettuce")!, salad isn't it?
   E: and "bonen" (= "beans")?
   S: *uh, bones?*
   E: beans
   S: *oh yes, beans, oh how stupid* ⟨*laughs*⟩
I: what, what are they?
S: uh "bonen" (= "beans")
I: what are they like?
S: "bonen" erm, little green ⟨draws a bean in the air⟩ uh 2 yes
I: vegetables, ja?
S: yes vegetables
I: mm
S: and erm 1 salade

3) S: ⟨laughs⟩, that's from French ⟨laughs⟩

I: mm
S: 1 erm, also flowers, uh dahlias (Dutch pronunciation)

4) E: is dahlias also English?
   S: *no!* 1 well I don't really know
   E: no okay but I just wanted to know whether you knew 1 it probably is, because she understands you
   S: oh, well yes *but she knows some Dutch*

The comments in 1) and 2) undoubtedly confirm the first identification based on the pauses and hesitations preceding "teels" (= "grows"), and the rather desperate exclamation "o jee" and the rising intonation, accompanying "boons" (= "beans").

On the other hand, there are also a few instances where the retrospective data kept us from incorrectly marking an utterance as a CpS. Extract 4 shows that the subject, a second-year student, who admittedly *did* have problems expressing the word "plooirokje" (= "pleated skirt"), was quite sure of "plies" (pronounced /plaiz/) as a correct English translation for "plooien" (= "pleats"). "Plies" should therefore *not* be considered as a CpS.

Extract 4

S: if he had uh, skirts with, plies

    1) S: "plooirok" (= "pleated skirt") I didn't know either
       E: you did know "plooien" (= "pleats")?
       S: yes, and skirt, so, at least, plies is "plooien" (= "pleats"), isn't it? it's not? ⟨laughs⟩ oh that
       E: ⟨laughs⟩ pleats
       S: what is that?
       E: uh, pleats, are "plooien"
       S: oh, mm

Likewise, "dahlias" in extract 3, comment (4) above would not have been marked as a CpS if the subject had answered *yes* instead of a definite *no!* to the experimenter's question whether "dahlias" is also an English word. Now, of course, "dahlias" *is* considered a CpS, certainly because the subject adds "well yes, but she knows some Dutch", thereby indicating why she assumed borrowing from Dutch might be successful with this interlocutor.

Summarizing, we can state that, although retrospection is not the only source of information, it does play a very important role in the identification of CpS. First of all, CpS can be identified more reliably if the subjects' comments provide independent support for the identification of the other two judges. Secondly, retrospective comments help us to identify CpS which would otherwise have remained unnoticed. And thirdly, they reveal CpS which were incorrectly identified as CpS.

A Quantitative Comparison of Two Methods of Identification

In order to illustrate the above claims quantitatively, part of the data collected in tasks III and IV (the data of 12 subjects, approximately six hours) has been examined more closely. Two different methods were employed to identify the CpS in these data. In the first method two judges independently identified the CpS while watching the video-recordings. They based their decisions on hesitation phenomena, gazes, mimetic gestures, intonation, in-between comments made by the subjects, and so on. However, they had no access to the retrospective comments. These were only used in the second method, which was employed by the experimenter, who based her decisions regarding CpS use on the information contained in these comments. The results of the two methods were compared and are summarized in Table 1.

TABLE 1   *The number of CpS identified without (−R) and with (+R) the use of retrospective data*

	Method 1 (−R)	Method 2 (+R)
students	28	69
5 VWO	113	175
3 VWO	128	202
Total:	269	446

With the first method, 269 CpS were identified, i.e. in 269 cases the two judges agreed that an utterance met the requirements of our definition of a CpS. The retrospective comments considered in the second method led to the identification of 446 CpS. Table 1 shows that the number of CpS decreases with proficiency level. Of course, it is quite likely that the most proficient group used fewer CpS. After all, they had fewer problems. It should be borne in mind, however, that this effect may have been reinforced by the fact that their CpS were more difficult to identify. Table 2 presents a more detailed overview of the retrospective comments. All in all, the 12 subjects whose data were examined gave 455 retrospective comments. Nine of these led to the rejection of CpS identified by method 1, and consequently these nine cases will be discarded from further analysis. In 183 cases, however, the method 1 identification was confirmed, that is to say, there was perfect agreement among all three judges. This justifies us in considering these utterances as absolutely clear cases of CpS (note that the remaining 77 CpS identified by method 1 were not commented on in the retrospective session). 263 comments related to CpS that had either been marked by only one of the method 1 judges or had not been marked by them at all. The addition of this last category to those CpS that had already been identified by means of method 1, and were not rejected by method 2, resulted in the total number of 523 clear cases of CpS reported in Table 3. In other words, the use of retrospective data in addition to the use of performance characteristics functioning as problem indicators, have enabled us to almost double the number of identified CpS.

TABLE 2   *A specification of the results of retrospection*

	Method 1 CpS confirmed	rejected	New CpS	Total number of relevant comments
students	17 (= 24.3%)	1 (= 1.4%)	52 (= 74.3%)	70
5 VWO	74 (= 41.6%)	3 (= 1.7%)	101 (= 56.7%)	178
3 VWO	92 (= 44.4%)	5 (= 2.4%)	110 (= 53.1%)	207
Total:	183 (= 40.2%)	9 (= 2.0%)	263 (= 57.8%)	455

TABLE 3   *The Results of Methods 1 and 2 combined*

	Method 1 (−R) (excluding rejects)	Method 2 (=R) (new CpS only)	Total number of "clear cases"
students	27	52	79
5 VWO	110	101	211
3 VWO	123	110	233
Total:	260	263	523

As we have pointed out 77 (269 − (183 confirmed + 9 rejected)) of the CpS identified in method 1, were not commented on in the retrospective session. So in these cases we will have to rely on method 1. Considering though that method 1 involved two independent judges, and that only those cases are considered as clear cases where there is agreement among these two, this is hardly problematic. It is even less problematic if it is taken into account that in the majority of these cases CpS use was so evident that the subjects did not feel called upon to comment on them. And, apparently, the experimenter, too, deemed it superfluous to ask for further comments at the time.

In this respect, it is important to note that the experimenter, who conducted the retrospective session more or less without preparation, had to be selective in her promptings. Too many obvious questions might have given the subject the impression of being under-estimated, with possibly irritation and/or boredom as the results. As the subjects' co-operation was an essential condition for the success of the retrospective sessions, it was occasionally felt that some questions that might have led to the identification of a CpS had better not be asked, in order not to disturb the session or irritate the subject.

The Influence of "Researcher Bias"

Earlier in this chapter it was pointed out that one of the objections to the use of retrospective data is that they are subject to researcher bias. We tried to control this disturbing factor as much as possible by refraining from leading questions. Although we are sure that the experimenter's probing was not always felicitous, there are three observations which seem to suggest that we were fairly successful in reducing the effect of researcher bias. One is that the comments which led to the identification of a CpS were, in 328 out of 446 cases, spontaneously given by the subjects. Only in 118 cases was the identification based on comments prompted by the experimenter (see Table 4).

The second is that the subjects seem to be very "honest"; there is no evidence that they tried to hide their shortcomings in an attempt to keep up appearances. One of these "honest" remarks comes from the girl in extract 3. She had answered "roses" when the experimenter asked her what flowers her father was growing in their garden, but in the retrospective session she admits that she does not really know what they have, "I don't think we have roses, but yes, I've got to say something ⟨laughs⟩".

TABLE 4   *The Number of self- and other-initiated comments that led to the identification of a CpS*

	Self-initiated	Other-initiated	Total number of relevant comments
Students	58	11	69
5 VWO	111	64	175
3 VWO	159	43	202
Total:	328 (= 74%)	118 (= 26%)	446

The last observation is that most subjects were very willing to provide retrospective data. In fact, there were 33 instances where the subjects spontaneously provided the experimenter with more detailed information. Usually these comments reveal the use of reduction strategies, which, as was pointed out in the introduction, are directed at avoiding problems. The most illustrative example of this phenomenon was given by a 3 VWO pupil in one of our pre-tests (cf. extract 5).

Extract 5

    I: and in what ways can you adjust your sails? I mean I I
    S: erm, the wind erm,

    1) S: what, what "touw" (= "rope") was, I didn't know either, it has, it has, we have special terms for it
       E: mm
       S: for instance where you, the, with which you pull the main the main sails, it's called the sheet, the main sheet it's called
       E: mm
       S: yes, well of course I had to say "touw" otherwise he wouldn't understand, and I didn't know "touw" so I was talking about a line
       E: ja
       S: ja, then he changed it again into something else, but well, that was, at that moment, not the most important matter, what it was about

    S: from uh below, from below, from behind
    I: all right that's more likely, certainly

2) S: the, "de wind van schuin van achter" (= "free wind") is the most easy way of sailing

E: mm

S: you can uh, you can also, if there's cross wind you can also sail like this, *but that's, again again a lot more difficult to explain*

E: mm

S: *so I just started with the most easy way*

E: yes

It looks as if the subject in this extract exploits the retrospective session to re-establish his personality. He seems to realize that because of his having had to reduce the message he did not really do his job properly. He now wants to make it clear that even if he did a bad job, this is due to language problems and not because he does not know the field. His expertise certainly shows in the above extract, where he gives details of how to sail. We think that one reason why the retrospective sessions turned out to be so informative is that the subjects enthusiastically grasped the opportunity to rehabilitate themselves.

Conclusion

In sum, the most important conclusions of our study are that the use of retrospection (a) increases the number of identifiable CpS by 49%; (b) confirms our method 1 identification in 68% of the cases, which increases its reliability; and (c) allows us to eliminate (the small number of) CpS incorrectly identified by method 1. Besides, the spontaneity with which the comments were given suggests that researcher bias did not play an important role. We therefore conclude that the results of this study support our point of view that retrospective data can be considered a reliable and valuable resource in the analysis of CpS.

Notes to Chapter 11

1. The data presented in this chapter were collected within the research project "The use of compensatory strategies by Dutch learners of English". This project is carried out at Nijmegen University and is financed by the university's research pool.
2. VWO is a Dutch type of secondary school education which prepares pupils for entrance into a university. Generally, 3 VWO pupils are 14/15 years of age, while 5 VWO pupils are approximately 17 years old. The students were all in their early twenties.

3. In fact, the same task was conducted three times following a suggestion by Erik Schils: twice in Dutch, followed by once in English. This was in order to maximize fluent performance in the L1 and reduce the cognitive load to a minimum by the time the subject came to perform in the L2. There is no evidence that subjects found this repetition irksome, nor that there was a great deal of variation in the two performances in the L1.

4. The interviewer in all cases was a 29-year-old woman from Ireland. She was married to a Dutchman and had lived in The Netherlands for six months. Her knowledge of Dutch was minimal. Before experimentation began she received instruction on the required interview techniques and was trained in a number of practice sessions.

5. We realize that by applying strict criteria as to what qualifies as a clear case, we may well have biased our collection of CpS. It is, for instance, possible that certain types of CpS consistently fail to be identified by our methods and do not therefore meet our criteria for inclusion in the corpus. While this may be true, we feel it is better to err on the side of conservatism.

6. In these extracts, S stands for Subject, I for Interviewer and E for experimenter. The retrospective data are distinguished from the actual test data by means of indentation. The numbers in the actual test data indicate the length of pauses in seconds. Pauses shorter than one second are marked by a comma. Question marks and exclamation marks have been used to indicate rising intonation and emphatic speech respectively. Relevant information on the subjects' behaviour is given between angular brackets. Dots (...) have been used to indicate the omission of irrelevant parts of the data. The most important lines of the extracts have been italicized to attract the reader's attention. Note that the retrospective comments were originally given in Dutch and are here presented in translated form.

7. The retrospective data have also revealed retrieval problems which, although possessing similar characteristics to the lexical problems leading to the use of CpS, should be distinguished from these. Of course, if the right word can be retrieved, there is no need for a CpS. It is only if retrieval is unsuccessful that the learner may have recourse to a CpS.

References

COHEN, A. & ROBBINS, M. 1976, Toward assessing interlanguage performance: The relationship between selected errors, learners' characteristics and learners' explanations. *Language Learning* 26:1, 45–67.

CORDER, S. P. 1967, The significance of learners' errors. *IRAL* 5, 161–70.

— 1973, The elicitation of interlanguage. In J. SVARTVIK (ed.), *Errata: Papers in Error Analysis*. Lund: Gleerup, 36–47.

DECHERT, H., MÖHLE, D. & RAUPACH, M. (eds) 1984, *Second Language Productions*. Tübingen: Narr.

ERICSSON, K. A. & SIMON, H. A. 1984, *Protocol Analysis: Verbal Reports as Data*. Cambridge, Mass.: MIT Press.

FÆRCH, C. & KASPER G. (eds) 1983a, *Strategies in Interlanguage Communication*. London: Longman.

— 1983b. Plans and strategies in foreign language communication. In FÆRCH & KASPER (1983a), 20–60.

GLAHN, E. 1980, Introspection as a method of elicitation in interlanguage studies. *Interlanguage Studies Bulletin*, 5: 1, 119–28.

GLUCKSBERG, S., KRAUSS, R. & HIGGINS, E. 1975, The development of referential communication skills. In F. D. HOROWITZ (ed.), *Review of Child Development Research* Vol IV. Chicago: Chicago University Press, 305–45.

KELLERMAN, E. 1974, Elicitation, lateralization and error analysis. *York Papers in Linguistics* 4, 165–89.

KRAUSS, R. & GLUCKSBERG, S. 1977, Social and nonsocial speech. *Scientific American* 236: 2, 100–5.

MÖHLE, D. 1984, A comparison of the second language speech production of different native speakers. In DECHERT, MÖHLE & RAUPACH (1984), 26–50.

NISBETT, R. E. & WILSON, T. D. 1977, Telling more than we can know: Verbal reports on mental processes. *Psychological Review* 84, 231–59.

POULISSE, N., BONGAERTS, T. & KELLERMAN, E. 1984, On the use of compensatory strategies in second language performance. *Interlanguage Studies Bulletin* 8: 1, 70–105.

RAUPACH, M. 1983, Analysis and evaluation of communication strategies. In FÆRCH & KASPER (1983a), 199–209.

SCHLUE, K. 1977, An inside view of interlanguage. In C. HENNING (ed.), *Proceedings of the Los Angeles Second Language Research Forum*. Los Angeles: UCLA, 342–48.

TARONE, E., COHEN, A. & DUMAS, G. 1976, A closer look at some interlanguage terminology: A framework for communication strategies. *Working Papers on Bilingualism* 9, 76–90. Reprinted in FÆRCH & KASPER (1983a), 4–14.

TARONE, E. 1977, Conscious communication strategies in interlanguage: A progress report. In H. BROWN, C. YORIO & R. CRYMES (eds), *On TESOL '77. Teaching and Learning English as a Second Language*. Washington, D.C.: TESOL, 194–203.

WIESE, R. 1984, Language production in foreign and native languages: Same or different? In DECHERT, MÖHLE & RAUPACH (1984), 11–25.

12 Investigating FL Reading Performance Through Pause Protocols[1]

MARILDA C. CAVALCANTI

The issue of methodology with respect to the investigation of (FL) reader–text interaction is complex due to the inadequacy of existing instruments to investigate a highly unknown process. The present chapter, which is divided into three parts, describes the choice, adaptation and utilization of an instrument of data elicitation, viz. verbal protocols, aimed at capturing the reader's point of view about pragmatic interpretation problems arising from reader–text interaction.

Tools for Tapping the Reading Process

Research in reading has a long tradition of *product* analysis done on a quantitative basis. This tradition reflects researchers' preoccupation with how much readers can grasp from text. It is evidenced in the use of measurable techniques of data collection and analysis which invariably take on the format of multiple-choice reading comprehension tests. These tests, which have been criticized for measuring either more or less than what comprehension may involve, measure behaviour which only indirectly reflects the comprehension process itself.

Another measurement of behaviour related to comprehension, often presented as advance over multiple-choice questions, is the Cloze procedure (see Taylor, 1953). Unlike multiple-choice comprehension tests, this type of procedure neither tests readers' short term memory capacity nor skill in understanding questions. It is dependent on readers' knowledge structure range with respect to the ease or difficulty encountered in blank filling. In other words, I am implying that blanks may be meaningfully filled without reading and/or fully understanding a passage.

In recent years, simultaneously with research into the product of reading, there has been a development of interest in the reading *process*. This development, which was aided by the emergence of Information Theory and fostered by the advent of the computer, is reflected in qualitative approaches to reading research which seek a description of behaviour for the purposes of inferring the process(es). The outcome of this trend is reflected, on the one hand, in reading models (such as Goodman, 1967), and, on the other hand, in the advancement and/or revival of tools for tapping the reading process. In this paper I focus on the latter. I view these tools as falling into a four-fold classification:

(a) *miscue analysis* as proposed by Goodman & Burke (1970);
(b) *recall tasks* as used by Kintsch *et al.* (1975) and Kintsch & van Dijk (1978);
(c) *reading monitors and/or recorders* as developed by Just & Carpenter (1977); Whalley (1977); Pugh (1978); Thomas & Augstein (1972, 1979);
(d) *introspective techniques* as advanced by Hosenfeld (1977), Olshavsky (1976–7), Kavale & Schreiner (1979), and Alderson & Short (1981).

I briefly consider each one of the instrument types above to justify my choice of an instrument of data elicitation for a study of adult Brazilian informants. Before doing this, however, I should point out that these instruments are assessed with the following set of requirements in mind to account for the preservation of reading as:

(i) a silent and (as much as possible) private activity yielding performance data;
(ii) part of a real situation with minimum use of electronic apparatus;
(iii) a process allowing for the capture of ongoing thoughts on the reader's part;
(iv) based on an authentic text laid out in its full extent and not in chunks; and
(v) done both in the L1 and the FL.

(a) *Miscue analysis*, a technique based on the analysis of "miscues" or errors made in oral reading, was the first instrument to be dismissed. It does not meet the requirement of preserving reading as a silent and private activity.

(b) *Recall protocols*, as used by Kintsch & van Dijk (1978), refer to tasks usually known as "written summaries" in the classroom tradition. It is important to emphasize that these writers view written summaries as "texts in their own right", in other words, their analysis of recall protocols accounts for the text base and for the recall protocols proper. I ruled out this instrument of data collection because it does not capture the reader's ongoing thoughts due to the time interval between the reading and the recall task.

(c) The area of research which uses *reading monitors* and/or *reading recorders*, in so far as the processing of extended[2] pieces of prose is concerned, is fairly recent. Furthermore, its instruments are especially developed and not easily available.

Thomas & Augstein (1972, 1979), for example, designed a reading recorder (the "Brunel Reading Recorder") which enables readers to see on a viewer an average of five lines at a time. This recorder provides print-outs of patterns of reading (e.g. hesitations and think sessions) and serves as the basis for counselling. To my mind, this recorder, which makes a very reduced amount of text available at a time, is likely to render the reading situation unreal and tiresome.

As to reading monitors, Whalley (1977), concerned with purposes in reading, developed an apparatus for monitoring reading. This apparatus requires a darkened booth and provides facilities for illuminating sections of the text being read at the reader's will. Although it allows for a book-reading situation in so far as the amount of text available is concerned, Whalley's monitor has a serious disadvantage, viz. the unrealistic reading atmosphere resulting from the darkened booth.

(d) *Introspective techniques*. Having examined these three types of tools for investigating the reading process, Hosenfeld's (1977) *think-aloud* (while tackling a reading task) technique suggested itself as promising in the search for a research instrument to meet the requirements I had initially set. *Think-aloud*, also referred to as *verbal protocols* in Problem Solving Theory (see Newell & Simon, 1972) where it was first introduced and developed as a research instrument, requires the subjects to verbalize their thoughts while solving a problem. This technique belongs to the broad context of *introspection*, which itself is as old as general psychology.

Introspective Techniques

Radford & Burton (1974: 395) nicely summarize the appeal and the status of introspective techniques by saying:

"Introspection gives us information about experience. It yields data otherwise inaccessible. It may, besides, bring to light facts that might otherwise be overlooked, or stimulate us to ask new questions. Like any technique, it has peculiar difficulties, especially when used in odd circumstances. These, however, are the hazards of science."

Introspective techniques are a controversial issue both in cognitive psychology and in other schools of thought in psychology. Ericsson & Simon (1980) suggest that the drawbacks attributed to these techniques are chiefly related to cognitive demands which include:

(a) capacity (i.e. the maximum amount of information and number of activities dealt with in short term memory);
(b) memory (i.e. demands from short term memory or long term memory);
(c) metacognition (i.e. subjects' capacity to observe and talk about cognitive processes in operation).

To these cognitive demands Mann (1982) adds social psychological demands, i.e. threat and pressure imposed by an unfamiliar situation. Despite these drawbacks, I view these techniques as promising as they are likely to encourage questions about aspects of "cognitive processes in operation" which are usually ignored when other techniques are used.

Introspective techniques are classified by Radford & Burton (1974) into three groups (see also Cohen, this volume, Chapter 4)

1. *Self-observation* (i.e. introspection proper). The trained analyst-observer reports on mental events.
2. *Self-reports* or self-perception (i.e. retrospection). The subjects tell the researcher-analyst about their experience, "but without trying to be objective" (p. 390).
3. *Think-aloud* (i.e. verbal protocols). The subjects verbalize their thoughts while tackling a task.

This classification seems useful from the point of view of data collection design. In practice, however, as has been pointed out by Radford & Burton (1974), the borderlines may not be very clear cut. The three groups in this classification, I believe, might be better understood as part of a continuum which ranges from *introspection* proper through *naive psychology*[3], to a version of *psychoanalysis* (in so far as the interviewing technique is concerned and not in terms of therapy). These three groups would fit on the continuum as shown in Figure 1.

Introspective techniques of one sort or another have always been used in reading research. In fact, *self-observation* is the one technique

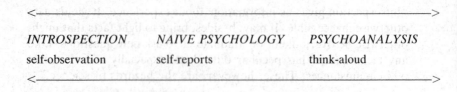

FIGURE 1   *Continuum of introspective techniques*

which characterizes theoretical approaches to reading (e.g. Thorndike, 1917 and Smith, 1971, *inter alia*).

Self-reports, which are not as common in reading research as self-observation, play a crucial role in the work developed (a) by the Göteborg group, i.e. Marton & Säljo (1976), (b) by Thomas & Augstein (1972, 1979), and (c) by Cohen *et al.* (1979).

Think-aloud emerged in reading research through the work of Hosenfeld (1977) in foreign language reading and of Olshavsky (1976–7) in first language reading. Before reviewing their work, I will discuss the strengths and weaknesses of the technique known as verbal protocols. This technique is the focus of attention throughout the remainder of this chapter.

Verbal Protocols

As originally developed in Problem Solving Theory by Newell & Simon (1972), verbal protocols require the subject to think aloud while tackling a task. This technique, which has become a hallmark of the Information Processing approach (see Ericsson & Simon, 1980: 217), is emphasized in Problem Solving Theory, which aims at getting enough data about each subject to identify what information he has got and how he is processing it. Newell & Simon (1972) mention that the first think-aloud tapes (on a logic task) were transcribed in 1957, and the tradition in the use of verbal protocols was started as a technique to check computer models of information processing, hence the emphasis on tasks based on chess and symbolic logic. Verbal protocols play a central and unquestionable role perhaps only in Problem Solving Theory. In other present or past theories and in different branches of psychology, verbal protocols (and introspection in general) remain a point of debate.

In the literature regarding learning strategies (and learning styles), for example, the use of verbal protocols or other forms of introspection was unusual and, according to Cohen (1981: 4), "frequently met with disfavour for not being reliable enough". This attitude towards the use of verbal protocols has changed favourably, and Cohen's (1984) study is an example of the use of an introspective technique to investigate learning strategies.

Besides Newell & Simon (1972), only two works in L1 reading research give a detailed account of procedures used to elicit verbal protocols, i.e. Olshavksy (1976–7) and Kavale & Schreiner (1979). This lack of information is not surprising since verbal protocols are never mentioned as a technique for data collection in books on research methodology. The two articles just mentioned, combined with Newell & Simon (1972) were, therefore, the starting point for the version of verbal protocols adopted in my research work.

Olshavsky (1976–7) chose to use verbal protocols after considering three types of techniques, viz. "introspection, retrospection and verbal protocols" (ibid. 661) to identify readers' strategies. She describes verbal protocols as requiring the subjects to think aloud while solving a problem. Olshavsky adapted the verbal protocol technique to study reading strategies by requiring her subjects to think aloud "after reading each clause of a short story" (ibid. 661). By placing a red dot at the end of every clause, the researcher reminded the subjects that they were supposed to talk about what they had just read and about what they were doing and thinking while they read. In her adaptation of verbal protocols, Olshavsky (1976-7) emphasizes and encourages clause reading. This, to my mind, is not very different from unrelated-sentence reading as done in psychological experiments (e.g. those carried out by Anderson & Bower, 1973, and Schank & Abelson, 1977). I believe that if readers interrupt their task at the end of every clause or sentence, reading becomes artificial, i.e. experiment-like.

Kavale & Schreiner (1979: 109), interested in the identification of reasoning strategies by average and above average readers, elicit verbal protocols by presenting their subjects with four different types of multiple-choice items. Their questions are based on a set of sentence-long-texts from various sources. Although their study is dated 1979, it falls into the category of research based on unrelated sentences which characterizes work published from 1970 to 1975, as pointed out by Golinkoff (1975–6) in a review of the literature on reading processes in good and poor comprehenders. Golinkoff (1975–6: 641–42) further adds that there is some questioning as to what a unit of reading is: a phrase, a clause, whole sentences or a combination of the three (see also the related discussion of translation units in Gerloff, this volume, Chapter 7). Although this question has not yet been answered, there has certainly been a move towards research based on whole texts and away from unrelated sentences (see Schrank & Abelson 1977: 6).

Both Olshavsky's (1976–7) and Kavale & Schreiner's (1979) studies investigate the reading processes of secondary school children. Both use a training phase before the actual elicitation of verbal protocols. Olshavsky (1976–7: 661) says that "the subjects learned this (think-aloud) before the study began so they read and respond in an ongoing manner with no time delay".

In FL reading, verbal protocols are best represented by the work developed by Hosenfeld (1976, 1977, 1979, 1984). Her early work focuses on the identification of reading strategies of successful and unsuccessful (non-native, high-school level) learners through the use of think-aloud data elicited individually in an interview-type situation. Her work is limited to the study of strategies related to the solution of word-meaning problems and to meaning retention while decoding. To analyse this data Hosenfeld developed a system of notation which displays the reading strategies identified as "reading maps". Hosenfeld's (1976, 1977) work is unique in that she proposes what could be described as a manual reading recorder which produces "computer print-outs".[4] Her system of notation, however, is too complex for mapping word-decoding strategies, let alone for mapping any other type of strategy.

More recently Hosenfeld (1979, 1984) carried out some case studies with non-sucessful (non-native) learners. In these studies she both identified their reading strategies and helped them acquire new reading behaviour. The case studies are based on think-aloud data stemming from reading (and grammar) tasks. Hosenfeld (1979) uses an inductive technique in remedial sessions with her subjects, i.e. the subjects go through a trial-and-error process to choose a model of a successful learner which is suitable to their style of reading. This model, which is summarized in a set of strategies, is used by the readers as a basis for the improvement of their strategies, and as a starting point for comparisons. The readers work in a learn-to-learn situation assisted by the researcher. Hosenfeld's findings (limited to word-decoding and meaning retention) demonstrate that unsuccessful readers, who used to do word-by-word translation and turned to the dictionary for the meaning of new words, acquired "effective strategies". These include translation into broad phrases, contextual guesses of the meaning of new words, and use of varied information sources in decoding (e.g. illustration, cognates, grammar).

In so far as verbal protocols are concerned, Hosenfeld's (1979) approach is very much based on interviewing techniques. In other words, in the elicitation of data the researcher intervenes as many times as necessary to prompt the subject to think aloud and move from retrospection to "introspection". In her early studies, Hosenfeld (1976, 1977) adopted an over-simplified view of introspection, i.e. she considered think-aloud as pure[5] introspection. Later Hosenfeld (see Cohen & Hosenfeld, 1981) adopted a new perspective, representing a move from retrospection to introspection, an interesting proposal for a methodological framework for researching mental states. This view of introspection is very comprehensive and accounts for the fuzzy borderline between introspection and retrospection.

Research context

The purpose of the research undertaken is to examine areas of pragmatic interpretation problems encountered by FL readers in tackling the introduction to an academic paper. Specifically it analyses the relationship between key lexical items and potential v. actual pragmatic interpretation problem areas. These areas are examined from three different points of view, viz. the researcher-analyst's, the materials designer's, and the FL reader's. Only the reader's point of view will be in focus in this chapter. Key lexical items are salient elements which recur throughout a text, holding it together through topic cohesiveness and serving as the basis for the creation of discourse coherence.

Pragmatic interpretation refers to the striving for equilibrium between reader-relevance and text salience. It is explained in terms of key lexical items for text salience, and contextually relevant clues for reader-relevance. Key lexical items function as indexical links between cohesion and coherence, and contextually relevant clues as indexical expressions representing the reader's point of view.

Reader-relevance is a construct accounting for the role of the reader in his/her interaction with the text. It indicates one pole of the reader–text interaction continuum. This pole describes what the reader finds relevant when interacting with texts as indexed by contextually relevant clues.

Text salience, finally, is a construct accounting for the role of the writer in his/her interaction with a text. It indicates the other pole of the interaction continuum. This pole describes the writer's manifestation in the text through salient items, i.e. key lexical items.

The reader's view, which is pinpointed through the items with which the reader chooses to interact, i.e. contextually relevant clues, stems from data elicited through an introspective technique from four Brazilian postgraduate students. This paper concentrates on the methodological issue of eliciting such reading performance data through an adaptation of verbal protocols.

Adaptation of verbal protocols: pause protocols

Since the verbal protocol technique is borrowed from Problem Solving Theory, an adaptation was necessary to make it fit the requirements and purpose of the reading tasks used for data elicitation. This adaptation was based on a series of four pilot studies, investigating:

(a) the type of text to be used;
(b) directions to be given to the subject-informants; and
(c) the role to be played by the researcher-analyst in the elicitation of data.

The verbal protocol technique developed from the pilot studies consisted of asking the subject-informants to read silently (for the purpose of making an oral summary) and to think aloud whenever they noticed a pause in their reading process. My aim in eliciting what I labelled *pause protocols* was to encourage the informants to read silently and discourage them from reading aloud, thus avoiding the problem of informants reading aloud and verbalizing only after having read large chunks of text. The readers were, therefore, asked to monitor their silent reading process and to start reasoning aloud on the basis of the pauses detected. Minimally, this reasoning should include elaborations on (a) the location of the problem encountered, (b) the nature of the problem, and (c) the way the problem was dealt with.

Pause protocols were used as a "breaching procedure" (Garfinkel, 1967), that is, the subjects were requested to face a familiar task (reading) in an unfamiliar way (thinking aloud when they detected the occurrence of a pause). The use of this procedure is based on the assumption that the identification of pauses, i.e. potential problem situations, caused either by the reader's inadequacy or hyperinterest in parts of the text (or in the topic as a whole), results from a natural slowing down of the processing of information. It represents a shift from "automatic"[6] to "controlled" processing in reading (see Shiffrin & Schneider, 1977).

The pause protocols were preceded by a training phase to guide the reader to focus upon pauses. The training phase aimed at providing practice in raising the reader's awareness towards the pauses that occur naturally in the reading process. It was developed as a warm-up exercise to lead the subjects from retrospection proper (i.e. retrospection about pauses made), to thinking aloud (when the pause was first noticed). This phase was designed as a result of the first pilot studies, which indicated that when asked to think aloud while reading, subjects usually ended up reading large chunks of text (or even the whole text) and then self-reporting. By the time they started doing these retrospections, they did not remember much of the process anymore. In the training phase, readers went from retrospective to think-aloud tasks, i.e. from tasks which required them to retrospect at the end of paragraphs to tasks which required them to think aloud while reading the paragraphs with a focus on pauses.

Utilization of pause protocols: data elicitation design and procedure

The final data elicitation design was divided into three phases (see Table 1). Phase I and Phase III are tests. The former had the purpose of checking the reader's "adequacy", a construct combining the reader's self-assessment in so far as linguistic confidence is concerned and the reader's proficiency as measured by the ELBA (English Language Battery) test. The latter, i.e. the Cloze test, functions as a comparative measure between the foreign language readers (i.e. the Brazilian–Portuguese native speakers) and EL1 readers (i.e. native speakers of English).

Phase II covers the actual elicitation of protocols from the FL readers. This phase was divided into three parts (see 3, 4, and 5 in Table 1). The elicitation of the protocols was introduced by a *structured interview* (see Cavalcanti, 1983) which represented the transition between Phases I and II. It had the double purpose of supplying some information about the reader's profile (e.g. attitudes, habits) and of serving as an ice-breaker for the data elicitation session as a social encounter. Following the structured interview, the readers had a *training phase* with a double-folded aim, viz. providing practice in raising the reader's awareness

TABLE 1 *Data elicitation design: Brazilian informants (EFL readers)*

	Source	Purpose	Medium
Phase I	1. Self-assessment	To check reader's adequacy ⎰ 1. Reader's linguistic confidence	Portuguese
	2. Proficiency Test	⎱ 2. Reader's proficiency	English
	3. Structured interview	To establish reader's profile	Portuguese
	4. Training phase	To lead reader from RETROSPECTION to THINK ALOUD	English/Portuguese
		To provide practice in raising reader's awareness towards occurrence of pauses in reading	
	5. Elicitation of protocols		
Phase II	5.1 FL reading		
	5.1.1 Title study task	As a control measure for topic knowledge and content anticipation (prediction)	English/Portuguese
	5.1.2 Pause protocol	To identify pragmatic interpretation problems	English/Portuguese
	5.1.3 Interventionist procedure	As a control measure for pause occurrence	Portuguese
	5.1.4 Oral summary	As a control and comprehension measure	Portuguese
	5.1.5 Selection of key lexical items	To check intersubjective agreement in reader-text interaction	English/Portuguese
	5.2 L1 reading		
	5.2.1 Title study task	As a comparison measure among EFL readers	P O R T U G U E S E
	5.2.2 Pause protocol		
	5.2.3 Interventionist procedure		
	5.2.4 Oral summary		
	5.2.5 Selection of key lexical items		
Phase III	6. Cloze task	As a comparison measure with EL1 readers	

towards the occurrence of pauses in the reading process and leading them from retrospective to think-aloud tasks. The former required the readers to retrospect about their processing of information at the end of paragraphs, the latter to think aloud while reading the paragraphs (focus on pauses). In other words, the think-aloud tasks required them to read silently and think aloud whenever they noticed a pause in the reading process.

The third part of Phase II involved the actual elicitation of *pause protocols*, first based on an English text, second on a Portuguese text. The pause protocols, used for the identification of pragmatic interpretation problems related to key lexical items, were combined with four control measures, viz. title study task, interventionist procedure, oral summary, and selection of key lexical items.

The *title study task* aimed at identifying differences/similarities in knowledge structures (schemata) in so far as the topic of the data base was concerned. This task was also used to check content anticipation, i.e. what the readers expected from the text.

The purpose of the *interventionist procedure* (see Appendix) was to induce a pause requiring immediate retrospection at about the same point (i.e. the second paragraph) in the text for all subjects. This induced pause was to serve as a basis for comparisons among the subjects since it was assumed that they would pause at different places in the text. The interventionist procedure (adapted from Cohen, 1981) consisted of a set of questions about ongoing thoughts/activities which were used to interrupt the readers 30 seconds after they had turned the first page of the text.

The *oral summary* (at the end of each paragraph and at the end of the text) corresponds to retrospective accounts of how the text was being processed from the point of view of content. In this sense, it is an informal measure of the negotiation of meaning throughout reader-text interaction. It is also a measure of control for comparative purposes since it occurs at pre-determined points in the text. These points were signalled by an arrow (←) to remind the readers of the task required of them.

Finally, the *selection-of-key-lexical-item task* had the objective of checking whether there was minimal basic inter subjective agreement in so far as key lexical items were concerned.

As illustrated in Table 2, the data elicitation design for the EL1 readers was a reduced version of the design for the FL readers. It started at Step 3 of Phase II (Table 1), skipped Step 5.1. altogether, and went straight into Steps 5.2. and 6.

TABLE 2 *Data elicitation design: English native speakers*

Source	Purpose
1. Structured interview	To establish reader's profile
2. Training phase	To lead reader from RETROSPECTION to THINK-ALOUD To provide practice in raising reader's awareness towards occurrence of pauses in the reading process
3. Elicitation of protocols	
3.1 Title study task	As a control measure: topic knowledge/content anticipation
3.2 Pause protocol	To identify pragmatic interpretation problems
3.3 Interventionist procedure	As a control measure
3.4 Oral summary	As a control and comprehension measure
3.5 Selection of key lexical items	To check notion of agreed basis in reader-text interaction
4. Cloze task	As a comparison measure with FL readers

For the data elicitation the only hardware instrument was a pocket-book size (15″ × 9″) Sony K-7 recorder combined with a micro clip-microphone. The software consisted of a set of typed instructions (see Appendix) for the tasks, and the two texts, one for the training phase and the other for the pause protocols.

Two introductions to academic articles from journals of political studies were used as texts, one in English and one in Portuguese. No readability formula was used to assess the texts, which were selected on the basis of the following criteria:

(a) the researcher's intuition about what could be of potential interest to Brazilian readers, viz. politics and Northern Ireland, although probably not part of their background knowledge;
(b) the research requirements in relation to
   topic — The text(s) should be from an area of study foreign to the informants. This requirement was part of the "breaching procedure" approach to reading through pause protocols and aimed at compelling the readers to process the information more slowly.
   organization — The text should be self-contained in so far as organization into the problem-solution structure was concerned.
   length — The texts should have an average of 650 words.

The researcher-elicitor acted as a "sounding board" during the protocol elicitation to foster reader-text interaction and avoid reader-text-elicitor interaction.

If necessary, however, the researcher-elicitor prompted the readers to think aloud in order to prevent the series of long silences which might otherwise have characterized some readers' protocols. It thus represented an additional measure to the adaptation of the think-aloud technique into pause protocols,

Data analysis

The primary data of this research, the EFL reading pause protocols, were analysed against the background data which consisted of the EL1 readers' pause protocols and the EFL readers' profiles. The latter includes information about their pause protocols based on the Portuguese text. The EFL pause protocols were translated from the Portuguese original into English. The primary data were prepared for analysis by:

i.   isolating the pause protocols from the other tasks;
ii.   searching for pauses which occurred naturally as part of the Oral Summary Task, i.e. at the end of paragraphs or at the end of the text;
iii. matching the pauses with the text; and
iv.   coding the pauses.

i.   Isolation of pause protocols. The pause protocols as raw data were already roughly identified and delimited in the transcriptions. The reason for this is that during the data elicitation the tape recorder had been switched off every time the readers had intonationally or verbally signalled the end of a pause.

ii.   Search for pauses in summaries. Before numbering the naturally occurring pauses, as well as the induced ones (stemming from the Interventionist Procedure Task), I looked for the occurrence of embedded pauses in the Oral Summary Task, i.e. in the SM and GSM. For example, as part of SI_1's (FL subject-informant 1) SM_4 (end-of-paragraph summary 4) the following was coded a pause:[8]

(.) ((MT)) but (.) wait a minute (.) there is something missing here/ (.3) Ah (.) that's what's missing/The underlined phrase "convincing explanation" is missing/[Missing? What's missing?] No/This was missing here/.

SI_1 had been summarizing the paragraph he had just read when he suddenly cut his summary short and made the remark above. This is an example of a pause during the summary task.

Pauses in summaries may also occur in a retrospective comment about the paragraph/text read. As an illustration, consider the pause in retrospection made by SI_4. The pause is mentioned in reply to the elicitor's probing:

[Any other pauses from that point onwards? Or any problem whatsoever?] Uh(.2) I paused briefly (.) at the word "lengthy" [uh] That's all ...

A more complex example of pause is transcribed below. The pause is embedded in an end-of-paragraph summary. SI_1 starts talking about the paragraph he has just read:

OK (.) I've finished the paragraph [uh (.) could you] As he says (.) this study addresses (.) addresses violence/He is concerned about the fact that people from the same background (.) etc. (.) behave differently [uh, uh] (.) right? (.) and that — that problems can be associated with social conditions [uh, uh] /The fact that people turn to political violence [uh]/

He then makes a 2 second pause preceded by a contrast connective, reads aloud, mutters (as if talking to himself), uses the same contrast connective again (signalling thinking time), and signposts the emergence of a problem:

But (.) ((RLV)) to go beyond (.) ((MT)) but (.) wait a minute (.) there is something here/ (.)

There is no overt problem marker in this case. The marker is implied, i.e. "There is something here" meaning "there is something I hadn't noticed" or "there is something I don't understand".

iii.   Matching pauses with text. Every pause was matched with the corresponding part of the text.

iv.   Coding the pauses. After the identification of naturally occurring, induced and embedded pauses, they were coded R(eader)-Problems, and R-Comments based on overt (or implied) markers, e.g. "I don't understand" = R-Problem, and "I think this is unsound" = R-Comment.

Only after the pauses had been coded were the data ready to be analysed in terms of what constituted the focus of the research, i.e. pragmatic interpretation and its relationship with key lexical items and contextually relevant clues, in addition to the question whether areas of potential reading problems were areas of actual reading problems in the data base.

Conclusion

To conclude I draw implications about the observational findings with respect to FL reader–text interaction and about the methodological approach used with respect to its strengths and limitations. The former presents pause protocols as a promising technique for research in reading, the latter entails suggestions for further research.

The primary data analysed were the EFL readers' pause protocols against the background data of the EL1 protocols. The EFL readers' L1 protocols were used first to investigate whether they approached reading differently in their native and in a foreign language. They were also used to check whether they would give more information about their L1 reading if the text were dense and the topic unfamiliar. The EFL readers were found to adopt the same reading style regardless of the language in which they read, but as was to be expected, they read faster in their L1. Furthermore, the EFL readers made fewer pauses in Portuguese than in English, although they made more pauses in their L1 reading than the EL1 informants did in their reading. It seems, however, that protocols based on L1 reading are less informative than protocols based on FL reading, something which was also found in the pilot studies, and which needs further investigation.

With respect to the areas of potential reading problems, these were found to be actualized in three out of four FL protocols. These areas of potential problems had been identified on the basis of key lexical items. Their actualization in FL reader–text interaction was verified through the occurrence of coinciding pauses based on contextually relevant clues.

The analysis of pauses coded as instances of pragmatic interpretation showed that mismatches stem from the reader's v. the writer's (via text) schemata and value systems. These mismatches in reader–text interaction, which result in R-Problems/R-comments, evince the striving for equilibrium between reader-relevance and text salience as captured in the protocols.

The methodological approach developed in this study constitutes an alternative in reading research. It tackles reading through an introspective technique, namely pause protocols, which results in performance data reflecting the reader's partially "frozen" process. This technique is promising as an attempt to capture the ongoing reading process. But pause protocols also have some limitations. They depend on the reader's awareness of his/her own processing of information, and this demands training. Pause protocols entail pauses which may be longer than in a real reading situation. Furthermore, these pauses may result in an over-elaboration of R-Problems/R-Comments and result in data which only indirectly represent the reading process. However, it can be argued that since the reading process is not overt to observation, it can of necessity only be reached via indirect routes, and that pause protocols represent one of these indirect routes yielding reading performance data.

The limitations of this study suggest that a more complex triangulated approach should be adopted in further research. The triangulation I have in mind should minimally add to my own research design the informant's view of the analyst's interpretation of the pause protocols, making the informant a research assistant. Furthermore, I suggest that the reader should also be asked to read on his own and audio record the pauses made. This type of real individual reading would serve as a measure to counterbalance over-elaborations and extra-long pauses which may occur in the presence of the researcher and the tape recorder. Finally, such a triangulated approach could be incorporated into a longitudinal case study.

Notes to Chapter 12

1. This is a revised version of a paper originally published in The ESPecialist 10 (1984), 9–31. A more detailed description of the research partially described here is contained in my PhD thesis (Cavalcanti, 1983), written under the supervision of Professor C. N. Candlin at the University of Lancaster. The first part of this research was funded by the British Council and the second and last part by CAPES/MEC, Brazil.
2. The research method of eye movement photography was strong during the 1950's and 1960's. It focused on the recording of eye movements to establish the number of fixations and the eye span with respect to words and sentences in isolation.
3. According to Berkowitz (1980: 203), naive psychology is associated with Heider's (1958) work in attribution theory: "Heider's theorizing is usually referred to as 'naive psychology' because of its emphasis on the phenomenology of the perceiver in his attempt to understand the causes of behaviour".
4. See Hosenfeld (1977) for examples of "reading maps", to which she refers as "computer print-outs".
5. This over-simplified view of introspection is also taken by Glahn (1980) in her research into oral FL communication. Specifically interested in grammatical phenomena, she had her subjects "introspect" to find out whether they "were at all capable of remembering what had been going on in their minds during the communication situation" (ibid. 119). The obvious inference is that Glahn uses a retrospective, and not an introspective technique, as she claims.

INVESTIGATING FL READING PERFORMANCE
247

6. Shiffrin & Schneider (1977) suggest that reading is a fast and automatic process which tends to slow down and become partly controlled when problems are encountered.
7. The problem-solution structure as proposed by Hoey (1979) is a framework imposed upon the organization of factual text. It suggests that a text can be analysed with respect to its situation, problem and solution. Each of these is overtly signalled by grammatical/ lexical items and by clauses.
8. The following conventions are used in the examples: Ps = pause; SM = end-of-paragraph summary; GSM = general summary at the end of the text; (.) slight pause; (.3) = a three-second pause; / = intonation boundary; [ ] = elicitor's intervention; ((MT)) = mutters; ((RLV)) = reads in low voice; and S = sentence. Other conventions used are described in parentheses in the text.

References

ALDERSON, J. C.& SHORT, M. 1981, Reading literature. Paper read at the BAAL Conference on Interpretive Strategies, University of Lancaster, September, 1981.
ANDERSON, J. & BOWER, G. 1973, *Human Association Memory*. Washington, D.C.: Winston–Wiley.
BERKOWITZ, L. 1980, *A Survey of Social Psychology*. New York: Holt, Saunders.
BORING, E. G. 1953, A history of introspection. *Psychological Bulletin* 50, 169–89.
BRUNER, J. C. *et al.* 1956, *A Study of Thinking*. London: Wiley.
CAVALCANTI, M. C. 1982, Using the unorthodox, unmeasurable verbal protocol technique: Qualitative data in foreign language reading research. In DINGWALL & MANN, 72–85.
— 1983, *The Pragmatics of FL Reader-Text Interaction: Key Lexical Items as Source of Potential Reading Problem*. Unpublished Ph.D. thesis, University of Lancaster.
CLARK, H. H. & CLARK, E. V. 1977, *Psychology and Language: An Introduction to Psycholinguistics*. New York: Harcourt Brace Jovanovich.
COHEN, A. D. 1981, Introspecting about second language learning. Paper prepared for presentation at the AILA Congress in Lund, Sweden, Aug. 9–15, 1981.
COHEN, A. D. & HOSENFELD, C. 1981, Some uses of mentalistic data in second language research. *Language Learning* 31:2, 285–313.
COHEN, A. D. *et al.* 1979, Reading English for specialized purposes: Discourse analysis and the use of student informants. *TESOL Quarterly* 13, 551–64.
COHEN, A. 1984, Studying second-language learning: How do we get the information? *Applied Linguistics* 5:2, 101–12.
COHEN, L. & MANION, L. 1980, *Research Methods in Education*. London: Croom Helm.
DINGWALL, S. & MANN, J. (eds) 1982, *Methods and Problems in Doing Applied Linguistic Research*. Lancaster: Department of Linguistics and Modern English Language, University of Lancaster.
ERICSSON, K. A. & SIMON, H. A. 1980, Verbal reports as data. *Psychological Review* 87:3, 215–51.
FLOYD, A. 1976, *Cognitive Styles*. Education studies: A second level course, personality and learning, Block 5. London: The Open University.
GARFINKEL, H. 1967, *Studies in Ethnomethodology*. Prentice-Hall.

GLAHN, E. 1980, Introspection as a method of elicitation in interlanguage studies. *Interlanguage Studies Bulletin Utrecht* 5:1, 119–28.

GOLINKOFF, R. R. 1975–6, A Comparison of reading comprehension processes in good and poor comprehenders. *Reading Research Quarterly* 11:4, 623–59.

GOODMAN, Y. & BURKE, C. 1970, *Reading Miscues Inventory*. New York: Macmillan.

GOODMAN, K. S. 1967, Reading: A psycholinguistic guessing game. *Journal of the Reading Specialist* 6, 126–35.

GOODMAN, K. S. & GOODMAN, Y. M. 1977, Learning about psycholinguistic processes by analysing oral reading. In L. J. CHAPMAN & P. CZERNIEWSKA (eds) 1978, *Reading: From Process to Practice*. Routledge & Kegan Paul in association with the Open University Press, 126–45.

HEIDER, F. 1958, *The Psychology of Interpersonal Relations*. Chichester: Wiley.

HOEY, M. 1979, *Signalling in Discourse* (= Discourse Analysis Monograph No. 6). Birmingham: English Language Research, University of Birmingham.

HOSENFELD, C. 1976, Learning about learning: Discovering our students' strategies. *Foreign Language Annals* 9, 117–29.

— 1977, A preliminary investigation of the reading strategies of successful and nonsuccessful second language learners. *System* 5: 2. 110–23.

— 1979, Cindy: A learner in today's foreign language classroom. In W. BORNE (ed.), *The Foreign Language Learner in Today's Classroom Environment*. Northeast Conference on the Teaching of Foreign Languages.

— 1984, Case studies of ninth grader readers. In J. C. ALDERSON & A. H. URQUHART (eds), *Reading in a Foreign Language*. London: Longman.

JUST, M. A. & CARPENTER, P. A. (eds) 1977, *Cognitive Processes in Comprehension*. Hillsdale, N.J.: Lawrence Erlbaum.

KAGAN, J. & HAVEMANN, E. 1972, *Psychology: An Introduction*. New York: Harcourt Brace Jovanovich.

KAVALE, K. & SCHREINER, R. L. 1979, The reading processes of above average and average readers: A comparison of the use of reasoning strategies in responding to standardized comprehension measure. *Reading Research Quarterly* 15:1, 102–28.

KINTSCH, W. & VAN DIJK, T. A. 1978, Toward a model of text comprehension and production. *Psychological Review* 85:5, 363–94.

LABOV, W. 1972, *Sociolinguistic Patterns*. Oxford: Basil Blackwell.

LINDSAY, P. H. & NORMAN, D. A. 1972, *Human Information Processing*. New York: Academic Press.

MANN, S. J. 1982, Verbal reports as data: A focus on retrospection. In DINGWALL & MANN, 87–104.

MARTON, F. & SÄLJO, R. 1976, On qualitative differences in learning: II. Outcome as function of the learner's conception of the task. *British Journal of Educational Psychology* 46:2, 115–27.

MILLER, G. A. 1956, The Magical Number 7, plus or minus two: Some limits in our capacity for processing information. In R. N. HABER (1968) (ed.), *Contemporary Theory and Research in Visual Perception*. New York: Holt, Rinehart and Winston.

MURPHY, G. & KOVACH, J. K. 1972, *Historical Introduction to Modern Psychology*. New York: Harcourt Brace Jovanovich.

NEWELL, A. & SIMON, H. A. 1972, *Human Problem Solving*. Englewood Cliffs, N.Y.: Prentice-Hall.

OLLER, JR., J. W. 1979, *Language Tests at School*. London: Longman.
OLSHAVSKY, J. E. 1976–7, Reading as problem solving: An investigation of strategies. *Reading Research Quarterly* 12, 654–74.
PUGH, A. K. 1978, *Silent Reading: An Introduction to its Study and Teaching*. London: Heinemann.
RADFORD, J. & BURTON, A. 1974, *Thinking: Its Nature and Development*. London: John Wiley & Sons.
RYLE, G. 1949, *The Concept of Mind*. London: Hutchinson.
SALMON, P. 1976, Doing psychological research. In F. FRANSELLA (ed.), *Personal Construct Psychology 1977*. New York: Academic Press.
SCHANK, R. C. & ABELSON, R. P. 1977, *Scripts, Plans, Goals and Understanding: An Inquiry into Human Knowledge Structures*. Hillsdale, N.J.: Lawrence Erlbaum.
SHIFFRIN, R. M. & SCHNEIDER, W. 1977, Controlled and automatic human information processing: II. Perceptual learning, automatic attending and a general theory. *Psychological Review* 84, 127–89.
SHIPMAN, M. 1981, *The Limitations of Social Research*. London: Longman.
SMITH, F. 1971, *Understanding Reading*. New York: Holt, Rinehart & Winston.
TAYLOR, W. L. 1953, Cloze procedure: A new tool for measuring readability. *Journalism Quarterly* 30, 415–33.
THOMAS, L. F. & HARRI-AUGSTEIN, E. S. 1972, An experimental approach to the study of reading as a learning skill. *Research in Education* 8, 28–46.
— 1979, Conversational investigations of reading: The self-organised learner and the text, Brunel University. MS.
THORNDIKE, E. L. 1917, Reading as reasoning: A study of mistakes in paragraph reading. *Journal of Educational Psychology* 8, 323–32.
WHALLEY, P. C. 1977, Aspects of purposive reading: The analysis of reading records. Paper presented to the Annual Conference of the British Psychological Society, Exeter.

Appendix

Protocol elicitation

(1) Pre-reading directions: Title study task
     Before you begin reading the passage, read the title only. What do you know about the subject? What do you think the text will be about?
(2) Reading directions
     1. You will be given the introduction to an article from a Political Science journal to be read silently. The reading purpose is a brief oral summary of the passage.
     2. The text should be read silently; however, this silent reading should be interrupted whenever you:
          2.1 detect a PAUSE[1](no matter how short) during your reading.
               2.1.1 Whenever your reading is interrupted because a *pause* is occurring/has occurred, you are asked to:
                    (a) locate the pause in the text, i.e. read aloud the word, expression or sentence that caused it;
                    (b) comment upon the reason for the pause, e.g. if it resulted

from something that called your attention or from any kind of problem encountered.

NOTE: If the pause demands solving a problem before reading is resumed, please try to *think aloud* while working towards a solution.

2.2 get to the end of each paragraph. (An arrow ← has been placed at the end of paragraphs as a reminder).

    2.2.1 When you finish reading each paragraph, you are asked to:

        (a) talk about what you will have just read, i.e. about the content of the paragraph;

        (b) comment upon what you will have been thinking about while reading the paragraph.

3. Continue reading the introduction to the article and talking about it until the end.

4. Try to read as if you were on your own. You will be interrupted only *once*.

5. The session will be tape-recorded.

(3) Interventionist procedure: please answer the following questions orally.

    (a) What are you thinking about?

    (b) Any thoughts in the back of your mind?

    (c) Are you repeating the content using own words (paraphrasing?)

    (d) Classifying the content?

    (e) Defining it?

    (f) Looking for an example?

    (g) Establishing associations?

    (h) Making comparisons?

    (i) Involved in any other kind of activity other than the ones listed above?

    (j) Any other comments?

(4) Post reading directions

    (a) (Summary) Please make a brief oral summary of the passage read.

    (b) (Key lexical item task) Suppose you had to summarize the passage again in two weeks' time. You are not allowed any time for taking notes. Instead you are asked to select three to five words (or expressions) from the passage to serve as memory activators for recall purposes. Which words (or expressions) would you choose?

    (c) Any comments?

---

[1] Pause. Moment when the reading activity is interrupted and you find yourself, for instance, *thinking* about a problem encountered, or about something that might have caught your attention.

13 Thin—— aloud a—— retrospective da—— in C-te—— taking: diffe—— languages – diff—— learners – sa—— approaches?

UTE FELDMANN AND BRIGITTE STEMMER

Methods of thinking aloud and retrospection have mainly been used to investigate the processes of translation of and communication in a foreign language. We have used this methodological approach in order to find out more about processes which take place in learners when working on a foreign language test. In studying the so-called C-test we have attempted to combine analytical–nomological methodology and exploratory–interpretative methodology (see Grotjahn, this volume, Chapter 3) to elucidate what the C-test really measures.

The C-test is based on the principle of reduced redundancy and on the construct of an internalized pragmatic expectancy grammar, and is conceived as an integrative measure of overall language competence in first, second and foreign languages (cf. Gaies, 1986; Klein-Braley & Raatz, 1984; Klein-Braley, 1985a, b). The current state of research on the C-test can be summarized as follows: the C-test is a very economical and, above all, a highly reliable measurement instrument. However, what it measures, i.e. its construct validity, is, in our opinion, thus far quite unclear. Since the C-test has already been used for practical purposes and since, because of the ease of construction, administration, and scoring, its use will probably increase in the near future, we think it imperative to find an answer to the question as to what it really measures.

A more detailed discussion of our methodological bases and our research design is given by Grotjahn in this volume. In this chapter we are mainly concerned with identifying and explaining processes which take place in German learners of French, and German learners of Spanish, when doing the C-test. A C-test consists of several short texts, each covering a different topic, in which the second part of every second word is deleted (for an example, see Appendix). We used the methods of thinking aloud and retrospective interview in our research design, which can be summed up as follows.

In an introductory phase, a subject (a German learner of French or Spanish) was introduced to the task individually. The subject was then left alone in the room to work through the C-test, having been asked to think aloud while doing the test. The subject's utterances were audio-taped. After this phase of the test, the interviewer and the subject listened to the audio-tape together. In this retrospective phase, the subject could spontaneously comment on his or her utterances and behaviour during the previous test phase and answer the interviewer's questions. The chapter is based on the transcribed and analysed protocols of 10 German learners of French and 10 German learners of Spanish.

Theoretical Assumptions

Human information processing made observable

How can processing, which takes place somewhere and somehow in our information processing system, be made observable, and what exactly is being processed? To answer the latter question first, a commonly accepted view is that of information being processed as certain patterns of knowledge which are stored in "chunks". As such mental patterns are not directly observable it may be possible to get at least some indication of their nature by observing their influence upon human behaviour (cf. Beaugrande, 1980). One way of doing this is by collecting and analysing thinking-aloud and retrospective data. As Ericsson & Simon (1984) point out, concurrent verbal reports and retrospective reports are direct verbalizations of specific cognitive processes. The concurrent report reveals the sequence of information heeded by the subject without essentially altering the cognitive process. Ericsson & Simon (1984) put forward a processing model which they apply to verbal reports. The core hypothesis assumes that "the information that is heeded during performance of a task, is the information that is reportable; and the information that is reported is information that is heeded" (ibid.: 167). In other words, only information in focal attention, and hence in short-term memory, can be verbalized and information which is verbalized is also in focal attention. Verbal reports are based on information currently held in short-term memory. In order to gain access to information in long-term memory, the information must first be brought into short-term memory and thus into focal attention. What part of the information in long-term memory finds its way into short-term memory is determined by the central processor which controls and regulates the non-automatic cognitive processes. In the case of automatic cognitive processing, intermediate steps occur which are not interpreted, and their associated input and output do not use short-term memory. Such intermediate steps do not enter short-term memory and are, therefore, unavailable for the production of verbal reports.

Identification of the retrieval cue

Two conditions must be met for information to be retrieved. Firstly, the processing system must be in a specific "retrieval mode" and, although little is known about this, we can assume that in our case the system is "on call". The second condition is that an appropriate retrieval cue must be present, and we assume that this is so. The problem is how do we identify the retrieval cue? There are cueing stimuli which cannot be inferred from the C-test text and consequently are not available for direct observation. Aside from such "invisible" cues the most obvious cueing stimulus in our C-test texts would appear to be the beginning of the incomplete item. However, the co-text and context of these items will certainly also serve as cueing stimuli. Which retrieval cues were actually effective in accessing memory structures we can only try to infer from the information gained by thinking-aloud and retrospective reports.

Processing and processing problems

The task our learner is confronted with provides the primary observable input on the basis of which further unobservable processing will take place. The processing capabilities of our learner's system might be limited in that the input data cannot be mapped on to the memory structure. Norman & Bobrow (1975) call this data-limited processing and distinguish two types of data-limits: signal data-limits and memory data-limits. Signal data-limits occur when the quality of the input confuses the mapping process. This might happen when there is some kind of noise that disturbs comprehension, as, for example, during telephone calls or when poor handwriting makes reading difficult. We have a similar situation in our C-test texts where the signal data-limit corresponds to the incomplete items. With memory data-limits the mapping process is obstructed for lack of appropriate memory structures, as, for example, if we try to understand Japanese but do not know any Japanese. Referring to C-test texts, a similar situation occurs when the learner is confronted with unknown or forgotten elements of the foreign language. In addition to data-limited processing we also have resource-limited processing where, according to Adams & Collins (1979: 6), "various, simultaneous demands for active control may exceed the system's capacity to cope". With respect to reading, a problem could arise when a good reader reads very specialized texts he or she is not familiar with, such as a legal document. In trying to understand the text, the reader tries to accomplish two things at the same time: to grasp the meaning of the whole text, while at the same time trying to comprehend the unfamiliar words or sentences. He or she might end up not understanding the meaning of the whole paragraph. Two simultaneously competing activities can be managed as long as there are no problems. But as soon as a problem arises, the amount of attention paid to it is at the expense of the other activity. Similarly, we can regard the C-test text as a very specialized kind of text. In focusing on the completion of a particular item, what the reader has so far grasped of the meaning of the text or the referent of the item might be completely out of the focus of attention. The particular item might not even be thought of as belonging to the text. Such a situation occurred when a learner simply tried to complete an item by adding letters or syllables without paying any attention to the context. Furthermore, having to talk aloud at the same time could be an additional burden.

Processing begins as soon as the learner starts reading the introductory part of the C-test text. This part does not contain any incomplete items. As a matter of simplification let us assume here that the learner also tries to comprehend this part. The learner then goes on to the mutilated text. The input is mapped against some existing patterns of knowledge which we will refer to globally as schemata. We will not distinguish here between schemata and frames but subsume both under the notion of schemata (cf. Anderson, 1981; Beaugrande, 1980; Minsky, 1975; Schank & Abelson, 1977; Winograd, 1975). As to the incoming information, the learner may identify small units such as phonological segments which are then gradually added together to larger units (e.g. words, sentence constituents, etc.) This type of processing is called bottom-up processing. Another possibility would be to take, as a starting point, higher level units (e.g. word knowledge which is activated by analysing a text) and work the way downwards. This is called top-down processing. A skilled reader will activate both top-down and bottom-up processing simultaneously. Adams & Collins (1979: 5) point out that "bottom-up processing ensures that the reader will be sensitive to information that is novel or that does not fit her or his ongoing hypotheses about the content of the text; top-down processing helps the reader to resolve ambiguities or to select between alternative possible interpretations of the incoming data". With reference to the C-test, it might be interesting to investigate whether or not the learners give preference to any of the two processing directions. And if they do, then when. We will return to this point later.

The incoming information which initiates processing is the C-test text, and like any other text it contains certain elements of information which could be omitted without disrupting the comprehensibility of the text. Such additional elements of information, which function as safeguards that ensure that the message is understood, are described as being redundant (e.g. Spolsky, 1973; Klein-Braley, 1985a, b; Raatz, 1985). As a C-test consists of many deletions, it is obvious that the deleted elements include some which are more, and some which are less, redundant. For example, in the sentence, "Les pet____ films public____ les intér____ parce qu'____ voit u____ maman ..." the plural ending of petits, publicitaires, intéressent as well as the e of the indefinite article "une" are redundant. Closely linked to the concept of redundancy is Oller's (1976) pragmatic expectancy grammar. Comprehension of input leads us to form certain expectations about what will come next, be it the next letter, the next word or the next sentence. Subsequent input may either confirm or refute such expectations. The native speaker of a language will be able to substitute a missing element much more easily than a non-native speaker. Contrary to the learner, the native speaker is able to make full use of the natural redundancy of a text and of pragmatic expectancy grammar. The learners face several problems. They are confronted with a defective text and on top of that they might have difficulty comprehending the non-defective input. This in turn could lead to difficulty in formulating expectations about what might follow and, thus, to failure in completing an item. The more competent learners are in the foreign language, the more they will be able to make use of the natural redundancy of the text. It would appear, therefore, that the more clues the learners are able to pick up, because of the natural redundancy of a text, and the more they are able to make use of their pragmatic expectancy grammar, the more developed is their foreign language competence and the better they will accomplish the task.

Analysis

General problem-solving behaviour

In order to elucidate the demands posed on the learners by the C-test and the way they cope with them, we investigated the verbal protocols. All 20 learners of French and Spanish started by reading the introductory part of the first text, i.e. the part which is still complete. They then did a number of different things: some continued directly to the first item, others re-read, translated or summarized the introductory part before going on to the first item. There are several reasons for these differences:

(a) in the former case, the learners either did not face any problems or simply ignored them. These possibilities seem rather unlikely, however, as most learners thought it important to understand the introductory part;

(b) in the latter case, where the learners re-read, summarized or translated the introductory text, there are again two possible explanations. Firstly, although the learners did not have any problems with the text, they wanted to make perfectly sure that they understood the first part; they "just wanted confirmation", to use their own words. Secondly, it is possible that — faced with problems — the learners activated various kinds of problem-solving strategies.

The importance most learners attached to the understanding of the introductory part is quite understandable, considering that it is from this non-defective part of the text that they hope to grasp the underlying schema and thus increase the redundancy of the following mutilated text at the semantic level, and to get some hints of what follows, in the sense of a "pragmatic expectancy grammar", as mentioned above.

As soon as the learner reads the first item, he or she begins to recover items. In principle, the learner could first skim through the whole text before returning to the first item and working sequentially through the text. From our 20 subjects, only two chose this procedure but gave up rather quickly, noticing that "it is impossible to skim through the whole text as there are only gaps". A similar observation is reported in Cohen, Segal & Weiss (1985), where subjects were told to read through the whole passage before attempting to fill in any blanks. The subjects reported that because of the close proximity of the blanks it was difficult to do this. The remaining 18 of our subjects worked on the items sequentially, i.e. they worked on one item and then moved on to the next. If the items in a sentence proved particularly difficult, the subject sometimes re-read the sentence over and over again before moving on to the next sentence.

Figure 1 gives a summary of the problem-solving behaviour as followed by our first 20 subjects:

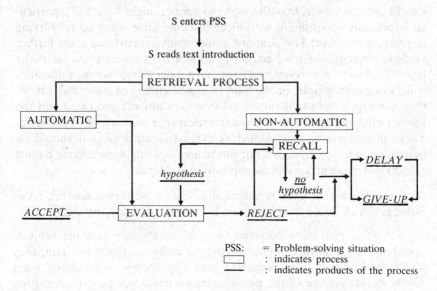

FIGURE 1. *A tentative model of the problem-solving process in C-test taking (taken from Stemmer (in preparation))*

There are basically two ways for the incomplete item to be recovered: by automatic retrieval or by non-automatic retrieval. In the first case the item was produced very quickly without "thinking" about it, so to speak. During thinking aloud, this item was produced without hesitation and the subject did not show any signs of reflecting on the item. In our data we deliberately set a time span of 2 seconds or less for an item to be categorized as being retrieved automatically. Although this might seem a rather long pause, considering the slow talking behaviour of our subjects while thinking aloud, we felt that an item being retrieved within this time span could still be categorized as being retrieved automatically. The subject usually did not give any comment on the item in the interview, and when asked to do so the typical response was "I don't know" or "that was spontaneous". In the case of non-automatic retrieval the subject used a recall strategy which could lead to an item being recovered or not. In the latter case, the learner either activated another recall strategy, gave up on the item, or delayed it until later. If the learner recovered an item, he or she could use an evaluation strategy so as to check on the appropriateness of the item. This procedure could also take place when the item was retrieved automatically. Evaluation of an item led to its acceptance or rejection. Acceptance usually resulted in completion of the item. One should note, however, that although the learner might have had a particular hypothesis about the item, difficulties could arise when actually trying to produce the item. This situation could result in activating some further kinds of strategy which we could call application strategies. As far as the first 20 subjects are concerned, we have only come across difficulties concerning orthography or the morphological ending of a particular item. One can argue here that the actual item was already produced and the learner merely checked on the outer appearance or concord of the item. These procedures were classified as evaluation strategies. It should be borne in mind, however, that our future analyses might necessitate a third category of strategies, such as application strategies.

In the case of item rejection, the learner activated another recall strategy which could lead to a new hypothesis, a delay, or a give-up.

A third possibility occurred twice in situations where the subjects could not make up their minds whether to accept or reject the item; they vacillated between two competing item hypotheses. What made them finally decide on one of the two hypotheses could not be extracted from the thinking-aloud protocol. In the retrospective interview both learners explained their decision as "intuition".

Specific problem-solving behaviour: Strategies

Having described the learners' more general approach to the problem-solving situation, we will now look more closely at the ways in which they tried to restore particular items.

An approach on the basis of strategies, as has been successfully used in interlanguage research, seemed promising. This field of research has been concerned mainly with the investigation of strategies used by the learner in language production (e.g. in interaction) and language reception (e.g. in reading a text). (Cf., for example, Cohen, 1984; Cohen & Hosenfeld, 1981; Cziko, 1980; Færch, 1984; Færch & Kasper, 1983; Haastrup, 1985; Kasper, 1984; Krings, 1986; Poulisse, Bongaerts & Kellerman, 1984; Ulijn, 1981). Like Færch & Kasper (1980: 60) we regard a strategy as "a potentially conscious plan for solving what, to the individual, presents itself as a problem in reaching a particular goal". Strategies should be regarded as dynamic rather than static plans, i.e. one strategy may interact with another. Research in the use of C-test strategies is restricted to work by Cohen, Segal & Weiss (1985) and our own work. Cohen, Segal & Weiss found the C-test to encourage micro-level processing and there being no clear pattern with respect to macro-level processing.

Before we discuss the list of strategies identified in the protocols of the learners when working on the first C-test text (see Appendix), some words of caution are necessary. Although we have listed all the strategies so far identified in these protocols, the list is, of course, an open one and will be extended and modified as necessary. In addition the list does not give the frequency with which the strategies occurred. Due to the small number of protocols so far investigated, no generalizations can be made. The same holds true for a comparison between the French and the Spanish data.

LIST OF STRATEGIES[1]
(taken from Stemmer (in preparation))

RECALL STRATEGIES

Recall strategies are employed in cases where the retrieval of an item is non-automatic. They are used as a strategic device in order to recover the looked-for item.

(1) Recall by structural analysis
    (a) Syntax analysis
        e.g.F.[2]   (subject is looking for item "que" in "je pense q____ "):
            S: je pense again a relative pronoun starts with qˆ ˆ ˆ
    (b) Formal indicators (apostrophe, comma)
        e.g.F. (subject is looking for item "on" in "parce qu'____ voit"):
            S: ˆles intéressent ˆ ˆ parce ˆ ˆ ˆ ˆ ˆ ˆ parce ˆ ˆ qu'il ˆ ˆ no parce ...
            Later in the interview:
            S: at this point I think I was thinking that this word must start with a vowel because of the apostrophe ˆ
(2) Recall by adding letters/syllables to item beginning
        e.g.S. (subject is looking for item "fastidia" in "el aire les fast____ "):
            S: el aire les fast ˆ ˆ fasto not fasta ˆ hmˆ I really don't know
        e.g.S. (subject is looking for item "contar" in "el recurso clásico es con____ un cuento"):
            S: el recurso clá clá ˆ I really don't know es conˆ con con con conocido consiguiente con ˆ con doesn't fit ...
(3) Recall by repetition
    (a) of given item letters
        e.g.S. (subject is looking for item "mucho"):
            S: todo el tiempo preguntan su falta mu muˆ mu mu I don' know
            ...

e.g.F. (subject is looking for item "retrouvent"):
    S: qu'elles retro ˆ ˆ ˆ that they retro ˆ retro ˆ
(b) of preceding/following word/s, sentences
    e.g.F. (subject is looking for "publicitaires" in "les petits films public___"):
        S: ˆ les pet films public ˆ les petits films public ˆ ˆ ation (?) yes les petits films publica
(c) of text (including re-reading of text)
(4) Recall of past situation
    e.g.F. (subject is looking for item "vaisselle"):
               Interview:
        S: that's an item which ˆ which I've seen in the teaching book once it's funny but I remember this situation very well and the item was described there
(5) Recall by search for meaning
    (a) translation to mother tongue
        – translation of directly following word/s
        – translation of directly preceding word/s
        – translation of prefix
        – translation of (further) co-text, preceding/following sentence (including introductory and final sentence of text)
        e.g.F. (subject is looking for item "parce" in "c'est pa___ qu'elles"):
           S: ehmˆ pa what's that pa ˆ no I don't know that one ˆ I think that ˆ this ˆ ˆ ehm partir no ˆ ˆ
        e.g.F. (subject is looking for item "retrouvent"):
           S: ... qu'elles retro ˆ ˆ ˆ that they retro ˆ retro ˆ back or something like that ehm ...
    (b) looking for mother tongue meaning equivalent or using (hypothesized) mother tongue meaning equivalent
        e.g.F. (subject is looking for item "retrouvent"):
           S: retro that doesn't get me anywhere at the moment ehm something like call back or remember or anything like that but I don't know the word ...
        e.g.S. (subject is looking for "fastidia"):
           S: ... el aire les fast ˆ that means get tired ˆ what's that in Spanish ˆ
        e.g.S. (subject is looking for item "permanecer"):
           S: ... y deben permˆ ˆ perma ˆ perma ˆ y deben ˆ per ˆ ˆ ma ˆ stay ˆ stay ˆ I would say in German but I can't think of the Spanish equivalent ...
    (c) looking for general meaning of text
        e.g.F. (subject is looking for item "parce que"):
           S: that must be something ˆ ˆ ˆ which gets the girl to do that ˆ ˆ ˆ
(6) Recall by looking for external help
    (previous test example, other C-test texts or introductory/final part of text)
    e.g.F. (subject is looking for "quotidienne" which was mentioned before in the test example):
        S: scènes de ˆ l quoti ˆ dienne
Later in the interview:
        S: I knew that from the earlier text
    e.g.S. (subject is looking for item "cantar"):

S: o hacerles can ˆ can ˆ hm ˆ let's read the last sentence I might find something there ...
(7) Recall by substitution
(subject substitutes the incomplete item by, for example, a filler)
    e.g.F. (subject is looking for "dirais" in "je dir____ " and uses "something" as a filler)
        S: je di dir something ... (continues reading)
(8) ???
(no strategy identifiable)

EVALUATION STRATEGIES

Evaluation strategies are used in order to check on the appropriateness and "correctness" of a retrieved item.
(1) Check on meaning of item
    (a)   translation of item into mother tongue
        e.g.S. (subject translates "se mueren de calor" into mother tongue):
            S: ... si están querradas ˆ ˆ ˆ s-s-e mueren de calor they die with h ˆ yes se mueren (writes 'se') de calor (writes 'de') ...
    (b)   translation of co-text +/−item
        e.g.F. (subject translates "des scènes de leur vie"):
            S: qu'elles retro des scè des scènes de leurs vie in the sense of scenes of their life
    (c)   comparing concurrent items
        e.g.F. (subject is looking for "que"):
            S: je dirait même que or même quand perhaps ˆ but ˆ ˆ ˆ ˆ that doesn't make more ˆ ˆ sense ˆ yes it doesn't look as if it gives much more meaning to the sentence ...
    (d)   incorporating meaning of co-text
        e.g.F.
            S: je pense que c'est parce qu'elles oh I see I think it is because parce ˆ
        Later in the interview:
            S: that came to my mind cause I noticed that this whole sentence refers to the preceding text somehow I think it is because ...
(2) Check on form of item
    (a)   structural analysis of item and/or co-text
        (also including adjustments to similar items in text)
        e.g.F (subject is checking on ending of "retrouvent"):
            S: ... pour elles ˆ ˆ représentent has to be plural ... or is représent la vie quotidienne ˆ ˆ no has got to be the scènes
        e.g.S. (subject is checking on "bajas"):
            S: ... las ventanas ˆ están ˆ ˆ ˆ oh I see below ˆ baj ˆ las ventanas están bajas ˆ exactly it depends on the nomen bajas ...
    (b)   translation of item into mother tongue
        e.g.S. (subject translates "estar en movimiento"):
            S: ... quisieran estar ˆ estar (writes) ˆ I'll write that down right away en mom mom movim-iento (writes) that is moving
    (c)   check by "sound" of item/s
        – repeated item articulation

     – repeated concurrent item articulation
     e.g.F. (subject checks on ending of "retrouvent"):
         S: ... for them^ représentent représent repré représentant tent tant
            tent représent quelque chose
  (d) recall of past situation
     e.g.F. (subject checks on item "publicaux"):
         S: ...^^ publical or something like that ^ no publicaux ^ ...
         Later in the interview:
         S: mmh er it was still in my mind from the French lessons that
            somehow it had to be publicaux
  (e) construction of example
     e.g.F. (subject checks on ending of "leur"):
         S: ... des scènes de leur de leur with s ^ de leurs vie yes with no
            ^^ I don't know^^ leur of their life their no without s leur vie ...
         Later in the interview:
         S: ... I was thinking of an example ... and then I thought it was
            without an s
(3) Other evaluation strategies which cannot (clearly) be assigned to (1) or (2) or
are a mixture of (1) and (2)
  (a) re-read of whole text or part of text
     (self-explanatory)
  (b) check by "sound" of item/s
     – repeated item articulation
     – repeated concurrent item articulation
     – reading item in co-text
     e.g.S. (subject is checking on item "llegar"):
         S: ... para lle ^ in order to arrive lle what does it mean llevar or
            llegar ^ llegar llegar ^ llegar ^ llevar ^ que lleve ^ well one is carry
            and the other is arrive ey ^ I'll never learn that ^ llegar ^ llegar
            llegar ^ no llevar ^ what was that again llegar ^ llegar ^ llegar
            (writes llegar)
  (c) check via other languages
     e.g.F. (subject is checking on "scènes"):
         S: ... ehm des scènes des des si:n^ yes I'd say des scènes ...
  (d) check via "look of written representation"
     e.g.F. (subject is checking on "publiques"):
         S: ^^ publiques well q e s (spells) let's see if that looks more familiar
            now
(4) ???
(no strategy identifiable)

    The question-marks in our list refer to those instances where we
were not able to discern the learner's strategy: the thinking-aloud protocols
usually showed long pauses finally resulting in the learner producing an
item or not. The retrospective protocols either did not reveal any comments on such instances or the subject was unable to give any explanation
of what was going on. An obvious interpretation would be that the subject

did not verbalize his or her thoughts and later forgot about them. Another possibility is that problem-solving simply did not take place in a verbal form and consequently, there was nothing to be verbalized. In short, some problem-solving behaviour took place but we could not get at it. And another rather human trait should also be considered: the subject might simply have been "dreaming".

Some strategies seem more likely to reflect bottom-up processing than others, whereas some seem to be intermediate between top-down and bottom-up processing. We have tried to summarize this situation in Figure 2.

Bottom-up and top-down processing is represented as a continuum on which the different strategic approaches are projected. The strategies have no fixed place on this continuum but might move to the left or right, depending on what the learner does. The kind of processing which is activated might also be related to the characteristics of the retrieval cue. It might be possible that the nature of the "invisible" retrieval cues can be inferred from the retrospective and thinking-aloud protocols, and in particular from the strategies which we have identified. For instance, when searching for an item by structurally analysing the sentence, not only the beginning of the item, but also the word schemata in the sentence can serve as a retrieval cue. Similarly, when re-reading parts of the text over and over again, retrieval seems to involve sentence or text schemata and not simply the beginning of the item. However, before drawing any conclusions, more data must be analysed and looked at from this point of view.

(1) Structural analysis	(3b) Repetition of words/ sentences	(3c) Repetition of part of text/ whole text	(4) Recall of past situation
(2) Adding of letters/ syllables	(5a) Translation to mother tongue		(5c) Looking for general meaning of tex
(3a) Repetition of item letters	(5b) Mother-tongue meaning equivalent		
	(6) External help		
	(7) Substitution		

Bottom-up processing ⟵⟶ Top-down processing

FIGURE 2. *Bottom-up and top-down processing represented as a continuum on which different strategic approaches are represented (taken from Stemmer (in preparation))*

Limits

The approach outlined above is one possible way of explaining problem-solving behaviour and (foreign) language processing, but it has its limits. For example, strategies cannot be localized unambiguously along the top-down — bottom-up continuum. Though the subject might try to retrieve an item by simply adding letters to the item under attention, the item itself is part of a meaningful sentence and text, i.e. co-text and context affect word recognition. One must also take into account the number of items the learner has solved prior to solving any particular item. The higher the number of items already solved, the more co-text and context the learners have at their disposal and the higher will be redundancy. This in turn might make item retrieval easier.

Some remarks should also be made about the French and the Spanish data. Due to the low number of protocols so far examined, we cannot draw any final conclusions. Nevertheless, we would like to put forward some speculations based on our observation that the learners of French and Spanish essentially used the same strategic approaches. There could be several reasons for this:

1. the strategic approaches may be similar because the languages are genetically and structurally closely related and therefore pose problems of a similar character;
2. the strategies so far identified are of such general character that any differences that may exist simply do not show up;
3. all the learners of French and Spanish knew English and at least one other language, which was another Romance language in more than half of the cases. Surprisingly however, no interlingual inferencing took place (except in two cases). This might simply have been due to the fact that very few of the items in the analysed text seemed suitable for interlingual inferencing.
4. and last, but not least, the number of protocols analysed could simply be too small to show any differences.

Outlook

In our investigation we have tried to obtain information about how mental knowledge patterns are activated in a problem-solving situation by describing specific problem-solving behaviour on the basis of strategies. It was, indeed, possible to distinguish different problem-solving strategies

and these were projected on a bottom-up and top-down processing continuum. Exactly how often a particular strategy was used, with which item
this strategy occurred, and whether or not this strategy led to finding a
correct item, are currently being analysed. We think that the
exploratory–interpretative approach described in this chapter, which aims
at the uncovering of strategies, in combination with analytical–nomological
procedures (cf. Grotjahn, in this volume, Chapter 3), will hopefully lead
to a more thorough understanding of what the C-test really measures.

Notes to Chapter 13

1. It should be noted that the German utterances of the subjects are translated into English.
   All "mistakes" made by the subjects in German as well as in French and Spanish were
   transcribed without correction.
   ˆ indicates a pause
   ˆ ˆ indicate a longer pause etc.
2. In the above examples e.g.F. refers to an example taken from the French data, e.g.S.
   refers to an example taken from the Spanish data. The C-test texts which the examples
   refer to can be found in the Appendix.

References

Arbeitskreis der Sprachzentren, Sprachlehrinstitute und Fremdsracheninstitute
    (AKS) (ed.) 1985, *Fremdsprachen und Hochschule (FuH)*, AKS-Rundbrief
    13/14. (Ruhr-Universität) Bochum:AKS.
ADAMS, M. J. & COLLINS, A. 1979, A schema-theoretic view of reading. In R.
    O. FREEDLE (ed.), *New Directions in Discourse Processing*. Norwood, N.J.:
    Ablex, 1–22.
ANDERSON, J. R. (ed.) 1981, *Cognitive Skills and Their Acquisition*. Hillsdale,
    N.J.: Erlbaum.
BEAUGRANDE, R. DE 1980, *Text, Discourse, and Process*. London: Longman.
COHEN, A. & HOSENFELD, C. 1981, Some uses of mentalistic data in second
    language research. *Language Learning* 31, 285–313.
COHEN, A., SEGAL, M. & WEISS, R. 1985, The C-test in Hebrew. *Fremdsprachen
    und Hochschulen*. AKS-Rundbrief 13/14, 121–27.
CZIKO, G. A. 1980, Language competence and reading strategies: A comparison
    of first and second language oral reading errors. *Language Learning* 30,
    101–6.
ERICSSON, K. A. & SIMON, H. A. 1984, *Protocol Analysis. Verbal Reports as Data*.
    Cambridge, London: MIT Press.
FÆRCH, C. 1984, Strategies in production and reception — some empirical evidence.
    In A. DAVIES, C. CRIPER & A. HOWATT (eds), *Interlanguage*. Edinburgh: Univer-
    sity Press. 49–70.
FÆRCH, C. & KASPER, G. 1980, Processes and strategies in foreign language learning
    and communication. *Interlanguage Studies Bulletin* 5, 47–118.
— (eds) 1983, *Strategies in Interlanguage Communication*. London, New York: Long-
    man.

GAIES, S. J. 1986, Validation of the noise test. In R. GROTJAHN, C. KLEIN-BRALEY & D. K. STEVENSON (eds), *Taking Their Measure: The Validity and Validation of Language Tests* (= Quantitative Linguistics 30). Bochum: Brockmeyer.

HAASTRUP, K. 1985, Lexical inferencing — a study of procedures in reception. *Scandinavian Working Papers on Bilingualism*. 63–86.

KASPER, G. 1984, Pragmatic comprehension in learner — native speaker discourse. *Language Learning* 34, 1–20.

KLEIN-BRALEY, C. 1985a, Reduced redundancy as an approach to language testing. *Fremdsprachen und Hochschule*, AKS-Rundbrief 13/14, 1–13.

— 1985b, C-tests and construct validity, *Fremdsprachen und Hochschule*, AKS-Rundbrief 13/14, 55–65.

KLEIN-BRALEY, C. & RAATZ, U. 1984, A survey of research on the C-test. *Language Testing* 1, 134–46.

KRINGS, H. 1986, Translation problems and translation strategies of advanced German learners of French (L2). In J. HOUSE & S. BLUM-KULKA (eds), *Interlingual and Intercultural Communication: Discourse and Cognition in Translation and Second Language Acquisition Studies*. Tübingen: Narr. 263–76.

MINSKY, M. 1975, A framework for representing knowledge. In P. WINSTON (ed.), *The Psychology of Computer Vision*. New York: McGraw-Hill.

NORMAN, D. H. & BOBROW, D. G. 1975, On data-limited and resource-limited processes. *Cognitive Psychology*, 7, 44–64.

OLLER, J. W. 1976, Evidence for a general language proficiency factor: An expectancy grammar. *Die Neueren Sprachen*, 165–74.

POULISSE, N., BONGAERTS, T. & KELLERMAN, E. 1984, On the use of compensatory strategies in second language performance. *Interlanguage Studies Bulletin* 8:1, 70–105.

RAATZ, U. 1985, Tests of reduced redundancy — the C-test, a practical example. *Fremdsprachen und Hochschule*. AKS-Rundbrief 13/14, 14–19.

SCHANK, R. & ABELSON, R. 1977, *Scripts, Plans, Goals and Understanding*. Hillsdale, N.J.: Erlbaum.

SPOLSKY, B. 1973, What does it mean to know a language: or how do you get someone to perform his competence? In J. W. OLLER JR. & J. C. RICHARDS (eds), *Focus on the Learner*. Rowley, Mass.: Newbury House, 164–76.

STEMMER, B. in preparation, *Processes in C-test-Taking*.

ULIJN, J. 1981, Conceptual and syntactic strategies in reading a foreign language. In E. HOPKINS & R. GROTJAHN (eds), *Studies in Language Teaching and Language Acquisition* (= Quantitative Linguistics Vol. 9). Bochum: Brockmeyer.

WINOGRAD, T. 1975, Frame representation and the declarative-procedural controversy. In D. BOBROW & A. COLLINS (eds), *Representation and Understanding: Studies in Cognitive Science*. New York: Academic Press, 185–210.

Appendix

Example of a French C-Test

"Mes filles aiment beaucoup la publicité télévisée. Elles sont très jeunes et c'est vraiment ce qu'elles préfèrent. Je dir____ même q____ cela 1____ passionne. J____ pense q____ c'est pa____ qu'elles retro____ des scè____ de 1____ vie quoti____ qui, po____ elles, représ____ quelque ch____. Les pet____ films public____ les intér____ parce qu'____ voit u____ maman fa____ sa vais____ ou pas____ son aspir____, une famille àtable, un enfant manger son fromage ou sa crème glacée."

Example of a Spanish C-Test

"Generalmente, un largo viaje en automóvil es un problema para los ninos. Ellos quisieran correr por el campo y tienen que estar sentados. Quisieran es____ en movim____ y deben perma____ inmóviles. S____ las venta____ están ba____, el ai____ les fast____. Si es____ cerradas, s____ mueren d____ calor. To____ el tie____ preguntan s____ falta mu____ para lle____ o piden baj____ para term____ con alg____ urgencia. E____ recurso clá____ es con____ un cue____ o hacerles can____ unas canc____ muy conocidas. Del cuento, que suele ser también archisabido, se aburren en seguida. Con las canciones pueden amenazar los oídos de los demás viajeros e inquietar al conductor, con serias consecuencias."

14 Two Successful Language Learners: An Introspective Approach[1]

BARBARA GILLETTE

Introduction

The study of successful language learners is not a novel idea today, and learner-oriented research has undergone great changes in outlook over the past two decades. In the 1960s, when a rationalist view of language began to displace behaviourist approaches to language teaching, learners became an important field of inquiry.

Initially, cognitive variables and more specifically language aptitude, as measured by Carroll (1981: 105), stood at the centre of investigation. Success in language learning was believed to be closely related to success in other subject areas, the best overall students constituting the most successful language learners. In 1972, the publication of *Attitudes and Motivation in Second-Language Learning* by Gardner & Lambert shifted the emphasis towards research in affective variables, which were found to be potent predictors of communicative skills in a second language.

Both aptitude- and attitude-oriented research seek to shed light on the same elusive question. Why do some learners achieve fluency in a second language, seemingly without effort, while others, under the same circumstances, struggle desperately to fulfil basic language requirements? Is the difference rooted in attitude, aptitude, or both?

Aptitude as a part of general intelligence has been shown to predict achievement in classrooms emphasizing conscious learning, while attitudinal factors are clearly related to successful language acquisition (Krashen, 1981: 19). The increasing preference for acquisition-based communicative methods such as Strategic Interaction and Silent Way in the 1980s is likely to generate still more interest in learners' attitudes and might eventually make aptitude testing obsolete. Nevertheless, the great variation found among language learners can hardly be explained by a single factor, however relevant it may be.

A New Trend in Learner-Oriented L2 Research

Learner studies as undertaken by Lambert & Gardner involve a massive body of data elicited by standard questionnaires. Statistical methods used to analyse them yield general traits only. Although subsequent researchers, such as Stern (1975) and Reiss (1985), explicitly focus on "the learner", they seem to implicitly mean "the learners". Much of even the most recent literature on language learners is quantitative in nature, and based on the assumption that language learners are a fairly homogeneous group displaying typical behaviour traits which can be measured and analysed.

Language is, however, a human activity which, as such, has rarely proved to be easily quantified. This limitation has inspired a new trend in the investigation of learning strategies — the use of introspective data. Self-observation is the research tool used in such journal studies as Kathleen Bailey's (1980) account of her own learning of French. Wilga Rivers (1983) describes in a daily diary how she, a life-long L2 pedagogue, learned a sixth language. Moreover, "thinking-aloud" techniques have yielded interesting information on students' actual behaviour during a number of specific language-learning tasks (Cohen & Hosenfeld, 1981). Finally, the unstructured interview has been found to be highly productive in eliciting valuable information on the language-learning process, not otherwise obtainable (see Hosenfeld, 1976 for a detailed description of this procedure, Cohen 1984, for a concise discussion of various types of verbal report data and their role in L2 research, and Ericsson & Simon, 1984 on the empirical validity of verbal protocols in general).

The use of introspective data in second language research leaves many a question unanswered if we seek measurable certainty. Introspection does, however, reveal aspects of language learning previously inaccessible to investigation. Moreover, such qualitative research is invaluable if our goal is to consider the individual learner as a whole person, not just a hypothetical entity in an anonymous language-learning process.

The Learners

Any choice of certain language learners over others for a study such as this requires a clear concept of what a good language learner is. For Stern (1975: 305), it is someone who approaches native proficiency, a goal unrealistic, to say the least, for most foreign language students. Such a high standard does, however, provide a useful assumption. Native speakers have intuitive knowledge of grammar and focus on meaning rather than form when they communicate. As this study will illustrate, this orientation is, indeed, characteristic of good language learners.

A second, and possibly less justifiable, criterion for choosing subjects has been teacher evaluation in the form of grades given. Often used in a discrete-point approach to language teaching, such a norm means nothing more than that the learner is highly controllable by his school environment and has conscientiously fulfilled all his obligations as a student.

R. and M. are no such obedient "straight A students" and they do not equal native speakers in any aspect of their competence. They do, however, communicate successfully at the intermediate level. More importantly, they themselves rate their French training as successful and satisfying. Both R. and M. also enrolled in an introductory Spanish course which is neither part of their language requirement (two to four semesters of obligatory language study stipulated by many American universities), nor closely related to their major fields of study, Political Science/English Journalism and Psychology, respectively. Both students have a personal, highly successful approach to language study which encouraged them to tackle another language on their own initiative. It is this satisfaction and confidence, as well as their above-average achievement, which makes R. and M. successful language learners.

Elicitation Format

R. and M. are well known to this author, in and out of class, thus informal discussions preceded and accompanied the investigation, sometimes helping to determine its course. Extensive classroom observation was possible in French, while information on progress in Spanish was made available by helpful colleagues and, of course, the learners. Classroom notes in both languages were used for analysis, but were provided only by R. — M.'s classroom strategies did not include taking notes.

An adapted version of Lambert & Gardner's standard questionnaire on attitude and motivation was completed by both students in October, 1984. Finally, a tape-recorded interview was given in the researcher's office at the University of Delaware. The interviews, lasting approximately two hours, were "unstructured", in the sense that students' answers determined their course, and questions were worded so as to minimize the possibility of accidentally forcing the learner's statement into a particular direction (Hosenfeld, 1976: 120). The information obtained through these procedures was compiled, analysed, and mapped against descriptions of good language learners currently available in L2 research literature.

Findings

(1) Motivation

Lambert & Gardner claim that successful language learners have to be psychologically prepared to adopt various aspects of behaviour which characterize members of another linguistic-cultural group (1972: 3). Such an orientation is defined as "integrative motivation", which, in their theory of second language learning, is opposed to "instrumental motivation", a utilitarian approach to language learning predicted to produce inferior results in L2 achievement.

More recently, the integrative/instrumental dichotomy has been viewed rather as a continuum. Genesee *et al.* stress that for social situations where L2 is learned as a foreign instead of a second language, the importance of integrative motivation may have been over-estimated (1983: 210). Rubin & Thompson report that pure pragmatism can be an excellent motivation for second language achievement, concluding that "some people are remarkably successful in mastering a language without feeling powerfully drawn to the country or the people who speak it" (1982: 6).

The findings of this study clearly support the position taken by Rubin & Thompson. Neither M. nor R. seeks psychological integration into the target language group. On the motivation questionnaire, both students gave the lowest rating to "I am studying French because I think it will help me better understand French people and their way of life" and the strongest endorsement for "I think it will some day be useful in getting a good job" (R.) and, even more instrumental, "I need it in order to finish college" (M.).

R. often stresses the importance of gaining a second perspective of the world: "I think knowing just one language is ethnocentric and very limiting". (Hereafter double quotes will be used for original student comments, single quotes for statements in the questionnaire.) His orientation, although clearly instrumental (R. wants to become a foreign correspondent), is closer to integrative on the continuum than M.'s, whose only contact with French speakers left him with the impression "snotty". Compare R.'s statement: "French has always been ... the intellectual language ... so much thought ... is French-based". Motivational intensity as measured by the questionnaire is, indeed, significantly higher for R. Both learners, however, claim they would 'learn French somewhere else if it were not taught at this school'. While M. would 'pick it up in everyday situations', R. would 'try to obtain lessons in French somewhere else', something he actually did during his final year in high school. These statements show above average interest in both students as well as their independence in pursuing personal goals.

During the interview, R. explained his own motivation as a great desire to communicate, in the particular instance with his Dutch-speaking host family in Belgium. Reiss, too, found the motivation to communicate strongest among the most successful language learners (1985: 517). It is the act of communication itself which provides the most tangible kind of motivation (Macnamara, 1973: 64) for learners like R.

(2) Personality

While extroversion has long been viewed as a prominent personality trait of good language learners, Reiss found that "the successful language learner is *not* necessarily uninhibited" (1985: 516). This fact is illustrated by M., a highly competent language learner who, during his interview, made the following statement:

> "I hate skits ... I'm paranoid with people I don't know ... I don't like to have to interact with people I don't know and I won't like it ... I just don't feel comfortable".

Confirming expectations in another area, both students had low scores on Adorno's F-scale measuring authoritarian traits, as opposed to high scores on Lambert & Gardner's "sensitivity for others scale". (Such high empathy combined with extroversion may explain R.'s typical class-room behaviour — while being very outgoing he frequently holds back to give others a chance to participate.) Empathy, related to the democratic/anti-authoritarian trend in both learners, has been found to successfully predict authenticity in foreign language pronunciation (Brown, 1980: 109).

High self-esteem, too, is reportedly linked to L2 success, especially with regard to oral production (Brown, 1980: 104). While global self-esteem as measured by the questionnaire is high only for R., M. has great confidence in his language learning ability, often calls language study "easy", and seems to benefit from situational as well as task self-esteem. It is task-specific self-esteem, regardless of inhibition in other domains, which correlates most highly with L2 production (Heyde, 1979).

Tolerance of ambiguity, another frequent characteristic of successful language learners, is shown by both R. and M. in their open-minded and confident approach to the (translation-free) Silent Way, the method of instruction used in Spanish courses at the University of Delaware. This personality trait is typical of learners who are relatively accepting of events and facts contradicting their own views (Brown, 1980: 94), an attitude related to other socio-cultural variables discussed below.

Finally, researchers in this field have discussed risk-taking or the "willingness to appear foolish as long as reasonable communication results" (Rubin, 1975: 47). R.'s approach is that of a classic risk-taker ("I don't care what sort of ... pidgin-French I have to use ... to be understood"), as opposed to that of a perfectionist L2 speaker. The advantage of risk-taking is not only increased oral practice, but also the generation of comprehensible input. R.'s frequent questions and comments make him what Seliger would call a "high input generator" (1983: 253), while M. rarely volunteers in the classroom and spends most of his time listening.

(3) Socio-cultural variables

So far, R. and M. have been shown to differ considerably in motivation and personality. They do, however, have much in common in another important domain, their socio-cultural background. Both students' families are reportedly "talkative", "very open-minded", and have "greater than average interest in politics and foreign affairs". Gardner discusses the potent role that parents play in the development of attitudes towards outgroups, and claims that the "family-wide orientation" has lasting effects, liberal attitudes being transferred to children and facilitating the acquisition of another language (1973: 239). Cultural sensitivity, developed in the home, leads to success in L2 according to Tucker & Lambert (1973: 249).

Interest in others, desire to travel, and great tolerance for outgroups, are prominent traits in both R. and M. When asked about French–

Americans in the questionnaire, both students strongly supported their minority rights. Although the learners are not familiar with this specific group, their acceptance of outgroups in general inspired them to give the clearest possible endorsement to a statement like 'The French–American has every reason to be proud of his race and his traditions'.

Ethnocentrism is extremely low for M. whereas R. endorses statements calling for America's superiority in a geopolitical sense. Considering the whole person, this fact is easily explained by his Reserve Officers' Training Corps scholarship and involvement in the U.S. military. This type of patriotism in no way diminishes R.'s cultural sensitivity, demonstrated in other areas of experience.

Genuine interest in socio-cultural matters is evidenced by R.'s and M.'s high scores on Gardner & Lambert's "social inquisitiveness scale", as well as their exceptional interest in history and everyday politics. R. went to great length to travel in Europe, with the explicit goal of meeting people, picking up languages everywhere, and consciously avoiding behaving like a tourist. During his stay, he felt "constantly thrilled and curious ... about learning so much". R.'s cultural sensitivity and inquisitiveness is equally pronounced in the classroom, where Spanish notes on new vocabulary include geographical as well as social restrictions on word usage, such as not to insult men in Spain by calling them "hermoso".

Both students prove that a favourable socio-cultural predisposition does not depend on encouragement to study a specific language (the parents' "active role") or the number of foreign friends parents have. What counts, instead, is the attitudinal atmosphere in the home, or the parents' "passive role" (Gardner, 1973: 235). It can encourage or discourage cultural sensitivity, an orientation so paramount for L2 success that Tucker & Lambert suggest it should be explicitly developed in the classroom to promote better language learning (1973: 249).

(4) Cognitive variables

Both students are good at "getting the big picture" without worrying about missing details which the new language might obscure, which is taken to be a sign of field independence. M., in particular, successfully discovers patterns in even advanced Spanish texts. He enjoys picking out salient information and infers meaning easily during Silent Way sessions. R.'s linguistic sensitivity (e.g. for the exact semantic range of an item like "hermoso" or for slight phonetic variations in Dutch), as well as the degree of empathy reported for both students are more characteristic of field dependence. Just like the traditional view of instrumental versus integrative motivation, the field-dependent/independent distinction is a continuum and not a strict opposition. Despite the dominance of field independence in R. and M. it is clear that both cognitive styles are highly developed and used appropriately by the learners.

Active thinking during class periods is demonstrated by R. as well as M. — they are students who "always know the answer", meaning they actively process information at all times, which helps them to retain what is said by others. An entry in R.'s Spanish notebook provides an example for such instant hypothesizing — "una regleta ... one cube (block?)". According to Reiss, a good language learner "answers questions mentally, whether called upon or not" and thereby becomes what she terms a "silent speaker". This inner activity may well explain why successful learners do not necessarily have to be extroverts (1985: 18). Krashen (1983) calls mental rehearsal "the din in the head", while Bedford (1985) describes it as "spontaneous playback". Both authors contend that such inner activity in a learner is an indication that natural acquisition is taking place.

The efficient organization of linguistic knowledge is an additional cognitive skill observed primarily in R., who frequently uses cognates to link new material to old, such as "des*nudo* — naked, *nude*" "*enterrado* — buried, *interred*" (my emphasis). R. successfully uses his French to infer meanings in Spanish, and often attempts to create new words — based on established patterns — in French. Instead of viewing a number of different languages in isolation, R. consciously works at combining all of his linguistic knowledge into one network.

Finally, high awareness of the learning process itself is characteristic of both R. and M. When Reiss compared strategies employed by good and by less successful language learners, she found striking differences in the terms students used to describe their own behaviour. While statements were very vague for poor students, the better students analysed their strategies in precise and detailed terms (1981: 125). The learners in this study know equally well how exactly they acquire L2 — alertness in class is the key for both — and are fully aware of the overall classroom situation. This is R.'s perception of his Spanish class:

> "The silent method is really a pretty decent method. I like the fact that we're doing things ... and associating the action and not the (English) word with the word. In that respect it's good".

While continuing to describe the method used to teach the learner's newest, and therefore, most exciting and best documented language, R.

acknowledges that he adapts it to his own style. Translation, although officially banned from the classroom, is his personal way to retain vocabulary. Indeed, it is quite natural that a learner in the early stages of mastering a foreign language will turn to his mother tongue for support (Leontiev, 1981: 29). What is remarkable is the independence of R.'s approach which is based on inner authority rather than outside expectations. This self-regulation is shared by M. and pervades all other strategies used by the learners.

(5) Learner strategies

Individual strategies are only symptoms of certain predispositions — motivational, personal, socio-cultural, and cognitive — and they have to be learner-specific in order to be successful. This last fact is often stressed by Rubin & Thompson who call the first strategy recommended in *How to Be a More Successful Language Learner*, "Find your own way" (1982: 49).

Such individualism comes naturally for R. and M., who do not concern themselves very much with outside norms such as grades, assignments (M.) or other-imposed word lists (R.) and concentrate instead on what works for them. M. does not take notes, never studies, and acquires French as a learner in a natural setting would, by listening and interacting. With a clearly internal locus of control (Lefcourt, 1982), M. is extremely self-regulated, uninfluenced by expectations of typical student behaviour, and very successful with his main strategy, attentive listening in class. Although M. has never studied L2 acquisition theory, he knows intuitively that he is learning by "absorption" or "osmosis". This learner has good instincts about what works for him and follows them — every other learner has to determine "what works" and take the same step for himself, with the same confidence and on his own initiative, in order to be successful.

Competent language learners such as R. and M. are not likely to use low-order, conscious strategies. In fact, the use of mnemonic devices is so uncommon among successful students, that it may be typical of poor language learners (Reiss 1985: 517) who rely excessively on learning. R. and M. are acquirers and often stress that they focus on meaning, not form, when they communicate. They do not use conscious rules to monitor spoken French — "How it sounds is what I go on" (R.), "I do what feels right" (M.) — but pay attention to form when reading or writing. Grammar is personal for these successful learners, not other-imposed, but developed from within, mainly through trial and error.

Trial and error is a strategy mentioned by both R. and M. independently. Significantly, the two students view error as a useful tool for learning rather than an embarrassment. Again, they know instinctively how to develop a new linguistic system — by hypothesis-testing — and carry it out in the classroom. Of course this involves risk-taking (R.: "I always give it a stab"), and active hypothesizing in the face of ambiguity (M.: "If I don't understand everything, I will try to make a hypothesis with what I've got"). R., when telling a story in class, demonstrates such high tolerance of uncertainty that he will initiate utterances fully aware that he does not know all the words necessary to complete it, The will to learn and the drive to communicate prevail in lines such as "J'ai acheté … un … a keg? … (un baril) … un baril de bière." Moreover, R.' views error as an aid to memory, predicting that the "mess-up" will lead to definite acquisition.

Grammar-based methods do not reward such insightful behaviour. Perfectionist, other-regulated students are more successful in achieving top scores on discrete point tests. Their linguistic behaviour is governed by explicit rules imposed by others, whereas R.'s and M.'s "rules" tend to be internalized like those of native speakers (R.: "I don't care *why* it's perfect.").

The approach R. and M. have to language is entirely their own, so it does not automatically stop when class is over. M., while still in high school, read French art books and soccer magazines on his own, subject matter he was truly interested in, ideal for acquisition. R. is still building his linguistic network when walking from one class to another, trying mentally to say the same phrase in English, French, Dutch, and Spanish (such language play even occurred in one of his dreams). He greatly enjoys French films, sometimes converses with a friend in that language, and reads parts of his French textbook regardless of specific assignments. These voluntary, pleasurable activities are "strategies" only in the sense that they constitute actual student behaviour as opposed to the predispositions discussed in earlier sections. They are not, however, means to an end, consciously employed to reach goals set by others. R. and M. intuitively behave in distinct ways, making errors work and moulding instructional givens to their own style, thereby taking charge of their own language studies instead of being controlled by others.

Conclusion

The two successful language learners at the centre of this study proved to be, above all, acquirers who focus on meaning rather than conscious rules. Moreover, R. and M. are willing to take risks in order to test hypotheses. Their orientations differ considerably with regard to both personality and motivation, an illustration of the fact that there may not be a single ideal predisposition for high achievement in a second language. The success both learners enjoy is more likely to be rooted in what they have in common — cultural sensitivity, alertness in class, as well as using errors constructively rather than trying to avoid them. Most importantly, R. and M. are in full control of their own learning process. Rather than being dominated by their school environment, R. and M. adapt it to their individual purposes and never look for language learning "recipes" developed by others. Consequently, it does not seem appropriate to pass on a list of "strategies" to be imitated. Instead, this study might encourage students to look more closely at their own behaviour in the foreign language classroom. Such awareness is an important step towards becoming a successful learner.

Note to Chapter 14

1. Originally presented at the Delaware Symposium VII on Language Studies, October, 1985. Professor J. P. Lantolf's guidance in this investigation is gratefully acknowledged.

References

BAILEY, K. M. 1980, An introspective analysis of an individual's language learning experience. In S. D. KRASHEN & R. C. Scarcella (eds), *Research in Second Language Acquisition*. Rowley, Mass.: Newbury House, 58–65.

BEDFORD, D. A. 1985, Spontaneous playback of the second language: A descriptive study. *Foreign Language Annals* 18, 279–87.

BROWN, H. D. 1980, *Principles of Language Learning and Teaching*. Englewood Cliffs: Prentice-Hall.

CARROLL, J. B. 1981, Twenty-five years of research on foreign language aptitude. In K. C. DILLER (ed.), *Individual Differences and Universals in Language Learning Aptitude*. Rowley, Mass.: Newbury House, 83–118.

COHEN, A. D. & HOSENFELD, C. 1981, Some uses of mentalistic data in second language research. *Language Learning* 31:2, 285–313.

ERICSSON, K. A. & SIMON, H. A. 1984, *Protocol Analysis: Verbal Reports as Data*. Cambridge: MIT Press.

GARDNER, R. C. 1973, Attitudes and motivation: Their role in second language acquisition. In J. OLLER, JR. & J. C. RICHARDS (eds), *Focus on the Learner: Pragmatic Perspectives for the Language Teacher*. Rowley, Mass.: Newbury House, 235–45.

GARDNER, R. C. & LAMBERT, W. E. 1972, *Attitudes and Motivation in Second Language Learning*. Rowley, Mass.: Newbury House.

GENESEE, F., ROGERS, P. & HOLOBOW, N. 1983, The social psychology of second language learning: Another point of view. *Language Learning* 33:2, 209–24.

HEYDE, A. 1979, The relationship between self-esteem and the oral production of a second language. Unpublished doctoral dissertation, University of Michigan.

HOSENFELD, C. 1976, Learning about learning: Discovering our students' strategies. *Foreign Language Annals* 9, 117–29.

KRASHEN, S. D. 1981, *Second Language Acquisition and Second Language Learning*. Oxford: Pergamon Press.

— 1983, The din in the head, input, and the language acquisition device. *Foreign Language Annals* 16, 41–44.

LEFCOURT, H. M. 1982, *Locus of Control: Current Trends in Theory and Research* (2nd ed.) Hillsdale, N.J.: Lawrence Erlbaum Associates.

Leontiev, A. A. 1981, *Psychology and the Language Learning Process*. Oxford: Pergamon Press.

MACNAMARA, J. 1973, The cognitive strategies of language learning. In J. OLLER, JR. & J. C. RICHARDS (eds), *Focus on the Learner: Pragmatic Perspectives for the Language Teacher*. Rowley, Mass.: Newbury House, 57–65.

REISS, M. A. 1981, Helping the unsuccessful language learner. *The Modern Language Journal* 65, 121–28.

— 1985, The good language learner: Another look. *The Canadian Modern Language Review* 4: 3, 511–23.

RIVERS, W. 1983, *Communicating Naturally in a Second Language: Theory and Practice in Language Teaching*. Cambridge: University Press.

RUBIN, J. 1975, What the 'good language learner' can teach us. *TESOL Quarterly* 9, 41–51.

RUBIN, J. & THOMPSON, I. 1982. *How to be a More Successful Language Learner*. Boston, Mass.: Heinle & Heinle.

SELIGER, H. W. 1983, Learner interaction in the classroom and its effect on language acquisition. In H. W. SELIGER & M. H. LONG (eds), *Classroom Oriented Research in Second Language Acquisition*. Rowley, Mass.: Newbury House. 246–66

STERN, H. H. 1975, What can we learn from the good language learner? *The Canadian Modern Language Review* 31:4, 304–18.

TUCKER, G. R. & LAMBERT, W. E. 1973, Sociocultural aspects of language study. In J. W. OLLER, Jr. & J. C. RICHARDS (eds), *Focus on the Learner: Pragmatic Perspectives for the Language Teacher*. Rowley, Mass.: Newbury House, 246–50.

Notes on Contributors

Theo Bongaerts studied at the universities of Nijmegen and Reading. He is currently senior lecturer in applied linguistics and English at the University of Nijmegen, where he received his Ph.D. in 1978. His current research interests include the relationship between L1 and L2 referential communication, syntactic development in second language acquisition, and the acquisition of a dialect as a second language.

Marilda Cavalcanti received her Ph.D. at the University of Lancaster, England, in 1983. She currently teaches as assistant professor at the Department of Applied Linguistics of the State University of Campinas (UNICAMP), Brazil. Her research interests are in the area of L1 and FL reading and writing. She was the recipient of the 1985 International Reading Association Institute for Reading Research Fellowship Award.

Andrew Cohen is Associate Professor of Applied Linguistics at the School of Education, Hebrew University of Jerusalem. He has conducted research and published in the fields of sociolinguistics and psycholinguistics, with particular emphasis on bilingual education, language testing, and language learning. For over a decade, his research has included the use of verbal report measures in an effort to better understand the cognitive processes involved in language learning.

Hans W. Dechert received his Ph.D. from the Johann-Wolfgang-Goethe-Universität at Frankfurt in 1954. He has taught at Rutgers University, New Brunswick, NJ, USA and the Justus-Liebig-Universität at Giessen, Federal Republic of Germany. At present he is Professor in the Department of English and Romance Languages and Literatures of the University of Kassel. During recent years the focus of his research in the Kassel Psycho- and Pragmalinguistic Research Group (KAPPA) has been the psycholinguistics of second-language speech production of adult learners of English and German.

He is vice president of AILA Commission on Psycholinguistics and Secretary General of the International Society of Applied Psycholinguistics.

K. Anders Ericsson received his Ph.D. in cognitive psychology from the University of Stockholm, Sweden, in 1976. In 1980, after three years as a post-doctoral fellow/research associate with Professor Herbert Simon at Carnegie-Mellon University in Pittsburgh, he moved to the University of Colorado at Boulder where he currently holds a position as Associate Professor of Psychology. His main area of empirical research concerns detailed analyses of exceptional memory performance and memory skills where protocol analysis plays an important role.

Claus Færch was Associate Professor of English Language at the Aarhus School of Economics, Denmark. From 1975 to 1986 he worked as an Assistant and Associate Professor at the University of Copenhagen, where he was director of the Project in Foreign Language Pedagogy (PIF) from 1977 to 1986. He has published widely in contrastive linguistics and interlanguage studies, the latter including work on communication strategies, language transfer and classroom research. From 1984 until his death in early 1987 he was chairman of the Danish Association of Applied Linguistics (ADLA).

Ute Feldmann studied Applied Linguistics, Spanish and English at the University of Bochum, FRG, where she completed her M.A. with a thesis on discoursal aspects in German learners' Spanish interlanguage. She is currently collaborating in a research project on the C-test, where she is particularly interested in introspective methods as an instrument of data elititation and test validation.

Pamela Gerloff received her Bachelor of Arts degree in French and Psychology from Michigan State University. She is currently a doctoral candidate at Harvard University, completing her thesis examining the translation process at various levels of language proficiency. She has previously taught first and second languages in Europe and the United States, and has also worked as a full-time professional translator.

Barbara Gillette, a native of Austria, received her M.A. in Modern Languages from the University of Graz in 1981, where her studies had included French and American literature as well as general and applied linguistics. Subsequently she taught English as a Second Language at

English Language Services (Case Western Reserve University) in Cleveland, Ohio. At present, she teaches French at the University of Delaware while working towards a Ph.D. in linguistics. Her research interests include second language acquisition in the classroom as well as introspective learner studies with a special emphasis on learner variability.

Rüdiger Grotjahn received his Ph.D. in linguistics from the University of Bochum, FRG, where he has taught linguistics and foreign language pedagogy since 1972. His main research interests are in the methodological foundations of second language research, language testing and quantitative linguistics, and he has published widely in these areas. He is co-editor of the series "Quantitative Linguistics" and currently co-directing a project on the C-test.

Kirsten Haastrup received her Ph.D. from the Royal Danish School of Educational Studies in 1975, where she worked as a part-time lecturer from 1975 to 1978. Between 1975 and 1985 she was employed as a part-time lecturer and research fellow at the Department of English, University of Copenhagen. Since 1985 she has been Associate Professor of Foreign Language Pedagogy at the Department of English, The Cophenhagen School of Economics and Business Administration. She has published on language testing, teacher training, and communication strategies. Her present research interests focus on receptive procedures in foreign language use and learning.

Anke Hölscher is a graduate from the Universiy of Kassel, FRG, where she studied English and French Language and Literature. In her M.A. thesis she examined translation processes by means of thinking aloud protocols. She is currently a secondary school teacher of English and French.

Gabriele Kasper received her Ph.D. from the University of Bochum, FRG, where she worked at the Department of Language Pedagogy from 1975 to 1980. Since 1981 she has been Associate Professor of Applied Linguistics at the University of Aarhus, Denmark. Her publications include work on pedagogic grammar, interlanguage pragmatics, communication strategies and classroom research. Presently her main interests are on cognitive processes of L2 learning and communication and cross-cultural pragmatics.

Eric Kellerman works at the English Department, Nijmegen University, The Netherlands. He studied at Brighton College of Education, and the Universities of Reading and York before moving to his present position in 1974. He has degrees in Education and Linguistics and recently ended a long-running battle with himself by finishing his Ph.D. He has taught in both primary and secondary schools, and his research interests revolve round second language acquisition in formal settings, particularly with regard to lexico-semantic development and the role of the native language. His leisure pursuits include cooking and eating, Californian wine, the history of landscape architecture, and getting on airplanes as often as possible.

Hans Krings received his Ph.D. in language pedagogy ("Sprachlehrforschung") from the University of Bochum, Federal Republic of Germany. He taught German, Italian and French in a number of institutions, worked as a professional translator in Italy and collaborated in a research project on the teaching of Spanish and Italian in German secondary schools at Bochum University. Since 1986 he has been a lecturer in the Department of German at the University of Paris X — Nanterre. His current research interests focus on psycholinguistic aspects of foreign language learning and on translation theory.

Dorothea Möhle received her Ph.D. from the University of Freiburg, FRG. For several years she taught at the College of Education at Göttingen. Since 1975 she has been Professor in the Department of English and Romance Languages and Literatures at the University of Kassel. She is a collaborator in the Kassel Psycho- and Pragmalinguistic Research Group (KAPPA). Her present research interests focus on psycholinguistic aspects of second-language learning and on the analysis of oral speech production of advanced learners of French.

Nanda Poulisse graduated at the department of English, Nijmegen University, The Netherlands, in 1982 on a study of the acquisition of deictic verbs of motion by Dutch learners of English. Since 1983 she has been working as a research assistant at the same university where she carries out a project on the use of compensatory strategies by Dutch learners of English. Besides second language acquisition, her current research interests include psycholinguistics.

Klaus P. Schneider studied English and Slavic Philology and Education at the Universities of Marburg, FRG, Edinburgh and Moscow. He received his Ph.D. in 1987 from the University of Marburg, where he currently works as a research assistant in English linguistics and collaborates in the project "Analysis of Lexical Errors". He has published on discourse analysis and second language research.

Herbert A. Simon is Richard King Mellon University Professor of Computer Science and Psychology at Carnegie-Mellon University, where he has taught since 1949. During the past 30 years he has been studying decision-making and problem-solving processes, using computers to simulate human thinking. He has published over 600 papers and 20 books and monographs.

Educated at the University of Chicago (Ph.D., 1943), his work has been recognized by honorary degrees from a number of universities.

He was elected to the National Academy of Sciences in 1967. He has received awards for his research from the American Psychological Association, the Association for Computing Machinery, the American Political Science Association, the American Economic Association, and the Institute of Electrical and Electronic Engineers. He received the Alfred Nobel Memorial Prize in Economics in 1978, and the National Medal of Science in 1986.

He has been Chairman of the Board of Directors of the Social Science Research Council, and of the Behavioral Science Division of the National Research Council, and was a member of the President's Science Advisory Committee.

Brigitte Stemmer completed her M.A. in Applied Linguistics. English and French at the University of Bochum, FRG, in 1981. Since then she has been travelling Asia and Africa, studying medicine, and working as a research assistant at the Universities of Bochum and Essen. Influenced by her medical studies, which are slowly approaching towards an end, she is currently examining from a non-anatomical perspective what happens in the head of foreign language learners when solving a language test.

Rüdiger Zimmermann received his Ph.D. from the University of Kiel, FRG, in 1968. He was associated to Queens College of the City University of New York 1969/70 and to the University of Wuppertal, FRG, 1970–72. Since 1973 he has been Professor of English Linguistics at the University of Marburg, FRG, where he currently directs a project on "Analysis of Lexical Errors". He has published in Historical, Contrastive and Applied Linguistics, the latter including second language research and manipulation in the language of mass media.

Index